Th[illegible] War

Conflict in Eu[illegible]a

Steve Phillips

Series Editors
Martin Collier
Erica Lewis

HEINEMANN ADVANCED HISTORY

HEINEMANN ADVANCED HISTORY

Heinemann Educational Publishers
Halley Court, Jordan Hill, Oxford, OX2 8EJ
a division of Reed Educational & Professional Publishing Ltd
Heinemann is a registered trademark of Reed Educational & Professional Publishing Ltd

OXFORD MELBOURNE AUCKLAND
JOHANNESBURG BLANTYRE GABORONE
IBADAN PORTSMOUTH NH (USA) CHICAGO

First published 2001

ISBN 0435 32736 4
03 02 01
10 9 8 7 6 5 4 3 2 1

Designed, illustrated and typeset by Wyvern 21 Ltd

Printed and bound in Great Britain by The Bath Press Ltd, Bath

Index compiled by Indexing Specialists

Photographic acknowledgements
The author and publisher would like to thank the following for permission to reproduce photographs: Agence France Press: 56, 93; Corbis: 9, 17, 47, 51, 64, 67, 82, 89, 96, 112, 151 (both), 163, 179, 187, 191, 201, 216; Hulton Getty: 40, 41, 108, 209; Ronald Grant Picture Collection: 231; Science Photo Library: 76.

Cover photograph: © Corbis/Sygma

Author's acknowledgements
I would like to thank the following for their help, advice and support during the writing of this book: Nicholas Wilmott, Ian Davies, my parents Margaret and Nigel Phillips, with particular thanks to Erica Lewis, Melanie Copland and Vicky Cuthill. I am grateful to Andrew Kerley for comments on early drafts and Peter Rooks for rooting out material. I would also like to thank those students I have taught at Somerset College of Arts and Technology, Taunton and the Gryphon School, Sherborne, especially Amy, Helen, Lauren, Christian, Rob, Tom, Peter and James, who have given me so many ideas and such inspiration during the writing of this book.

CONTENTS

Containing communism: the USA in Asia 1945–73

HOW TO USE THIS BOOK

This book is divided into distinct parts. The parts on The Cold War in Europe 1945–91 and The Cold War in Asia and the Americas 1949–75 are designed to meet the requirements of AS Level History. Both parts give an analytical narrative of events to explain what happened during this important period of history. There are summary questions at the end of each chapter to challenge students to use the information to develop their skills in analysis and explanation, and to reinforce their understanding of the key issues. This part of the book will also provide a solid foundation in preparation for the deeper analytical work expected at A2 Level.

The A2 part of the book is more analytical in style. It contains interpretations of the key issues of this period and examines aspects of historiography central to the study of history at this level. These interpretations should be read in conjunction with the relevant AS chapter. In this way the student will be able to relate the information covered in the AS chapters to the more thematic and analytical interpretations in the A2 sections. The latter will also enable AS students to extend their understanding of the subject.

At the end of both AS and A2 parts there are assessment sections which have been designed to give guidance on how students can meet the requirements of the new AS and A2 specifications provided by the three awarding bodies – Edexcel, AQA and OCR – when answering questions.

It is hoped that the book will also be useful to the general reader who wants to find their way around what is a sometimes complex, yet fascinating, period of history.

Europe and the Iron Curtain during the Cold War period.

AS SECTION: THE COLD WAR IN EUROPE 1945–91

INTRODUCTION

Key questions

- What were the causes of the Cold War?
- How did the USA attempt to contain communism?
- How secure was the USSR's hold on eastern Europe?
- Why did the Cold War end?

During the Second World War the USA and Britain had been allies of the USSR against Nazi Germany, Fascist Italy, and Japan. This alliance did not survive the war. International relations from 1945 until the collapse of the Soviet Union in 1991 were dominated by the superpower rivalry that existed between the USA and its allies on one side and the Soviet Union and its satellite states on the other. This period of tension has been termed the Cold War; a war where the two sides did not come into direct armed conflict but attacked each other through propaganda, non-cooperation and economic measures. Although the hostility between the superpowers stopped short of direct military conflict, the Cold War did, nevertheless, see tension fluctuate considerably.

The defeat of Nazi Germany at the end the Second World War had left a power vacuum in Europe in 1945. The tension which developed between the USA and the USSR was in large part due to attempts by both countries to fill this vacuum. The USSR saw control over eastern Europe as necessary to safeguard their country from further attack from a hostile capitalist West. The USA saw a strong need to prevent Europe falling into the hands of communism, a political system which was seen as a threat to the freedoms of capitalism in the West. Thus Europe became a battleground between two different political ideologies.

The lack of trust and misunderstanding that marked relations between the two superpowers were to add to the growing hostility between them. The result was not only a deterioration in relations but a hardening of the division between eastern and western Europe. The countries of western Europe were supported by generous amounts of US aid which ensured rapid economic recovery and a consolidation of capitalism after the economic devastation brought about during the Second World War. In contrast, the countries of eastern Europe were brought under the control of the Soviet Union and had communist governments imposed on them. The Berlin Blockade of 1948–9 hardened the position of both sides and, by 1950,

A British cartoon showing Churchill peeping under the Iron Curtain.

the 'Iron Curtain' between East and West was firmly established in Europe.

The death in 1953 of Stalin, the leader of the Soviet Union, led to a gradual improvement in relations between the two sides but this 'thaw' in relations was easily disrupted by events that threatened to upset the balance between East and West. The Soviet Union took direct military action to prevent both Hungary, in 1956, and Czechoslovakia, in 1968, breaking free of Soviet control. The building of the Berlin Wall in 1961 was to become a symbol of the division of Europe into two distinct camps.

The division of Europe, and that of Germany, seemed to have become permanent features of the continent by 1980. Nonetheless, by 1989 Soviet control over eastern Europe had weakened considerably. Mikhail Gorbachev, who had become Soviet leader in 1985, had no wish to forcibly impose rigid communism on any country. His foreign policy, while promoting a more friendly relationship with the West, allowed the governments of eastern Europe greater flexibility to pursue their own policies. Greater freedom in the USSR as well as most parts of eastern Europe was to lead to popular demonstrations calling for democracy and an end to communism. In those countries, such as East Germany and Romania, where the government refused to change, Gorbachev made it clear that Soviet forces would no longer be used to prop up unpopular governments. Stripped of support both at home and abroad, the communist regimes across eastern Europe collapsed, including the Soviet Union itself. The end of the Cold War saw an end to the Iron Curtain which had divided Europe for half a century.

CHAPTER 1

The seeds of conflict 1941–5

The Cold War, a period of international tension between the USA and the **USSR**, developed out of the end of the Second World War in 1945. It dominated international relations for over forty years. Although the tensions between the two superpowers came to the fore after 1945, the seeds of conflict were in existence before 1939. The Second World War may have smoothed over the causes of tension but it was only a temporary development. Far from removing the factors which produced tension, the Second World War ultimately created an environment in international relations which generated far more tension, hostility and rivalry between the USA and the USSR than had been seen before 1939.

WHAT DIFFERENCES IN IDEOLOGY WERE THERE BETWEEN CAPITALISM AND COMMUNISM?

The origins of Cold War conflict can be traced back to the Bolshevik Revolution of 1917. The Bolshevik seizure of power in Russia was to lead to the establishment of the world's first socialist state, a state whose government saw the ideas of communism as their guiding principles. Lenin, the leader of the Bolshevik Revolution, represented all that was feared by the governments of **the West**: a threat to the freedoms of democracy and capitalism. Thus, underlying the hatred which was to develop between the West and the Soviet Union, as Bolshevik Russia became, was a conflict between opposing **ideologies**.

Based on the ideas of Karl Marx, communism provided a framework of economic and political principles that directly opposed those traditionally held in the West. Communism was, in essence, a threat to the power structure of western society.

Economic differences

To the followers of Marx, capitalism was seen as being responsible for the division of society in the West into

KEY CONCEPT

The Cold War is the term given to the conflict that existed between the USA and the USSR after the Second World War. It was a conflict that involved economic measures, non-cooperation and propaganda but no direct armed fighting between the two sides. Thus, despite a breakdown in relations between the superpowers, 'hot' war was avoided. With the advent of nuclear weapons, both sides used a range of less destructive methods of conflict.

KEY TERMS

USSR The Union of Soviet Socialist Republics, also known as the Soviet Union, was introduced in 1923 as the official title of the areas of the old Russian Empire that were now under communist control. It was made up of fifteen different republics but was dominated by Russia, the largest in size and population. The USSR collapsed in 1991.

The West is the term given to the capitalist countries of western Europe and North America during the Cold War. The USA was the principal power of the West.

Ideology A set of ideas and beliefs which form the basis of an economic or political system. The Cold War involved conflict between two competing ideologies: communism and capitalism.

different classes. The emphasis on private ownership of businesses was seen as producing the division between the rich factory owners and the poorer working classes. To do away with this inequality, communists believed that all factories, businesses and land should be taken over by the government on behalf of the people. This process of nationalisation would enable the goods generated by the economy to be more fairly distributed according to need. The principle of a state-owned economy is the opposite of private enterprise, which is encouraged by capitalism, whereby individuals have the freedom to own their own businesses and keep the majority of the profits. In capitalist economies the incentive of individual gain is a direct contrast to the community responsibility encouraged by communism. To the owners of businesses, factories and land, the process of nationalisation represented a threat to their wealth, status and power and it was these people who dominated the governments of countries in the West.

Political differences

As well as differences in economic ideology, there was an important contrast in terms of political system.

- **Liberal Democracies.** The USA saw itself as the upholder of liberal democracy. This political system was valued because it upheld important freedoms, such as the freedom to vote, freedom of speech, freedom of worship and a free press. In this sense liberal democracy gave people a choice of government and the chance to vote an unpopular government out of office.
- **The Communist State.** To the communists, political parties were the result of different and conflicting classes. In a communist state, where a classless society was being created, there was no need for different political parties. Thus, a communist system was a one-party state, with the Communist Party ruling on behalf of the people. In this respect the freedoms enjoyed in many countries of the West were under threat.

One other part of the ideology of communism which was to provide a source of fear in the West was the belief that conflict between capitalism and communism was inevitable because they represented completely opposed systems.

If communism was to succeed it had to be a worldwide revolution and this meant the collapse of capitalism. In March 1919 Lenin had stated 'We are living not merely in a state, but in a system of states: and it is inconceivable that the Soviet republic should continue to exist for a long period side by side with imperialist states.' In order to further the cause of communism and aid the collapse of capitalism the **Comintern** was set up. Its role was to coordinate communist groups throughout the world and support their attempts to undermine capitalism by all available means, including revolution. Thus, the ideology of communism was inherently hostile to the West and the values it stood for.

KEY TERM

Comintern An organisation set up in 1919 to facilitate contacts between communist groups throughout the world. The Soviet government was able to control its activities and the West feared it was being used to undermine capitalism and spread communist revolution.

Communism's emphasis on government control over the economy and a one-party state to further the interests of the industrial workers provided a sharp contrast with the economic and political freedoms taken for granted in the capitalist democracies of the West.

The hostility of the West towards communism seemed to be confirmed by its intervention against the Bolsheviks during the Russian Civil War of 1918–21. The Bolshevik Red Army faced opposition from conservative forces in Russia who became known as the Whites. The Whites wished to prevent the establishment of Bolshevik rule and in this aim they were supported by the Allied governments of Britain, the USA, France and Japan, who also wanted to reverse Lenin's decision to pull Russia out of the First World War against Germany. When the First World War ended in November 1918, Allied intervention to support the Whites in the Russian Civil War started to dry up and by 1921 the Bolsheviks had won the Civil War. Although the Bolshevik regime of Lenin survived the Civil War, the experience highlighted the hostility of the West towards communism and the fact that the West would contemplate military action against communism whenever the opportunity might present itself.

Tensions in the 1930s

Relations between the Soviet Union and the West remained poor throughout the inter-war years, with important consequences for international relations in

Capitalism and Communism: Ideological differences

Capitalism	Communism
Upheld as the guiding values of the West. • Private enterprise: businesses, factories and land owned by individuals or groups of individuals with the minimum of government interference. • Liberal democracy: a political system where each person has the freedom to vote, freedom to stand for election, freedom of speech, freedom of worship and freedom of the press.	*Upheld as the guiding principles of the Soviet Union.* • State-owned economy: an economy where all industries and agriculture are owned by the government on behalf of the people. • One-party state: a political system where there is only one political party to represent the people. In the Soviet Union all political parties other than the Communist Party were banned. Elections were contested between individuals who had to be members of this party.

Europe when Hitler's foreign policy threatened to engulf the continent in a major conflict at the end of the 1930s.

The refusal of the Soviet regime to honour the debts owed by previous Russian governments to the West was a source of tension in international relations. The Soviet government's policy of nationalising key sectors of the economy resulted in many foreign companies losing their investments. This particularly affected France, where investors in the Russian economy put pressure on the French government to recover these losses. The British government had, in addition to financial interests, a more personal reason for hostility: the Bolshevik government had executed the Tsar of Russia and his family. **Tsar Nicholas II** was a cousin of King George V and the British King was reluctant to undertake any communication with his cousin's murderers. Thus, when faced with the rise of an aggressive Germany under the leadership of Hitler, any attempts by Britain, France and the Soviet Union to form a united front against German expansion were undermined by mutual mistrust and hostility.

KEY PERSON

Tsar Nicholas II (1868–1918) The Emperor of Russia from 1894 until the Revolution of 1917. Executed by the Bolsheviks in 1918.

In dealing with Hitler's demands for territory, Britain and France pursued a policy of **appeasement** which involved negotiation and accommodating German demands where they were seen as reasonable. To the Soviet government this was a policy which raised suspicions about the seriousness of Britain and France in dealing with the threat of fascism. When Hitler demanded parts of Czechoslovakia in 1938 and 1939, Britain and France had proved ineffectual in standing up to Hitler. To Stalin, the Soviet leader, an accommodation with Hitler was necessary to limit the threat of a German invasion of the Soviet Union and to give him time to prepare for a war he believed was inevitable. The result was the Nazi–Soviet Pact of 1939. Although condemned by Britain and France, Soviet actions in signing the Pact were the result of their own half-hearted attitudes and ineffectual policies. For Stalin it was a 'marriage of convenience' that gave the USSR the opportunity to gain parts of Poland and to sign a non-aggression pact, which would delay a German invasion and give the USSR time to prepare. To Britain and France the Nazi–Soviet Pact seemed to confirm the untrustworthiness of Soviet foreign policy, in much the same way that the policy of appeasement seemed to demonstrate the double-dealing of Britain and France to the Soviet Union.

STRAINS IN THE GRAND ALLIANCE

When Hitler launched his invasion of the Soviet Union on 22 June 1941, the Second World War was transformed. The USSR found itself on the same side as Britain in resisting the might of Nazi Germany. When Japan bombed the US naval base at Pearl Harbor in December of the same year, the USA joined the war against the fascist powers. Thus, by the end of 1941, the Soviet Union, the USA and Britain were allies against Germany, Italy and Japan. Previous hostility between East and West was to be temporarily forgotten, or at least swept under the carpet, until the defeat of the fascist powers was secured by the formation of what was to become known as the **Grand Alliance**.

KEY TERMS

Appeasement The policy adopted by Britain towards Germany in the 1930s. It involved negotiating with Hitler and trying to reach accommodation with his demands for territory where they seemed reasonable. This method of dealing with Hitler failed to prevent the outbreak of the Second World War. Churchill and Truman associated appeasement with weakness and believed a hard-line approach, which involved standing up to foreign aggressors, would be more effective in the future.

The Grand Alliance The alliance of Britain, the USA and the USSR from 1941 to 1945, formed to defeat Germany and her allies during the Second World War. The leaders of the alliance – Churchill, Roosevelt and Stalin – were sometimes referred to as the **Big Three**.

KEY PERSON

Winston Churchill (1874–1965) Prime Minister of Britain during the Second World War. Strongly anti-communist, he was nonetheless prepared to work with the Soviet Union against Nazi Germany. He met Stalin several times and established a sound working relationship with the Soviet leader. Churchill was removed as Prime Minister after a general election in 1945, which took place during the Potsdam Conference. In the post-war world Churchill was deeply suspicious of Stalin's motives and in 1946 his *Iron Curtain* speech called for an alliance between Britain and the USA to prevent Soviet expansion.

KEY EVENT

Teheran Conference, 1943 The first meeting of the 'Big Three' (Churchill, Roosevelt, Stalin) during the Second World War. They discussed how to pursue the war against Germany, Italy and Japan.

Winston Churchill, the British Prime Minister, immediately offered help to the Soviet Union when the Germans invaded. The US President, Franklin D. Roosevelt (see page 15), was to do the same. Churchill recognised that the war could not be won without an agreement with the Soviet Union and was prepared to cooperate with Stalin, the Soviet leader (see page 14). Relations between Churchill and Stalin were helped by a mutual respect, although they certainly did not trust each other. Roosevelt was a realist who wished to concentrate on winning the war rather than arguing about what would happen afterwards, an issue where disagreements would be much more obvious. Thus, the three leaders were to establish a working relationship in order to secure victory against fascism. The 'Big Three' met in **Teheran** in November 1943 to agree on several issues concerning Poland. Yet, despite this level of cooperation, divisions remained between the three leaders and continued to be a source of tension in the relationship.

What were the strains in the Grand Alliance?

The Second Front. One key strain in the Alliance was over the timing of opening up a Second Front against Germany. Stalin was concerned first and foremost with the security of the Soviet Union. Since June 1941 the Soviet

The 'Big Three' (Churchill, Roosevelt, Stalin) at the Yalta Conference, 1945.

Union had borne the brunt of the fighting against Germany and had suffered severe losses both in human and material resources. To Stalin the need to open up a second front in western Europe against Germany in order to relieve the pressure on the USSR in the east was a pressing necessity. Yet the refusal of Britain and the USA to do so until the time was right led Stalin to be suspicious of their motives. Did they wish to see Nazi Germany defeat Soviet Russia before the defeat of Germany? Although there is no evidence that this was ever seriously considered by the British and US governments, Stalin's suspicions remained. Even when told of the decision to launch the D-Day landings to open a second front in June 1944, Stalin continued to be sceptical: 'Yes, there'll be a landing; if there is no fog. Until now there has always been something else. Maybe they'll meet with some Germans! What if they meet with some Germans? Maybe there won't be a landing then, but just promises as usual.'

The issue of Poland. Strains also developed when discussion of post-war arrangements got down to specific details. As the tide was turned against Germany these issues came to the fore. One of the most prominent issues was that of Poland. Britain had officially gone to war against Germany in 1939 to uphold the independence of Poland. Its fate was therefore a question of the utmost significance for the British. Due to its geographical position, Poland was of immense importance for the security of the Soviet Union.

- Poland had been the route of three invasions of Russia in the twentieth century.
- The Soviet Union was not prepared to see an unfriendly government in Poland.
- A provisional Polish government had been set up in exile in London by those who had fled the country in 1939 but there was also the Union of Polish Patriots, a prospective government based in the Soviet Union.

To complicate matters further, there was the traditional hostility between Poles and Soviets. This came to the fore in April 1943 when German troops discovered a mass grave in the Katyn Forest near Smolensk. The grave contained the bodies of over 10,000 Polish officers murdered when captured by the Soviets in 1939. The Soviets claimed the atrocity was the result of German actions and although the truth could not be established at the time, many Poles suspected that Soviet troops were responsible.

The Warsaw Rising. The disagreement over the future of Poland caused increased tension in 1944 when the Warsaw Rising took place. On 1 August Poles in the city who had links with the government in exile in London rose up against the German forces occupying the city. With the German army retreating in the east, the Poles saw an opportunity to liberate the city before the arrival of Soviet troops. The Soviet army, which had reached the River Vistula outside Warsaw, halted its advance against the Germans. Despite heroic efforts, the Poles were crushed by the Germans as the Soviet forces stood by and refused to help. Stalin claimed that increased opposition from German forces delayed the Soviet advance into Poland but, in the West, this refusal to help the Poles was seen as heartless. By the time the Soviet army captured Warsaw in January 1945 the Poles were in no position to offer resistance to any outside power. Stalin's ability to impose a settlement on Poland that was more to his liking was greatly enhanced and the West could do little more than offer verbal protests.

Harry Truman. These events added voices to the critics of the Grand Alliance. In the USA there were those, such as Vice-President **Harry S. Truman**, who hated communism and were uncomfortable with the whole idea of working closely with the Soviet Union. In 1941 Truman stated 'If we see that Germany is winning the war we ought to help Russia, and if Russia is winning we ought to help Germany, and in that way let them kill as many as possible.' This was not a view shared by President Roosevelt but it did represent the viewpoint of a sizeable part of the American public.

Breaking point. Despite the appearance of the Grand Alliance as a union of states fighting together against common foes, the mistrust and tension that had been

KEY PERSON

Harry S. Truman (1884–1972) US President after the sudden death of Roosevelt in 1945 until 1952. A member of the Democratic Party, he served as Roosevelt's Vice-President after 1944. His political career had been concerned with domestic issues and he knew little about foreign affairs when he suddenly became President. Under pressure from critics of Roosevelt's approach to Stalin, Truman adopted a more hard-line attitude to the Soviet Union. He took firm action during the Soviet blockade of Berlin during 1948–9 and entered the Korean War in 1950 to prevent the spread of communism in the Far East. At the end of his presidency he was under pressure from Red hysteria, a wave of strong anti-communist feeling promoted by Senator Joseph McCarthy.

evident before the Second World War remained. The Alliance was a temporary arrangement whereby disagreement and hostility was disguised rather than swept away. As the war drew to an end in 1945 the strains in this relationship came to the fore. When discussion of the details of a post-war settlement could not be avoided any longer these strains stretched to breaking point.

CONCLUSION

By early 1945 the seeds of the Cold War were in place. Long-term causes of conflict had existed since 1917: two superpowers had emerged that represented directly opposed ideologies and the defeat of Nazi Germany had created a power vacuum in Europe into which both countries were drawn to protect their own interests. Nonetheless, despite the existence of these factors, the Cold War was not yet inevitable. It was the attitudes and policies that both the USA and the USSR developed towards each other during and after 1945 that led to the final breakdown in relations.

SUMMARY QUESTIONS

1 Explain the differences in ideology between the West and the USSR.

2 Why was the Grand Alliance formed?

3 What factors caused strains in the Grand Alliance?

CHAPTER 2

The Cold War in Europe 1945–50

The period 1945 to 1950 saw the Cold War develop, with the central issue being who would dominate post-war Europe. The defeat of Nazi Germany, which at one stage during the Second World War had controlled most of the continent, had left a power vacuum. Large areas of Europe had been left devastated by the war and in many parts of the continent administration and government had ceased to function. This presented an unusual and in many ways unique situation into which both the USSR and the USA were drawn. The manner in which they dealt with each other caused the outbreak of the Cold War.

WHAT WERE THE ATTITUDES OF THE MAIN POWERS TOWARDS THE SITUATION IN EUROPE IN 1945?

The actions taken by both East and West after 1945 were conditioned in large part by their attitudes towards, and perceptions of, each other and the situation posed by the end of the war. These attitudes were to provide the most important short-term causes of the Cold War.

Soviet attitudes in 1945

Stalin's foreign policy was based on the aim of taking advantage of the military situation in Europe to strengthen Soviet influence and prevent another invasion from the west. This policy resulted in establishing pro-Soviet governments in as much of eastern Europe as possible. To the West this was seen as evidence of the expansionist nature of communism, but Soviet aims were based on attitudes that were more complicated than this.

Ever since the Bolshevik Revolution of 1917 Soviet foreign policy was concerned with two key aims: first, protecting the new state from hostile neighbours and ensuring its very survival, and second, aiming to promote the spread of world communist revolution. The Soviet Union had, since 1917, been working from a position of weakness. In the immediate aftermath of the Bolshevik Revolution there was a genuine feeling on the part of the Bolsheviks that world communist revolution would spread. World revolution, as predicted by Marx, was to be encouraged by the Third International, known as the Comintern, an organisation set up by the Bolsheviks to coordinate communist groups throughout the world. Yet by 1924 it was clear that the prospects for world revolution were very slim indeed.

As the prospects for world revolution faded, the Soviet Union's foreign policy became much more concerned with ensuring the survival of the new regime. Surrounded by potentially hostile nations, to whom communism represented a threat to both their political and economic systems, the Soviet government began to adopt more traditional aims.

Stalin was preoccupied with safeguarding Soviet security. Russia had been invaded from the west three times during the twentieth century: by Germany during the First World War; by those helping the Whites during the Russian Civil War; and by Germany again during the Second World War. Each time Soviet losses were substantial but the sacrifice required during the Second World War was unprecedented. Over 20 million Soviet citizens were killed during the war, on top of the vast economic losses incurred during the fighting. To Stalin the need to ensure such a devastating war was not again inflicted upon the Soviet Union was undoubtedly a weighty and pressing concern. One tactic which the Soviet Union was in a position to use in 1945 was to establish a buffer zone of Soviet-influenced states in eastern Europe, which would act as a barrier against further invasion of the Soviet Union from the west. This Soviet obsession with security was difficult for the US government to understand. To the US government, the USSR was more interested in spreading communism. While it would be understandable for a communist state to want to spread its own ideology when the opportunity presented itself, this does not seem to have been Stalin's prime concern. In fact Stalin himself raised doubts about the suitability of applying communism to some of the

KEY PERSON

Joseph Stalin (1879–1953) emerged as leader of the USSR after the death of Lenin in 1924. He was able to introduce harsh policies of industrialisation in the 1930s which turned the USSR into a world power. Stalin's use of terror against opponents within the USSR made western leaders critical of his government. His status in the Soviet Union was enhanced by his leadership against Germany in the Second World War. Deeply distrustful of the intentions of the West towards the Soviet Union he was determined to safeguard the country against foreign attack. After the Second World War he wanted to use eastern Europe as a buffer zone against future attack. To secure Soviet safety against attack Stalin believed that it was essential to have pro-soviet governments in eastern Europe. Stalin's leadership of the USSR was unchallenged until his death in 1953.

KEY PEOPLE

Franklin D. Roosevelt (1882–1945) President of the USA from 1933 until his death in April 1945. He was a member of the Democratic Party and liberal in attitude. Roosevelt was struck down by polio in 1921 and was thereafter confined to a wheelchair. A man of energy, enthusiasm and optimism, he was prepared to negotiate directly with Stalin during the Second World War. He was optimistic that this arrangement could continue after the war, a view not shared by his successor Truman.

George Kennan (b.1904) Deputy Chief of Mission in the US Embassy in Moscow in 1946. Kennan's analysis of Soviet foreign policy was given in the *Long Telegram* of 1946. He saw the USSR as aggressive and suspicious, and recommended firm action by the USA against what he viewed as Soviet expansion in eastern Europe. The *Long Telegram* was highly influential on Truman's foreign policy and led to the policy of containment. Kennan later returned to the Soviet Union as US Ambassador 1952–3.

states of eastern Europe, including East Germany. As before the war, Stalin saw survival as more important than spreading revolution.

US attitudes in 1945

When the USA joined the Second World War in 1941 President **Roosevelt** issued a statement which highlighted Four Freedoms that the USA was fighting for. The Four Freedoms were: Freedom from Want, Freedom of Speech, Freedom of Religious Belief and Freedom from Fear. These were to form the basis of US war aims against Nazi Germany. As the war drew to a close these freedoms could also be applied to the aims of the USA in the post-war world. Just as they were criticisms of Nazism in Germany, they could equally be used to criticise communism in the USSR. Although US hostility towards the Soviet Union hardened at the end of the war, Roosevelt was realistic enough to recognise that the USA had to seek some sort of working relationship with the USSR. Unless Americans were ready to commit substantial resources to Europe and were prepared to go to war to prevent Soviet expansion, an accommodation with Stalin was necessary. With the Soviet Red Army stationed in most of eastern Europe and in the atmosphere of war-weariness which enveloped the USA in 1945, Roosevelt saw negotiation and compromise as the most effective methods of safeguarding western interests. Roosevelt's personal relationship with Stalin may well have seen this approach succeed but Roosevelt was not a well man. When he died in April 1945 Roosevelt was replaced as President by Harry S. Truman. As Vice-President, Truman had been kept out of foreign affairs and as a result he found himself suddenly catapulted into a position he was not prepared for. This gave Truman a sense of weakness, which was increased by the growing pressure exerted within the USA by anti-communist groups. The result of Truman trying to assert his authority was the adoption of a more openly hostile attitude towards the Soviet Union.

Truman's hard-line approach to the Soviet Union found its justification in George Kennan's *Long Telegram* of February 1946 (see page 236). **George Kennan** was the USA's Deputy Chief of Mission at the US Embassy in

Moscow. His *Long Telegram* provided an analysis of Soviet foreign policy which emphasised the role of communist ideology. He saw the Soviet leadership as suspicious and aggressive; insecurities that stemmed from their view of the outside world. Given this outlook, there could be no compromise with the USSR. The *Long Telegram* formed the firm basis behind the belief that only a hard-line approach towards Stalin and the Soviet Union would work in containing communism and therefore safeguarding the USA's interests. From this point the US government dropped the prospect of compromise in favour of a policy of **containment**.

KEY TERM

Containment The US policy of actively seeking to prevent the spread of communism. It was heavily promoted by George Kennan's *Long Telegram* and became the basis of US foreign policy under Truman.

There were other factors that pushed Truman into dealing firmly with the Soviet Union. His hard-line approach, which was to become known as the 'Iron Fist', was a reaction against the policy of appeasement that had been pursued by the British against Nazi Germany. Appeasement had involved negotiation with Hitler and compromise when his demands seemed reasonable. Yet appeasement seemed to encourage Hitler to ask for more concessions and the outbreak of war in 1939 was seen as evidence of the ultimate failure of appeasement. Truman believed, like many other politicians in 1945, that the same mistake should not be made again when dealing with an aggressive state.

US industry was also anxious about the threat of communism in 1945. The consumer-based US economy was concerned to see a revival in Europe to ensure a free market for US goods. Fears of an economic recession made US industrialists keen to protect this potential market from being closed off by the spread of communism. One sector of the US economy that was particularly threatened by the end of the Second World War was that which had been geared towards war production. The development of the Cold War kept international tension high and continued the demand for weaponry. This attitude was shared by US armed forces. It is, perhaps, no coincidence that the navy, which was most threatened by post-war demobilisation, was the most vocal in raising fears regarding the Soviet Union.

Harry S. Truman, US President 1945–52.

US hostility towards the USSR was inflated by a failure to understand the Soviet obsession with security. US security had not been threatened directly during the Second World War and, geographically isolated from enemies, the amount of fighting on US soil had been negligible. There was no comparison with the extreme suffering and hardship endured by the Soviet Union. The failure of the US government to comprehend the Soviet demand for security from further attack led them to interpret every action as part of the USSR's desire to dominate Europe and spread world communism. This misinterpretation added to the hostility that developed during the Cold War.

The actions of the Soviet Union in tightening its hold over eastern Europe made the US government suspicious of its real intentions.

Why was the USA so hostile to communism after 1945?

- The USSR was seen as representing a political system that was a direct threat to the freedoms of western capitalism.
- Truman had become President when Roosevelt died and was, by his own admission, an amateur in foreign affairs. He needed to assert his authority by adopting a hard-line approach to the Soviet Union.
- The *Long Telegram* saw the USSR as aggressive and expansionist. It was a view that greatly influenced the US government.
- A hard-line approach was needed because appeasement of aggressive leaders was seen to have failed against Hitler in the 1930s.
- US industry wanted to protect its markets in Europe, which were threatened by the spread of communism.
- The US military and industrial concerns based on military production wanted to protect their own position. They highlighted the dangers of Soviet expansion in order to put pressure on the US government to keep arms levels high.
- The US government failed to understand the Soviet Union's obsession with security against attack.

British attitudes in 1945

The attitudes of the British government in 1945 were more hostile to the Soviet Union and more suspicious of its intentions than those of the US government. The end of the Second World War saw Britain economically bankrupt. In terms of commitments, responsibilities and experience, Britain was still a great power but one that lacked the resources to sustain this role. Britain was now very much a junior partner to the USA and, despite public declarations to the contrary, the British government was aware of its weakness. Without US support there was little the countries of western Europe could do to stem any Soviet advance. Churchill feared the Americans, tired of fighting, would return to a policy of isolationism, as they had after the First World War. He realised that even with US support there was little the West could do to prevent Stalin doing as he wished in eastern Europe. This explains why Churchill hoped that a personal agreement with Stalin might limit his actions. The two leaders met in Moscow in 1944 and agreed to recognise spheres of influence in Europe: the Soviet Union would have a 90 per cent influence in Romania and 75 per cent in Bulgaria, while Britain would have 90 per cent influence in Greece; they would go 50:50 in Hungary and Yugoslavia. Churchill was fearful of Soviet expansion and, alongside this attempt to limit Stalin by personal agreement, he tried to secure US promises of a commitment to Europe in the post-war world.

In July 1945 Churchill was ousted as Prime Minister of Britain after a general election that saw a landslide victory for the Labour Party. The foreign policy of the new government, headed by **Clement Attlee**, differed very little in terms of how the Soviet Union was viewed. Attlee's impression of Stalin was 'No principles, any methods, but no flowery language'. Ernest Bevin, the foreign secretary, never showed the slightest sympathy with communism, at home or abroad. Bevin made several attempts to get the USA to make a greater commitment to Europe by pointing to the danger of the Soviet threat to Iran as well as to eastern Europe. By 1946 the foreign policies of Britain and the USA were more in step with each other over the need to stand firm against the threat from the Soviet Union.

KEY PERSON

Clement Attlee (1883–1967) As leader of the Labour Party, he was Prime Minister of Britain between 1945 and 1951. He had been Deputy Prime Minister to Churchill in the wartime coalition government, when he was concerned with domestic policies. Attlee did not share any sympathies with communism or the Soviet Union. He replaced Churchill as Prime Minister during the Potsdam Conference, after the 1945 election. Like Churchill, he distrusted Stalin's motives and worked to secure a firmer commitment from the USA to help western Europe fight the spread of communism.

In 1945 the attitudes of the three main powers were hardening as they started to focus on post-war issues. When the two sides tried to reach agreement on the details of the post-war settlement, hostility, coupled with misunderstanding and distrust, quickly led to a breakdown in relations.

HOW DID THE COLD WAR DEVELOP IN EUROPE BETWEEN 1945 AND 1949?

The alliance of the Big Three lost its reason for being as soon as Nazi Germany was defeated in 1945. The tensions and differences that had been kept below the surface came quickly to the fore. By 1947 there was a deep rift between East and West, which led to the first major crisis of the Cold War in June 1948: the **Berlin Blockade**. Within the space of four years the division between East and West became so deep that it proved difficult and, in the short term, impossible to heal.

KEY TERM

Berlin Blockade, 1948–9
The USSR cut off all road, rail and canal links to West Berlin in an attempt to force the West to leave the city, which was within the Soviet-controlled zone of Germany. The West was able to beat the blockade by flying supplies into the city until restrictions were lifted in 1949.

The Yalta and Potsdam Conferences, 1945

In August 1941 Britain and the USA had agreed to the Atlantic Charter, a general statement of liberal principles on which the post-war international settlement was to be based. These principles included economic collaboration, a general security system and the drawing of national boundaries with regard to the wishes of the local population. These were broad principles that the Soviet Union had little trouble in supporting. But Stalin's attitude to fine principles was one of ambivalence:'A declaration I regard as algebra, but an agreement as practical arithmetic. I do not wish to decry algebra, but I prefer arithmetic.' Differences in the interpretation of general principles became obvious when, at the Yalta Conference of February 1945, the leaders got down to the business of refining details.

Yalta, February 1945. Stalin was on home soil when he met with Churchill and Roosevelt at Yalta in the Soviet Union. The personal relationship between the three leaders was still sound enough to result in some significant agreements:

- agreement on the establishment of the United Nations;

- the division of Germany, Berlin and Austria into temporary zones of occupation;
- the principle of free elections in eastern Europe.
- the Soviet Union also agreed to join the war against Japan, which was still going on, in return for receiving some of Japan's islands in the Far East.

The main source of disagreement was over Poland. When the Soviet Red Army liberated Poland from Germany, a communist government was set up, based at Lublin. This was despite the fact that there was a government in exile in London, which was ready to return to Poland as soon as it was safe to do so. At Yalta, Stalin agreed to allow members of the London-based government into the new Lublin administration. The West hoped that Stalin's promise to uphold free elections would reduce the influence of the communists in the government. In return for this concession the USA and Britain would allow the Soviet Union to keep areas of Poland gained in 1939 at the start of the Second World War.

Despite the agreements reached at the Yalta Conference, relations between East and West were to deteriorate quickly thereafter. When Roosevelt died in April 1945 his enemies accused him of being soft on communism. Soviet actions in eastern Europe after the conference seemed to indicate that Stalin's word could not be trusted. Truman, the new US President, was determined not to make the same mistake. Less than a fortnight after taking over the presidency Truman told **Molotov**, the Soviet Foreign Minister who was visiting the USA, that the Soviet Union must keep to the agreements reached at Yalta. Truman is said to have used 'the language of a Missouri mule driver' and Molotov complained that he had never been spoken to in such a manner before. Truman's reply was that if the Soviet Union carried out its commitments he would 'not get talked to like that' again.

Potsdam, July 1945. When the former wartime allies met later at Potsdam in July 1945 attitudes had hardened still further. The conference marked a severe cooling of relations. Stalin now faced Truman, who was still struggling to come to grips with the demands of the presidency, and

KEY PERSON

Vyacheslav Molotov (1890–1986) Soviet Foreign Minister from 1939 to 1949. He was a leading supporter of Stalin and was rewarded with the post of Foreign Minister. A hard-liner able to argue forcibly with western foreign ministers, he lived up to his name which meant 'hammer'. Inflexible and obstinate, he was, however, a skilful politician who infuriated those in the West who had to deal with him. He was not known as having a sense of humour.

Churchill, who was ousted as British Prime Minister by a general election and replaced by Attlee while the conference was taking place. Faced with two relative newcomers to foreign affairs, Stalin had a clear advantage.

- Truman and the British were annoyed with the actions the Soviet Union was taking in eastern Europe. Stalin had been allowed to incorporate some Polish territory into the Soviet Union and preceded to transport Poles who now found themselves in the USSR, behind the Polish border.
- Although the USA and Britain finally agreed to move the western frontier of Poland to the Oder-Western Neisse line, 5 million Germans were expelled from Poland and forcibly moved west into Germany.
- Throughout eastern Europe communist groups were being positioned in important government roles.

These actions worried Truman in particular and he determined not to inform Stalin of the decision to drop the first atomic bomb on Japan, an event that happened only four days from the end of the conference.

KEY EVENT

Hiroshima, 6 August 1945 The USA dropped an atomic bomb on Hiroshima, Japan, in order to bring the war in the Far East to an end. It was the first time an atomic bomb had been used in wartime. It devastated two-thirds of the city and killed over 70,000 people. A second bomb was dropped on Nagasaki three days later. The Japanese surrendered soon afterwards.

The use of the atomic bomb. The bombing of **Hiroshima** was the result of calculations made by the Americans in terms of how to bring the war against Japan to an end with the minimum of losses to US lives. Yet Truman was fully aware that the atomic bomb could be a powerful weapon by which pressure could be exerted on the Soviet Union. The enormous destructive damage caused by the bomb on Hiroshima shocked the world. Truman called it 'the greatest thing in history'. It was hoped that Stalin would take notice and become more amenable in Europe. Stalin saw the failure of Truman to at least inform him of the bomb as a deep insult and, far from making Stalin more amenable, it increased his suspicions and distrust of US motives. Stalin was, after all, a wartime ally of the USA and, it could be argued, had a right to be informed. When a second atomic bomb was dropped on the Japanese city of Nagasaki on 9 August, the USA was able to bring about the surrender of Japan without the need for Soviet assistance. Stalin was therefore denied a part in the occupation of Japan.

Events were to prove that the atom bomb had little impact on Stalin's policies. While encouraging the Soviet Union to develop its own atomic bomb as soon as possible, he regarded it as a weapon of bluff which was unlikely to be used in Europe because of its huge destructive power. Thus, the threat of the USA using its atomic bombs was to harden Stalin's attitude without softening his policies.

Russian influence in eastern Europe 1945–7

At the end of the Second World War the Soviet Red Army was stationed in large parts of eastern Europe. Given the political and military vacuum that existed after the defeat of Nazi Germany, the Red Army was well placed to exert influence in eastern Europe. Its presence was a source of much anxiety on the part of the West who realised that it provided Stalin with a powerful weapon with which he could stamp his policies on the region. In actual fact, the Soviet Union was to be demobilised rapidly from an army of over 11 million in May 1945 to about 2 million in early 1948. Sixty Red Army divisions remained in eastern Europe to fulfil a policing role. Although not aimed against the West, these divisions played an important role in imposing communist regimes on the region. Pro-communist governments were set up in Poland, Hungary, Romania, Bulgaria and Albania. The events that led to this situation differed slightly in each country but the usual pattern was one of pressure applied by the Soviet Union to allow communist politicians to hold key positions in **coalition governments** before elections were held. With posts such as that of interior minister, which was responsible for the police force and law and order, in communist hands, elections could then be manipulated to ensure communists controlled the levers of power. To strengthen communist parties, they were often encouraged by Stalin to merge with other, often bigger, socialist groups who found merger to be in reality a takeover. By the end of 1947 every state in eastern Europe was controlled by a communist government, apart from Czechoslovakia.

KEY TERM

Coalition government
A government made up of the representatives of more than one political party. They were often set up in the countries of eastern Europe immediately after the Second World War in the interests of national unity but provided a useful foothold for the communists to gain control.

Stalin had gained control over what he considered to be a legitimate sphere of influence for the Soviet Union. To have governments unfriendly to the USSR on its borders was seen as unacceptable because it was unlikely to guarantee security against future attack. The USA viewed this development differently. Stalin had failed to keep his promise to hold free elections in eastern Europe. The US government was suspicious of Stalin's intentions and was worried that there was a threat of Soviet expansion across Europe. These fears were also raised by Churchill.

KEY TERMS

Iron Curtain The name given to the figurative line that divided the communist East from the capitalist West in Europe. The term was made popular by Winston Churchill in 1946 when it was used in a speech at Fulton, Missouri.

Iron Fist A term used by Truman to describe a tougher approach to the USSR. It was a reaction to the approach adopted by Roosevelt, his predecessor, which was seen by Truman as too soft on communism.

Churchill's Iron Curtain Speech, March 1946

The call for firmer action by the West against the threat of communism was made by Churchill, the ex-Prime Minister of Britain. In a speech delivered at Fulton, Missouri, in the USA, Churchill declared that 'From Stettin in the Baltic to Trieste in the Adriatic an **Iron Curtain** has descended across the continent.' In order to meet this Soviet expansion, Churchill called for an alliance between Britain and the USA. Churchill gave the speech as a private individual; Attlee was not informed of its content beforehand but did not disagree with its message and later thanked Churchill. Truman had read the speech before it was delivered and was present when it was given. Public opinion in the USA was not favourable to the call for a wartime alliance but Churchill had stated what Truman and his advisers privately

Extract from Churchill's Iron Curtain speech, 1946

An iron curtain has descended across the continent. Behind that line lie all the capitals of the ancient states of Central and Eastern Europe. All these famous cities, and the populations around them, lie in the Soviet sphere, and all are subject in one form or another, not only to Soviet influence, but to a very high and increasing measure of control from Moscow. The Russian-dominated Polish Government has been encouraged to make enormous and wrongful inroads upon Germany, and mass expulsions of millions of Germans on a scale grievous and undreamed of are now taking place. The Communist parties, which were very small in all these Eastern States of Europe, have been raised to leadership and power far beyond their numbers, and are seeking everywhere to obtain totalitarian control. Police governments are prevailing in nearly every case, and so far, except in Czechoslovakia, there is no true democracy.

thought and it fell into line with Truman's **Iron Fist** approach: 'Unless Russia is faced with an iron fist and strong language another war is in the making.'

In Moscow the speech received a hysterical response. Stalin saw it as deliberately provocative and accused Churchill of being a **warmonger**. Relations between East and West reached a new low.

KEY TERM

Warmonger Someone who wishes to provoke war. Stalin accused Churchill of this after his *Iron Curtain* speech.

The Truman Doctrine and the Marshall Plan, 1947

To the West, which was looking around constantly for further evidence of Soviet expansion, events in Greece in 1947 confirmed their worst fears. Since 1944 there had been a civil war in Greece between the monarchists and the communists. After the defeat of Nazi Germany the Greek royal government had been restored to power with the help of the British, despite resistance from the communists who were strong in the countryside. Stalin seems to have kept to his agreement with Churchill that Greece was an area of British influence and did nothing to directly help the Greek communists, although the communist governments of Yugoslavia and Albania did send aid. Nonetheless, the West became convinced that this was another sign of Soviet expansion. Firm action was needed and this was something the British were finding hard to sustain.

By 1947 the draining impact of the Second World War was being felt. The British government owed £3000 million in debts incurred during the war against Germany. The British economy was in a state of crisis, made worse by the severe winter weather of 1946–7. The British government was forced to admit that it could no longer sustain its overseas commitments. In February 1947 they warned the USA that they could not maintain troops in Greece. Faced with the prospect of a British withdrawal leading to a communist takeover in another country of key strategic importance, the US President issued the **Truman Doctrine**.

KEY TERM

Truman Doctrine A policy statement issued by the US President in 1947. It stated that the US would aid any country or government under attack by armed minorities. It was aimed at preventing the spread of communism. It was used to send aid and military advisers to Greece to help the monarchist government against the communists.

In March 1947 Truman issued a statement which declared that 'it must be the policy of the United States to support free peoples who are resisting subjugation by armed minorities or by outside pressures'. (See page 236.) The

KEY TERM

Marshall Plan A plan to provide US financial support to war-torn Europe. It was drawn up by George C. Marshall, the US Secretary of State, in 1947. All countries in Europe were eligible for Marshall aid but the conditions attached made it impossible for the communist states of eastern Europe to apply. Over $17 billion were provided to Europe and by 1952 western Europe's economy was experiencing sustained growth.

KEY PERSON

George C. Marshall (1880–1959) The US Secretary of State from 1947–9. Responsible for launching the Marshall aid programme of financial help for Europe. Later served as US Secretary of Defense.

Truman Doctrine, as it became known, was a response to the situation in Greece but it was clear to all that it was designed to have wider application. Truman saw a straightforward choice between two alternatives: communism and democracy. Wherever communist forces were attempting to overthrow a democratically elected government the USA would take action. In practice Truman was prepared to support any government providing it was anti-communist.

US aid and military advisers were sent to support the Greek government and the communists were defeated. To Stalin this was evidence of US imperialism, a view reinforced by the launching of the **Marshall Plan.**

The Marshall Plan. In the spring of 1947 **George Marshall**, the new US Secretary of State, travelled through western Europe and was shocked by the devastation and economic suffering he witnessed. He recognised that economic support and assistance were desperately needed and the result was the launching of the Marshall Plan. The plan committed large sums of US financial assistance to Europe. It was, according to Churchill, 'the most unselfish act in history'. While providing much-needed aid for economic recovery and reconstruction, the motives behind Marshall aid were more than merely humanitarian. There were concerns that unless the economies of Europe recovered there would be a danger of economic recession in the USA. Without financial assistance, Europe would not be able to act as a market for US goods. In addition to this economic motive there was also a political consideration: the Americans saw poverty as the ideal breeding ground for communism; a prosperous Europe was less likely to fall for its attractions.

In theory Marshall aid was available for any European country to apply for but in practice it went to western Europe only. The conditions attached to receiving the aid – to provide economic records and open up their economy to US capitalist interests – were such that it was impossible for communist states to do so without a fundamental change to their system. The Soviet Union viewed Marshall aid as nothing more than an attack on communism.

Molotov condemned it as foreign interference in the states of Europe and labelled the plan **dollar imperialism**. Under Soviet pressure, the countries of eastern Europe declined the offer of financial aid.

The USSR effectively declared war on the Marshall Plan by tightening their hold over eastern Europe through the setting up of **Cominform**, an organisation to coordinate communist parties and groups throughout Europe, and **Comecon**, an organisation that provided economic assistance to the countries of eastern Europe. Thus, the Truman Doctrine and Marshall aid resulted in a Soviet response that made the division of Europe more entrenched.

The Czechoslovakian Crisis, 1948

At the beginning of 1948 Czechoslovakia was the only remaining democratic country in eastern Europe. Elections were due in May during which the communists were expected to do badly. The failure of Czechoslovakia to receive Marshall aid was blamed on communists in the coalition government. Before the election was held the communists staged a **coup d'état**. The police force was taken over by the communists and purged of non-communist personnel. Representatives of political parties other than the communists were removed from government in February. The only remaining non-communist in the government, **Jan Masaryk**, suffered defenestration: he was thrown from a window, probably by members of the security police. President Beneš was forced to resign, to be replaced by the communist **Gottwald**. The Czech communists had taken over the country with little bloodshed and without direct help from the Soviet Union.

The Czechoslovakian Crisis was of important psychological significance for the West. In addition to increasing the fear of communist expansion it played on feelings of guilt, particularly in Britain, because nothing had been done to prevent Hitler taking Czechoslovakia during 1938–9. Ten years later there was again little the West could do to thwart the stamp of oppression on a country which might have provided a valuable bridge between East and West.

KEY TERMS

Imperialism Building an empire of dependent states.

Dollar imperialism A term used by Molotov to describe Marshall aid. He saw the financial aid as a mechanism by which the USA would gain control over Europe and exploit it for US economic interests.

Cominform An organisation controlled by the USSR, set up in 1947 to coordinate communist parties throughout Europe.

Comecon An organisation controlled by the USSR, set up in 1949 to coordinate the economies of communist countries.

'Coup d'état' A violent or illegal takeover of government.

KEY PEOPLE

Jan Masaryk (1886–1948) Served as Foreign Minister of Czechoslovakia from 1945–8. Opposed communism and died in suspicious circumstances during the communist coup of 1948.

Klement Gottwald (1896–1953) Communist leader of Czechoslovakia from 1948 until his death in 1953.

THE BERLIN BLOCKADE, 1948–9

The Cold War in Europe was to reach its first major crisis with the Berlin Blockade of 1948–9. Although disappointed with the increase in Soviet influence in countries such as Romania, Bulgaria and other parts of eastern Europe, the West could eventually 'forget' them; but Germany was different. Here the troops of both sides stood directly opposite each other: they could not avoid one another. The so-called 'German problem' would not go away because the arrangements agreed at the conferences at Yalta and Potsdam were temporary. At some point, the long-term future of Germany would have to be settled. The Berlin Blockade was one of the Soviet Union's most drastic attempts to influence this future.

Causes of the Berlin Blockade

At the Yalta and Potsdam conferences in 1945 it had been agreed to divide Germany and its capital city Berlin each into four zones to be administered on a temporary basis by the wartime allies (see map below) The western zones, run by Britain, the USA and France, benefited from an influx of Marshall aid. The eastern zone, run by the USSR, was plundered for resources, taken as reparations for war damage caused during the Second World War. Denied access to Marshall funds, living conditions in East Germany remained low and were slow to recover. By 1948 the difference in living standards between West and East

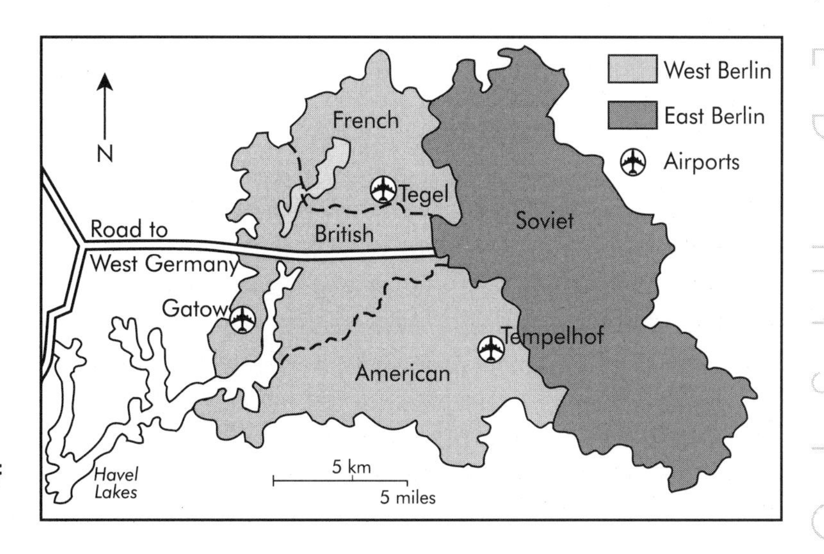

Divided Berlin: zones of occupation.

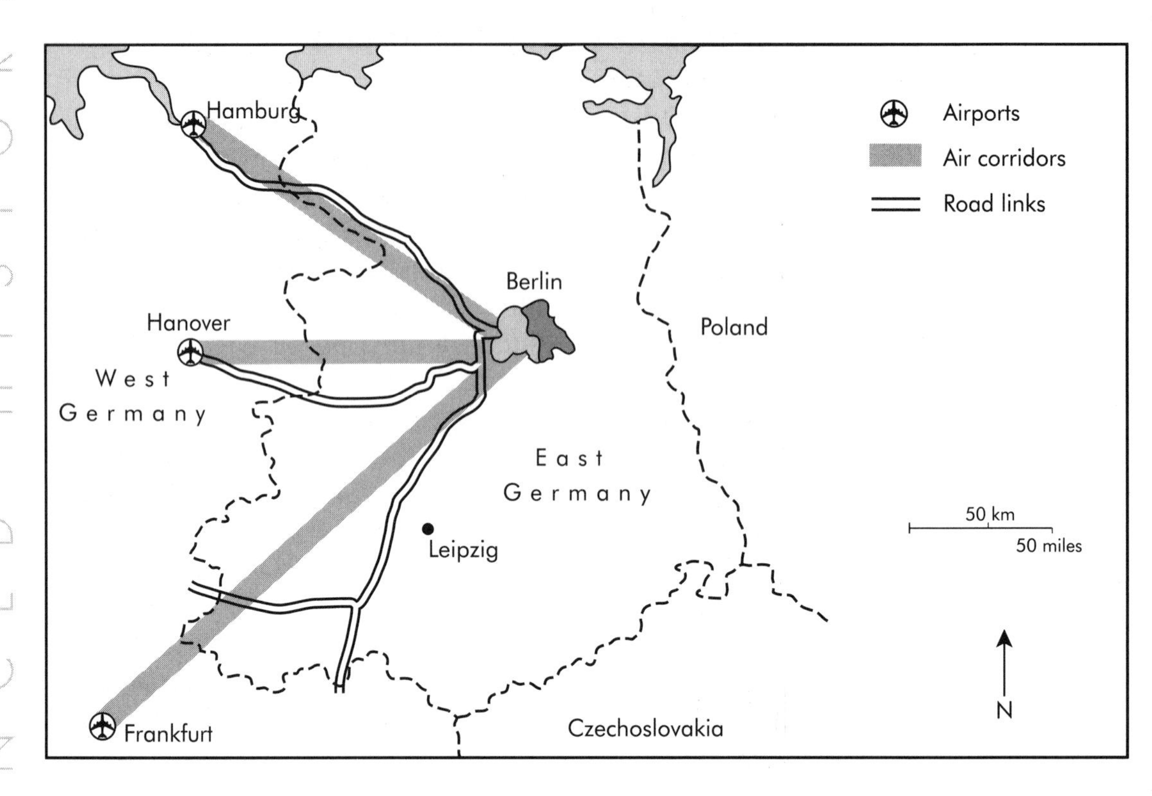

Links between West Berlin and West Germany.

Germany had become embarrassingly obvious. It was in Berlin that this difference was brought into sharp focus. West Berlin had become an island of prosperous capitalism in a sea of communism. As a symbol of this increasing prosperity, the western powers decided to introduce a new currency in their zones. The new Deutsche Mark would, it was hoped, provide economic stability and aid recovery. For Stalin this was the last straw.

The issue of Germany was to highlight the different attitudes of the superpowers to the post-war world. Talks in Moscow and London in 1947 between the two sides over the future of Germany broke down as both sides put obstacles in the way of an agreement. The USA did not fear a revived Germany due to its geographical position; in fact it saw Germany's economic revival as essential to US financial interests. In contrast, the Soviet Union had much to fear from a German revival that might lead to a repetition of the suffering caused during the two world wars. Thus, when the new currency was introduced in

West Berlin in June 1948, Stalin took action. All road, rail and canal links with West Berlin were severed. The blockade of the city was interpreted by the US government as the first stage of an attack on West Germany. This is unlikely. Stalin may have wished to starve the West out of Berlin, but he probably wanted to prevent the emergence of a separate West German state under US influence.

KEY EVENT

Berlin airlift, 1948–9 The actions of the West in response to the Berlin Blockade. All supplies were flown into West Berlin to prevent the population starving. It was a massive feat of organisation during which 2 million tons of supplies were airlifted into the city.

Results of the blockade

- **Berlin airlift.** The West responded to the blockade by organising an airlift of supplies into Berlin. All food and fuel supplies for over 2 million Berliners were flown into the city. It was an expensive operation executed with impressive organisational skill. Despite constant shortages, the city was able to survive. By May 1949 Stalin was forced to concede defeat and he lifted the blockade. The actions of the West had been successful and it was an important boost to their morale after the events in Czechoslovakia.

- **Creation of NATO.** The Berlin Crisis had illustrated the need for a more coordinated approach by the West in order to prepare for the possibility of Soviet aggression. In April 1949 the USA opened talks with Canada and the countries of western Europe with the aim of committing itself to a military alliance. The result was the setting up of the North Atlantic Treaty Organisation (**NATO**). This was an enlargement of the Brussels Treaty of 1948, which had been signed by Britain, France, Belgium, the Netherlands and Luxembourg to establish military cooperation in the event of war. The significance of NATO was that it involved the USA in a military alliance during peacetime and, therefore, made it clear to the Soviet Union that there would be no return to **isolationism**. The guiding principle of NATO was that an attack on one of its members would be seen as an attack on all. A NATO command was set up to coordinate the defence of its members. Thus, NATO was a defensive organisation to protect the West and its interests. Stalin viewed the creation of NATO as a deliberately provocative action but he was able to enhance the capability of the Soviet Union by breaking

KEY TERMS

NATO The North Atlantic Treaty Organisation, a military alliance of the USA, Canada and most of western Europe. Set up in 1949, it was an organisation to defend the West during the Cold War.

Isolationism A policy of keeping out of conflicts in foreign affairs and not getting involved in military alliances. After the First World War the USA had adopted a policy of isolationism towards Europe. The British feared the USA would return to isolationism after the Second World War.

the US nuclear monopoly. The Soviet Union exploded its first atomic bomb in August 1949, earlier than the West had expected. Despite this increase in Soviet power, the Berlin Crisis and the formation of NATO had taken any initiative in Cold War relations away from the USSR.

- **Creation of FDR and GDR.** Another significant result of the Berlin Crisis was the end to any hope of an agreement between East and West over Germany. The temporary division of the country, laid down at Yalta and Potsdam, was now to become a more permanent feature. In August 1949 the three western zones of Germany joined together to become the Federal Republic of Germany (commonly known as West Germany). In response, the Soviet zone became the German Democratic Republic (East Germany) in October. As capitalism flourished in West Germany, communism was imposed upon East Germany. It was a division that was to last for forty years.

The Berlin Crisis of 1948–9 marked the first major flashpoint of the Cold War. Relations between the USA and the USSR, former allies against Nazi Germany, reached such a low position of distrust and suspicion that it became difficult to have any meaningful dialogue, let alone agreement. Conflict and tension were to remain constant features of East–West relations for another forty years with important consequences for Europe and the rest of the world.

SUMMARY: HOW DID THE USA ATTEMPT TO CONTAIN COMMUNISM IN EUROPE 1945–9?

- **By agreement** – e.g. at the Yalta and Potsdam conferences. Roosevelt favoured this method. Truman felt that Stalin would not keep to any agreements and preferred other methods.
- **By the deterrent of nuclear weapons.** Between 1945 and 1949 the USA was the only country to possess the atomic bomb.

- **By applying the Truman Doctrine** – i.e. by sending military aid and advisers to those governments facing the threat of communism. This method was used in Greece.
- **By economic measures under the Marshall Plan.** Economic recovery would restore prosperity to Europe and make the spread of communism less likely.
- **By propaganda.** Communist actions in Czechoslovakia and elsewhere in Europe were condemned by the West. It was hoped that this would shame them into limiting the spread of communism.
- **By non-cooperation with the USSR.** The USA put obstacles in the way of reaching agreements over the future of Germany.
- **By firm action.** This was what Truman termed the Iron Fist approach. The West's refusal to give in during the Berlin Blockade by organising the airlift was evidence of this in action.
- **By military alliance.** The involvement of the USA in the formation of NATO showed that the USA were not going to return to isolationism.

SUMMARY QUESTIONS

1 Why did the USA develop the policy of containment?

2 Explain how the attitudes of the USA and the USSR in 1945 helped cause the Cold War.

3 Explain the role of economic rivalry in the growing tension between the USA and the USSR during the period 1945–9.

4 By what methods, and with what success, did the USA attempt to contain communism in Europe between 1945 and 1949?

CHAPTER 3

The Soviet orbit: eastern Europe 1945–80

Two key factors were responsible for the incorporation of eastern Europe into the sphere of Soviet control. The first was the presence of the Red Army in eastern Europe at the end of the Second World War; the second was Stalin's concern for Soviet security. In order to safeguard the Soviet Union against future attack, Stalin would not contemplate governments in eastern Europe that were unfriendly towards the USSR. Although Stalin was willing to accept coalition governments in the years immediately after the Second World War, the tension generated by the Cold War resulted in the trend towards the imposition of communist governments on the countries of eastern Europe. Thus developments in this region of Europe were greatly influenced by the international situation between the superpowers.

Soviet control over eastern Europe was exercised through a range of different yet interrelated methods, helped by a degree of support for communist parties that was not insignificant in some countries. Although it is tempting to see Soviet control over eastern Europe as complete, there were challenges to the communist regimes in the region, most notably in Hungary (1956) and Czechoslovakia (1968). These challenges were dealt with by the direct use of Soviet intervention. Until the 1980s the Soviet bloc in eastern Europe looked secure and the Iron Curtain which divided Europe was seemingly a permanent feature.

BY WHAT METHODS DID THE SOVIET UNION IMPOSE CONTROL OVER EASTERN EUROPE?

The establishment of communist regimes across eastern Europe was aided by a substantial degree of sympathy with, if not support for, the policies put forward by communist groups. Communist parties called for radical change from the situation that had existed before the Second World War. This was in tune with the mood of popular opinion; there was little desire to restore the old regimes. The desperate need for reconstruction after the devastation of the war fitted in with the communists' message of building a new society. Communists advocated land reform, a policy particularly popular with the peasants. The communists had often played a leading role in resisting the German occupation during the war and had gained respect in doing so. In Yugoslavia the local communist resistance under Tito had helped liberate the country before the arrival of the Red Army. The Bulgarian Kostov had become a crippled hunchback after leaping from a prison window to escape his torturers. Despite these factors, which had resulted in support for communist groups in eastern Europe, it would be misleading to exaggerate the level of support. In 1945 the communists were not the only political group calling for radical change. In the countryside, peasant parties were popular and posed a significant threat to the communists' ability to do well in elections. This was a danger that Stalin recognised, and communist parties were forced to adopt political measures in order to gain a hold over the governments of the region.

Immediately after the Second World War, communist groups in eastern Europe were encouraged by the Soviet Union to form agreements and coalitions with other left-wing parties, such as socialists and peasant groups. Stalin thought this would be more acceptable to the West than communist one-party states. When relations with the West deteriorated in 1947 the communist hold over the governments of eastern Europe was tightened.

KEY TERM

Salami tactics The term, given by the Hungarian communist Rakosi, to describe the political tactics of communist parties in eastern Europe after the Second World War. It involved forming coalitions with other left-wing groups and then accusing them of being anti-Soviet or pro-fascist in order to discredit them. The result was to make the communists strong enough to take over government by themselves. These tactics were particularly effective in Hungary.

Hungary

In Hungary, the communists worked with the peasant Smallholders' Party. Then, in what was to become a common pattern, the communists applied what Matyas Rakosi, the Hungarian communist leader, termed **salami tactics**. These involved provoking splits and divisions among coalition partners who were then accused of being anti-Soviet, pro-fascist or other such trumped-up charges. Purges followed. In Hungary in 1947 the communists accused the leadership of the Smallholders' Party of offences against the Red Army and dissolved their party. By the end of the year all other political parties in Hungary had been abolished.

Bulgaria

In Bulgaria the communists formed a coalition with the Peasants' Party. In 1947, Nicolai Petkov, the leader of the peasant-based Agrarian Party was hanged for allegedly plotting a coup.

Poland

In October 1947, those ex-members of the Polish government in London who had been allowed into the new coalition government by Stalin at Yalta were removed from office. The communists had secured their grip on the government and dissolved other political parties.

Romania

Rigged elections in 1946 helped the communists secure their hold on power. In 1947 the Peasant Party was dissolved and King Michael was forced to abdicate.

East Germany

In the eastern zone of Germany the communists had been instructed by Stalin to merge with the much bigger Socialist Party to form the Socialist Unity Party (SED). The communists then purged members of the former Socialist Party from the SED. The communists had succeeded in taking over a much larger organisation and were in a position to rule East Germany for forty years.

Czechoslovakia

It was only in Czechoslovakia that the process took a little longer and required a coup to remove non-communist elements from the government in 1948. Thus, by 1950 all of the countries of eastern Europe were either one-party states or were countries where the Communist Party dominated over small local parties, whose share of seats in parliament was pre-determined before elections.

By 1948, the governments of eastern Europe were in the hands of communist parties that had strong links with the Soviet Union. The credentials of many of the leaders of eastern Europe illustrated these links. Boleslaw Bierut, President of Poland from 1945 to 1952, had spent the years 1938–43 in Moscow. Walter Ulbricht, the East German leader, spent several years in the USSR. They remained hard-line Stalinists.

Cominform

Soviet control over the direction of the east European regimes was tightened by the setting up of Cominform in 1947. The Communist Information Bureau (Cominform) was an organisation set up by the USSR to coordinate communist parties throughout Europe. It was the Soviet response to the Truman Doctrine and attempted to provide unity among the socialist bloc. Through Cominform the USSR could influence the direction of policy within the individual states of eastern Europe.

- The countries of eastern Europe were expected to fall into line behind Soviet foreign policy.
- It encouraged the adoption of the Soviet model of economic development, such as collectivisation in agriculture and nationalisation of industry, and rejected the idea that there could be different 'roads to socialism' depending on local conditions.

These measures were not accepted by all communists in eastern Europe and led to a purge of those who disagreed with Moscow. The main victims included Gomułka in Poland and Kádár in Hungary. Yugoslavia posed a particular problem. Its leader, Tito was always more independent, the result of the country not being reliant on the Red Army for liberation from Nazi occupation. Tito's unwillingness to slavishly follow the Soviet line led to the expulsion of Yugoslavia from Cominform in 1948. To prevent a reoccurrence of this questioning of Soviet dominance, a further wave of purges of Communist Party members took place throughout eastern Europe to remove those suspected of 'Titoism'.

Comecon

The Soviet response to Marshall aid was the setting up of Comecon, another instrument of Soviet control over eastern Europe. Comecon, the Council for Mutual

Economic Assistance, was founded in 1949. It was supposed to give assistance to the socialist economies of eastern Europe but it tended to work to the advantage of the USSR, which gained access to the economic resources of the region. It provided support for collectivisation in agriculture and the development of heavy industry on Stalinist lines but, in its aim of providing financial assistance, it achieved little in its early years. Later, in the 1950s, the USSR used Comecon to try to encourage economic specialisation within the Soviet bloc. Czechoslovakia and East Germany would concentrate on heavy industry, while Romania, Hungary and Bulgaria would focus on the production of food and raw materials. The USSR would provide the technology needed for economic development. This policy caused resentment in Romania where it was seen as unwarranted interference.

The presence of the Red Army

The imposition of communism on eastern Europe was seen in the West as the result of pressure exerted by the presence of the Red Army. This view is misleading. The Red Army was demilitarised relatively quickly after 1945 and, with the exception of Romania, the communist takeover of eastern Europe was achieved without direct involvement from Soviet troops and personnel. In Czechoslovakia in 1948 there were only 500 Soviet troops. Yet if the actual presence of the Red Army was limited, the fear that local communists might call them in to help secure their position was undoubtedly real. Military intervention by Soviet forces was used in Hungary in 1956 and Czechoslovakia in 1968 when the unity of the socialist bloc was threatened. Soviet military intervention in the socialist bloc was justified in 1968 by the **Brezhnev Doctrine**: the USSR reserved the right to intervene in the affairs of another socialist country if the interests of world socialism were endangered.

The Warsaw Pact

Soviet control over eastern Europe was coordinated in a military sense through the organisation of the **Warsaw Pact.** The Pact was the eastern bloc's reply to the admittance of West Germany into NATO. Formed in 1955, it was an agreement to coordinate the defence of the

KEY TERMS

Brezhnev Doctrine A policy statement issued by the Soviet leader, Brezhnev, after the USSR had invaded Czechoslovakia in 1968 to reverse the reforms of Nagy's government. It stated that the USSR believed it had the right to intervene in the domestic affairs of eastern Europe when the interests of world socialism were threatened. It was an attempt by the USSR to justify its actions in Czechoslovakia.

Warsaw Pact A military alliance of the communist states of eastern Europe. Set up in 1955, its aim was to coordinate the defence of the socialist bloc. In reality the organisation was dominated by the USSR.

socialist bloc. An attack on one of its members would be deemed an attack on socialism and all other members would come to their aid. In practice, the Pact strengthened the position of the Soviet Union in eastern Europe by making its members reliant on Soviet forces for protection against both external and internal threats. As a result Soviet troops were stationed across eastern Europe although, with the exception of East Germany, not in large numbers. The organisation of the Pact was based in Moscow under a Soviet Supreme Commander. The dominant role of the Soviet forces was also highlighted by the fact that, although by the end of the 1950s the eastern bloc countries possessed nuclear warheads, it seems that it was only on Soviet authority that they could be used. It was troops from several Warsaw Pact countries that invaded Czechoslovakia in 1968 to deal with the 'threat to socialism'. The military hardware, tanks and guns, used by member states were supplied by the USSR. Meetings of the leaders of Warsaw Pact countries were useful demonstrations of socialist unity, but tensions existed between member states. Romania resented Soviet interference and usually took no role in military manoeuvres organised by the Pact. Albania left the organisation in 1968.

Soviet domination over eastern Europe was secured by a range of strategies: political, economic and military. Yet Soviet control was as much a product of circumstances as it was of direct Soviet intervention. The unique situation that eastern Europe found itself in after the Second World War gave local communist groups a distinct advantage. It was obvious that change was needed and the communists were able to align themselves with this popular mood. Events after 1947 showed that the future of the region was tied to developments in international relations. Soviet domination over eastern Europe was an inescapable result of Cold War tensions between the USSR, desperate to secure a buffer zone against attack, and the West.

SUMMARY: WHAT METHODS DID THE USSR USE TO GAIN CONTROL OVER EASTERN EUROPE?

Political:
- Encouraged the communist takeover of governments
- Close links with political leaders, many of whom had been trained in the USSR
- Political pressure exerted by Soviet leaders – e.g. during the Hungarian Crisis, 1956
- Cominform

Economic:
- Comecon

Military:
- Presence of Red Army troops
- Fear of Soviet military intervention
- Military intervention – e.g. Hungary, 1956 and Czechoslovakia, 1968
- The Warsaw Pact
- The Brezhnev Doctrine

WHAT CHALLENGES WERE THERE TO SOVIET DOMINANCE IN EASTERN EUROPE BETWEEN 1950 AND 1980?

Moscow saw the Soviet hold over eastern Europe as an essential feature in the security of the USSR. Whenever this security was threatened the Soviet Union took action. After the death of Stalin in 1953, developments in the USSR under Khrushchev encouraged some communist groups in eastern Europe to push for change. During the period from 1953 to 1980 events showed that the Soviet Union was not prepared to allow any changes that threatened its hold over the region.

1953

The death of Stalin in 1953 led to the emergence of **Nikita Khrushchev** as Soviet leader. Khrushchev adopted a new style of leadership, which affected both domestic and foreign affairs. His policy of **destalinisation** led to a more relaxed atmosphere within the Soviet Union as the government moved away from heavily repressive measures.

KEY PERSON

Nikita Khrushchev (1894–1971) emerged as leader of the Soviet Union after the death of Stalin in 1953. Although he was a committed communist, Khrushchev wanted to move away from the brutal policies of Stalin. He criticised Stalin's policies and encouraged destalinisation. In international relations Khrushchev adopted a softer tone than Stalin towards the West. He believed that the superpowers should accept each other's existence and put forward the idea of 'peaceful coexistence'. Yet when Soviet power was under attack, Khrushchev made threats to the West. The Soviet climb down during the Cuban Missile Crisis of 1962 was a personal embarrassment from which he never recovered. He was sacked by the Soviet Politburo in 1964 and died in 1971.

KEY TERMS

Destalinisation The attempt by Khrushchev, the Soviet leader, to move away from the policies of Stalin. Khrushchev criticised Stalin's use of terror and his economic policies of concentrating on heavy industry and forced collectivisation in agriculture. Khrushchev's actions encouraged those in eastern Europe who wanted reform to push for change, though there were limits to the extent of destalinisation.

In foreign policy he wished to promote better relations with the West. Khrushchev's criticism of Stalin's hard-line approach encouraged some communists in the eastern bloc to push for liberalisation in their own countries. Those leaders of communist regimes who adopted a Stalinist line came under increasing pressure.

- In June 1953 there were riots in Czechoslovakia during which symbols of Soviet power were attacked. At Pilsen Soviet flags were burnt and the town hall was sacked. The riots were quickly put down but the unrest encouraged those in East Germany who were unhappy with the government.
- Strikes broke out across East Germany when the government tried to impose wage cuts. Soviet troops were needed to restore order, leading to the arrest of 25,000 people of whom 400 were executed. This threat to the East German regime could have been serious. The existence of East Germany was seen by many of its own citizens as artificial because it was a product of Cold War tension between the superpowers. Yet without the agreement of the West for a unified Germany to be neutral, the USSR had little choice but to ensure the survival of this 'temporary' state.

The Soviet response. Despite the ruthless suppression of unrest, the Soviet government saw the need for political relaxation in eastern Europe. Purges were stopped and some of those politicians who had previously been removed were returned to positions of power. In Poland **Władysław Gomułka,** the Deputy Prime Minister who had been purged in 1948, was readmitted to the Communist Party in 1956. Soviet insistence on collectivisation in agriculture was dropped in East Germany and Poland. When Khrushchev gave his '**Secret Speech**' in 1956, criticism of Stalinist policies gathered momentum. Those eastern European governments that did not relax policies quickly enough to satisfy public opinion, had pressure applied by popular demonstrations. In Poland workers rioted, demanding an end to food shortages and an end to communism. The rioters were crushed but the Polish government appointed the moderate communist Gomułka as party leader in an attempt to calm tensions. The Soviet Union was unhappy

KEY PERSON

Władysław Gomułka (1905–82) Leader of the Polish Communist Party after the Second World War until he was purged in 1948 for criticising Stalin. Returned to power in 1956 after destalinisation, he remained leader of Poland until 1970.

KEY TERMS

Khrushchev's secret speech, 1956 This speech was delivered at the twentieth Communist Party Congress in the USSR. In the speech, Khrushchev criticised Stalin's policies. This encouraged reform, both in the USSR and in eastern Europe.

with Gomułka's return to power but did not feel able to intervene given the traditional hostility between Poland and its larger neighbour. Soviet nerves were partly reassured by the fact that, although Gomułka was a Polish nationalist, he was also a communist. The impact of destalinisation in Hungary was, however, a different matter.

The Hungarian Rising, 1956

Destalinisation led to calls for reform in Hungary. Encouraged by the Polish example, Hungarian reformers started demonstrations in order to put pressure on the government. The hard-line Hungarian government of Gerö could not control the resulting violence. Soviet troops stationed in Budapest, the Hungarian capital, were forced to leave the city. Under Soviet pressure, Gerö was replaced by the more moderate **Nagy**, who the Soviet leadership hoped would be more acceptable to the reformers. Nagy's attempts to introduce moderate reforms, known as the New Course, failed to satisfy the increasing demands of popular opinion. In order to keep a hold on events, Nagy gave in to demands to introduce multi-party democracy and to leave the Warsaw Pact. These measures were too much for the USSR. Soviet forces were sent into Hungary and a new government under Kádár was established. Order was restored but at the loss of over 35,000 lives, including Nagy, who was executed. The Soviet bloc remained intact but the resulting bitterness and resentment was to be long lasting.

KEY PERSON

Imre Nagy (1896–1956)
Leader of the Hungarian Communist Party, Nagy spent several years in the USSR before returning to Hungary after the Second World War. He was critical of Stalin's style of leadership and economic policies. He became leader of the Hungarian government in 1956 and introduced reforms. His proposal to take Hungary out of the Warsaw Pact led to a Soviet invasion of the country. Nagy was removed and replaced by the more hard-line Kádár. Nagy was seized by Soviet forces and taken to Romania. He was later executed.

Budapest citizens attack symbols of Soviet influence during the Hungarian Crisis of 1956.

The Berlin Crisis, 1961

The failure of the USA, the USSR and Britain to agree on a permanent solution to the problem of Germany after the Second World War gave the border between West and East Germany additional significance. Here, East met West. West Berlin remained an island of prosperous capitalism surrounded by communist East Germany; West German television and radio channels could be received along East Germany's border with the West. On the basis of this information, many East Germans decided to flee to the West. To stem this flow the East German government closed the frontier between East and West in 1958. But the number of people escaping to West Berlin continued to rise. By July 1961, 30,000 East Germans were fleeing each month. Most of these refugees were young, skilled people whom East Germany could not afford to lose. Since 1949 nearly 3 million people had left East Germany. The country could not sustain this degree of loss for much longer. The survival of East Germany as a separate country was threatened. The solution to this problem was the building of the **Berlin Wall**.

KEY TERM

Berlin Wall Built in 1961 to halt the flood of refugees escaping from communist East Germany into capitalist West Berlin, this huge concrete structure became the ultimate symbol of the East–West divide. The order to build the wall was given by Ulbricht, the East German leader and implemented by Erich Honecker who later became East Germany's leader. The East German government referred to the wall as the 'anti-fascist protective barrier' and avoided calling it a wall. In the 1980s Honecker occasionally referred to it as the 'so-called wall', just as West German newspapers usually referred to East Germany as the 'so-called DDR', indicating that they did not accept its existence.

The Berlin Wall. Walter Ulbricht, the East German leader, had wanted this solution for some time but had been overruled by Khrushchev. As the situation grew more desperate, Khrushchev changed his mind and in August security constructions of the border' were built in a military-style

Sightseers climb onto a bus to look over the newly-built Berlin Wall, February 1964.

operation. The Berlin Wall was a huge concrete structure over three metres high. Referred to in the West as the 'wall of shame', the East German government preferred to call it the 'anti-fascist protective barrier'. It was to be a physical symbol of a divided continent. With a secure border established between itself and the West, East Germany was stabilised. The flood of refugees was halted, although about 5000 people risked their lives escaping over, through or under the wall. Not all were lucky: 191 people died in the process. East Germany became notorious as the country whose population had to be penned in to stop them escaping. It was not a good advert for communism.

Czechoslovakia, 1968

Events in Czechoslovakia in 1968 were to some extent a repeat of those in Hungary in 1956. A liberalisation of communism within a country of the eastern bloc led to an armed military response from the Soviet Union. Despite these similarities there were differences in the course of events which resulted from the particular situation in Czechoslovakia.

Antonin Novotny had become Czechoslovakia's leader in 1957. A hard-liner whose inflexiblity upset those communists who wished to introduce reforms, Novotny was not the leader to introduce destalinisation into Czechoslovakia. By 1963 reformers within the Communist Party were able to force Novotny to resign and he was replaced by **Alexander Dubček**, a convinced communist, but one who believed in reaching agreement by compromise rather than force. The resignation of Novotny encouraged the reformers to press for more change and Dubček gave the impression he was willing to listen to new ideas. Reforms were implemented. Censorship was abolished and the media called for democracy. The dominant position of the Communist Party was threatened. The pressure for reform gathered pace in what became known as the '**Prague Spring**'. The Soviet Union became concerned at this threat to the Socialist Bloc, while the East German government worried over the possible spread across the border of the call for reform. After a meeting between the Soviet and Czechoslovak leaders failed to satisfy these concerns, the Soviet Union mobilised the forces of the Warsaw Pact and invaded Czechoslovakia.

KEY PERSON

Alexander Dubček (1921–92) lived in the USSR for thirteen years. On returning to Czechoslovakia he worked his way up the ranks of the Communist Party, becoming leader in 1968. Dubček was not a natural reformer but he preferred to work by negotiation and compromise. When the USSR put pressure on Dubček to reverse reforms, he gave in. He was expelled from the party but re-emerged as a symbol of reform during 1989.

KEY TERM

Prague Spring The events of 1968 in Czechoslovakia, when reformers within the Communist Party tried to introduce liberal measures. The Prague Spring came to an end when the country was invaded by Warsaw Pact troops and Dubček was removed from power.

KEY TERMS

Martial law The implementation of military government during which normal laws are suspended.

Normalisation The process of ensuring the hold of the Communist Party on government was not weakened by reformers.

On 20 August 1968 over 200,000 Warsaw Pact troops invaded Czechoslovakia and imposed **martial law**. Their aim was to bring about '**normalisation**', which meant ensuring the hold of the Communist Party was not weakened. Socialism needed to be protected and it seemed that this could be achieved only by closer supervision of the country by a Soviet military presence. Dubček, who had seen events in Czechoslovakia run out of his control, gave in to Soviet demands. All the reforms introduced during the 'Prague Spring' were reversed. The Czechoslovak Communist Party was purged and Dubček was replaced in 1969. The country had little option but to fall into line behind the USSR. Unlike Hungary in 1956, there was no rioting and fighting in the streets. In the face of armed intervention, protest against the invasion was muted but Jan Palach, a twenty-year-old student, gained international publicity when he burnt himself to death in Prague's Wenceslas Square in protest at events.

The Soviet invasion was justified by the Brezhnev Doctrine, issued in September 1968. There was no doubt that the USSR was willing to take action when it felt the interests of socialism were threatened within its sphere of influence. From a Soviet viewpoint their actions were successful. The new Czechoslovak government became a loyal supporter of the Warsaw Pact. The invasion also sent a message to those who wished to push reform too far in other eastern bloc countries. There was to be little serious unrest in the region until the early 1980s.

KEY PERSON

Lech Wałesa (b. 1943) An electrician at the Lenin shipyard in Gdansk, Poland. In 1980 he played an important role in organising shipyard workers protesting against the government. He became leader of the trade union Solidarity and pressed the government to allow workers the right to form their own free trade unions. After the collapse of communism in Poland, Walesa was elected President 1990–5.

Poland, 1980–1

The Polish workers had a history of protesting against government measures that affected their living standards and the crisis that developed in 1980 was initiated by protests against price rises ordered by the government. Thus, protest in Poland was the result of discontented industrial workers rather than communist reformers. Strike action centred on the Lenin shipyard in Gdansk where the workers were led by **Lech Wałesa**. His demands included the organisation of independent trade unions; a criticism of workers' organisations dominated by representatives of the Communist Party. Wałesa's call for workers' solidarity in the face of government action led to a high degree of support, which the government could not ignore. In August 1980 the government agreed to recognise **Solidarity** as the first independent trade union in the communist bloc. To the embarrassment of the government Solidarity quickly became a mass organisation of over 9 million members and started to pose a serious threat to the stability of a communist government, which claimed to represent the people. The USSR became concerned and organised military manoeuvres along Poland's border. In October, General **Wojciek Jaruzelski**, the Polish Prime Minister and Party leader decided to take stronger action against Solidarity. The organisation was suspended by the government and martial law was declared. Solidarity's leaders were arrested. Although strikes continued, the unrest was contained. Jaruzelski's actions had done enough to avoid a Soviet invasion.

KEY TERM

Solidarity An organisation of Polish workers, which was set up illegally in 1980. It was the first independent trade union, free from communist control, in eastern Europe.

KEY PERSON

Wojciek Jaruzelski (b. 1923) A general in the Polish army and member of the Communist Party, Jaruzelski rose through the ranks to become Prime Minister in 1981. He struggled to contain the threat posed to communism by Solidarity. He declared martial law and in doing so reassured the USSR that stability would be maintained. Jaruzelski's actions were unpopular in Poland but prevented a Soviet invasion to restore order. He remained leader of Poland until 1991.

CONCLUSIONS

During the period 1950–80 challenges to Soviet dominance and communist control over eastern Europe were quashed by a mixture of Soviet pressure and the actions of the communist governments within their own countries. Attempts at reform that failed to observe the defined limits of destalinisation were reined in and 'normalisation' was imposed by hard-line communists who knew that if events became serious they could count on the support of the Soviet military.

SUMMARY QUESTIONS

1 What methods did the USSR use to impose their control over eastern Europe?

2 How effective were these methods?

3 What challenges were there to Soviet domination over eastern Europe during the period 1950–80?

4 How did the USSR deal with these challenges?

CHAPTER 4

The collapse of Soviet control over eastern Europe 1980–91

Attempts to challenge Soviet control over eastern Europe during the period 1948–80 had been unsuccessful, in part due to the weaknesses of the challengers although the main factor was the support that the communist governments of eastern Europe could call on from the USSR. In this sense communism had been imposed on the region by outside influences generated by the Cold War. This situation changed radically in 1985 when Mikhail Gorbachev became Soviet leader. His policies had an enormous influence on the course of events in eastern Europe, acting as an encouragement to those who wished to reform government. Gorbachev also pursued a different policy towards the West that brought about an end to the Cold War and, along with it, the reasons for Soviet dominance over eastern Europe disappeared.

WHAT FACTORS LED TO THE COLLAPSE OF COMMUNIST REGIMES IN EASTERN EUROPE?

Pressure for change in eastern Europe came from both internal and external factors. The 1980s saw both of these factors combined to bring about change. Internal weaknesses became more pronounced and public opinion in eastern Europe was more critical of the regimes. Gorbachev encouraged those who wished to press for reform and made it clear that the Soviet Union would no longer intervene in the affairs of other socialist states.

Internal factors

There were many reasons for popular discontent against the governments of eastern Europe.

Economic issues. By the 1980s there were clear signs that the socialist economies of eastern Europe were unable to deliver the degree of prosperity evident in the West.

- The state-controlled industries of eastern Europe were inefficient both in terms of quality and quantity of goods produced. Since the 1950s most of the countries of eastern Europe had concentrated their resources on heavy industry rather than consumer goods and, as a result, food, clothing and housing were in short supply and often inadequate. Industrial pollution was bad enough to have a serious impact on the health of the people of the region. Management had become a privileged group with little concern for innovation as long as their position in society was maintained. The increase in oil prices in the mid-1970s had made it difficult for governments to get credit for foreign exchange and investment. By the 1980s the technology used in the region was rapidly becoming out of date. The USSR was slow to develop new technologies, such as personal computers, robotics and video equipment. Eastern Europe had become reliant on Soviet technology and, as a consequence, also fell behind the West.

- Living standards in eastern Europe had long fallen behind those of the West but by the 1980s the expectations of its population were different. On the borders of East Germany and Czechoslovakia, West German television stations could be received with images of life under capitalism. Western music, cinema and fashion also had some influence on the people of eastern Europe. The mass consumer society of the West provided a sharp contrast with living standards in the East. Not only did western-style capitalism seem more attractive, but the failure of socialism to provide the living standards expected was evident to more and more of those citizens living in eastern Europe.

- A sense of impending economic crisis was helped by the slowdown in the rate of growth in industrial production. By 1985 all of the socialist economies of the eastern bloc had growth rates which were virtually negligible, including the more developed economies of East Germany and Czechoslovakia. All led to the impression of a vast bureaucratic economic system grinding to an inevitable halt.

Calls for political reform. Criticisms of the regimes of eastern Europe were not restricted to economic issues; there was often a conflict between those leaders who wished to maintain a hard-line communist approach and others, including Communist Party members, who pressed for reform. The leaders of the communist parties of the eastern bloc were often portrayed in the West as uninspiring, mediocre men, more interested in their personal power than the needs of their country. Although there is some truth in this view, it underestimates the conviction of some communist leaders who had suffered for their beliefs before 1945 and had, like Todar Zhivkov, the Bulgarian leader, played an important role in resisting the German occupation during the Second World War. But by the 1980s the regimes of eastern Europe were led by men who were increasingly out of touch with the needs of their country and had been in position long enough to enjoy the trappings of power. They were leaders who were reluctant to change a system that worked for them. In 1985 Janós Kádár had been leader of Hungary since 1956, Gustáv Husák had dominated Czechoslovak politics since 1968 and Zhivkov had led Bulgaria since 1956. With communist parties dominant and the use of a repressive police network, opposition in these countries was severely limited.

East Germany. The regimes of East Germany and Romania illustrate these common themes in East European politics as well as some distinct features peculiar to the individual situation within each country. Since 1971, East Germany (the DDR) had been led by **Erich Honecker**, an uninspiring, hard-line communist. Honecker was not a man comfortable in presenting a grand vision for the future to inspire his people but he could recite by heart the number of indoor toilets in every region of the country. Of all of the economies of eastern Europe, that of East Germany was the most successful (or least unsuccessful), but even here living standards were well below those of West Germany. Regarded by the West as an artificial country, East Germany struggled to find a sense of its own identity. Under Honecker the regime attempted to instil a sense of national pride through sporting achievements. A programme of rigorous selection, training and in some cases force-feeding with drugs, produced considerable

KEY PERSON

Erich Honecker (1912–94) East German leader from 1971 to 1989. Honecker had been responsible for implementing the building of the Berlin Wall in 1961. He was a hard-line communist against reform. Popular protests forced him to resign as leader in 1989. Despite attempts to arrest him and put him on trial for abusing his power, Honecker was allowed to go into exile in the USSR.

success in swimming and athletics. At the 1980 Moscow Olympics East Germany took 11 of the 13 gold medals available in women's swimming. In athletics the world record for the women's 400 metres was set in 1985 by Marita Koch who ran 47.60 seconds. It is unlikely to be beaten. Successes such as these provided a focus for national pride but its effectiveness was hampered by popular resentment at the privileges and pampering given to athletes by the government. The government's failure to create national unity was evident in its extensive use of police spies. The **Stasi**, East Germany's secret police, kept files on 5.5 million East Germans through an elaborate system of informers. Over 600,000 people were employed directly by the Stasi with an additional 100,000 informers. When government files were opened after the country collapsed it was clear that husbands were informing on their wives who, in turn, were informing on their husbands. The East German government was very well informed! Unfortunately, a lot of the information was critical of the regime. Jokes were often a good indicator of popular opinion and by the 1980s many were at the expense of Honecker. Anne McElvoy, the *Times* correspondent in East Berlin heard one such joke:

> After having breakfast, Honecker is lying on the beach when the sun says, 'Good morning. I wish you an agreeable day and will shine as well as I can for you'.
>
> In the evening, the sun begins to sink and Honecker says, 'Thank you, dear sun, for shining all day for me'.
>
> 'Kiss my ass you old fool,' replies the sun, 'I'm in the West now'.

By the mid-1980s the East German leadership had failed to gain the respect of a large section of its own people. Pressure was growing within the Party to push Honecker aside before it was too late to reform. Honecker remained, however, inflexible and seemingly unmoveable.

Romania. In Romania the leadership of **Nicolae Ceauşescu** was firmly entrenched by the early 1980s. Ceauşescu had been courted by the West because of his independent stance in foreign affairs. He was not prepared to blindly

KEY TERM

Stasi The East German secret police.

KEY PERSON

Nicolae Ceauseşcu (1918–89) Communist leader of Romania from 1965 to 1989. He pursued policies of forced industrial development and heavy repression. He developed a cult of personality to extreme proportions and, by the mid-1980s, most of his support was manufactured rather than real. His rule was not merely ruthless but also vindictive. In 1989 popular unrest led to the overthrow of Ceauşescu. He and his wife were executed on Christmas Day, 1989.

accept the policy of the USSR and was therefore seen as a possible chink in the Iron Curtain. The West was prepared to overlook some of Ceauşescu's less pleasant policies at home. He was accorded state visits to France, where he stole some silver from the presidential palace, and Britain, where he upset the Queen by having his own food taster at meals given at Buckingham Palace. His behaviour was a sign of growing paranoia and megalomania.

Ceauşescu's regime was one of the most repressive in eastern Europe.

- His secret police, the **Securitate**, ruthlessly crushed any opposition. Coal miners who went on strike in 1977 were severely dealt with. After an agreement with the government ended the strike, most of the miners' leaders were killed in 'road accidents' or died of premature disease. Securitate doctors later admitted to giving the miners medicals, which involved five-minute X-rays to ensure the development of cancer.
- In addition to repression, there was a very tight system of censorship, which involved the registration of all typewriters by their owners every year. Government propaganda was the only source of information for the vast majority of Romanians.
- As Ceauşescu's hold on power grew, so did his ability to push through more extreme policies. In the mid-1980s he introduced a policy of **systematisation**, which involved the demolition of whole villages, to be replaced by agro-industrial complexes. Ceauşescu seems to have chosen villages for this policy on a whim and it was very unpopular.
- Attempts to pay off Romania's foreign debts resulted in severe shortages. Only one forty-watt bulb was allowed per room. Alongside these restrictions a new palace was constructed in the centre of Bucharest at enormous cost.
- Ceauşescu and his wife, Elena, had got used to playing the role of dictators. The Romanian government was packed with family members who lived in relative luxury. Ceauşescu's many palaces were decorated with lurex fabrics and porcelain figurines of ballerinas in tutus and deers skipping through the forest: critics termed it 'comrade kitsch'. By 1985 Ceauşescu had alienated virtually the entire population, with the exception of the Securitate.

KEY TERMS

Securitate The Romanian secret police under Ceauşescu.

Systematisation Ceauşescu's policy of creating large agro-industrial complexes, where agricultural and industrial activity would be jointly undertaken. Old villages were demolished and their population forcibly moved to build these new centres. They were very unpopular and an economic failure.

Thus, the nature of the governments of eastern Europe and their policies produced discontent and latent opposition. External factors gave encouragement to these forces.

External factors

In 1985 **Mikhail Gorbachev** became leader of the Soviet Union. His policies had a considerable impact on eastern Europe and on the attitude of the USSR towards the socialist bloc. He was from a younger generation than the previous Soviet leaders and had a different outlook on communism and the Soviet state. He recognised that the whole Soviet system, which had become so entrenched, was performing badly. As a committed communist, Gorbachev made a genuine attempt to rejuvenate the Soviet Union. His policies included:

- *Perestroika.* A restructuring of the economy, which involved a measure of private enterprise to promote production, efficiency and higher-quality goods.
- *Glasnost.* A policy of openness that encouraged the population to put forward new ideas and show initiative.
- *Democratisation.* An attempt to get more people involved in the Communist Party and political debate.

These policies led to a more critical approach towards communism and this encouraged reformers to push for further liberalisation. Within four years popular opinion in the Soviet Union shifted towards an adoption of some aspects of the political and economic ideas of the West: others called for a wholesale rejection of communism. Gorbachev's policies encouraged reformers in the communist parties of eastern Europe to press for similar measures.

Another important aspect of Gorbachev's new approach was his attitude towards international relations. Gorbachev believed that the Soviet economy would be made more productive and improve living standards only if the USSR reduced its vast military spending. The Cold War had produced an arms race in both nuclear and conventional weapons that was an immense drain on the Soviet economy. When the USA started to plan for defensive weapons systems in space, the so-called **Star Wars**

KEY PERSON

Mikhail Gorbachev (b.1931) Leader of the USSR from 1985 to 1991. Gorbachev represented a younger generation of Soviet politicians who believed socialism needed to be reformed. His policies aimed to make the Communist Party more responsive and to liberalise the economy. He encouraged those in eastern Europe who wished to make similar reforms. In international relations Gorbachev recognised the inability of the USSR to compete with the USA in the arms race and called for limitations on nuclear weapons and an end to the Cold War. Gorbachev's political career came to an end with the collapse of the USSR in 1991.

KEY TERM

Star Wars Officially referred to as the Strategic Defense Initiative (SDI), Star Wars was the name given to the proposals of the USA in 1983 to develop nuclear defence systems in space.

Mikhail Gorbachev, Soviet leader 1985–91.

programme, Gorbachev realised the Soviet Union did not have the technology or finance to compete. Thus, in order to safeguard Soviet security, Gorbachev decided to abandon the arms race in favour of negotiated disarmament. The USA was relieved not to have to devote so much of its own resources to defence: Americans had come to appreciate that trade was a more effective mechanism of control. A series of summits between Gorbachev and the US president Ronald Reagan established a level of trust that made agreement on limiting weapons possible. By 1989 the relationship between the two superpowers was such that the Cold War had ceased to exist. Without the tensions generated by the Cold War, there was no longer a need for the USSR to exert control over eastern Europe. Without Soviet backing the governments of eastern Europe found their position increasingly precarious.

Gorbachev's new political thinking

It is no longer possible to draft a policy on the premises of the year 1947, the Truman Doctrine and Churchill's Fulton speech. It is necessary to think and act in a new way. What is more, history cannot wait; people cannot afford to waste time. It may be too late tomorrow and the day after tomorrow may never come.

The fundamental principle of the new political outlook is very simple: nuclear war cannot be a means of achieving political, economic, ideological or any other goals… Nuclear war is senseless; it is irrational. There would be neither winners nor losers in a global nuclear conflict: world civilisation would inevitably perish. It is suicide, rather than a war in the conventional sense of the word.

Security can no longer be assured by military means – neither by the use of arms or deterrence, nor by the continued perfection of the 'sword' and the 'shield'. Attempts to achieve military superiority are preposterous… The only way to security is through political decisions and disarmament.

From Mikhail Gorbachev, *Perestroika: New Thinking for Our Country and the World*, published in 1987

THE COLLAPSE OF COMMUNISM IN EASTERN EUROPE

Gorbachev's reforms in the USSR led to attempts by some governments in eastern Europe to reform in response to the changes, as well as increasing the pressure for change from the public. This trend gathered momentum and the pace of events took many by surprise. Those governments that resisted these trends quickly became isolated.

Poland

In Poland General Jaruzelski had suppressed the independent workers' organisation, Solidarity, in 1981 and declared a state of martial law. Support for Solidarity remained high, even though its organisation had to operate illegally, due to a failure of the government to solve economic difficulties. This support included the endorsement of the Catholic Church. By 1988 the government had lifted martial law and was prepared to introduce some reforms in response to Gorbachev's policies in the USSR. Solidarity was legalised and, in an important step, the government decided to allow it and any other political groups to stand in elections. In the general elections of 1989 Solidarity was able to defeat the Communist Party by a landslide. In the face of this lack of support, the Communist Party collapsed as an organisation and by 1990 it held no position in the coalition government formed after the election of 1989. The USSR had done nothing to stop these events happening, indeed Gorbachev seemed to approve of Poles deciding on their own future. The message was clear to all those pressing for change in other east European states: the USSR no longer had any wish to impose itself on the internal affairs of eastern Europe.

The communist collapse spreads

In Hungary the pressure for reform came from within the Communist Party and in 1988 Kádár, the hard-line leader since 1956, was sacked. The government, now dominated by reformers, decided to allow other political parties to contest elections. By 1990 the communists had lost control of the government after doing badly in elections. In Czechoslovakia the government was forced to make concessions in response to public demonstrations calling for reforms. An organisation called Civic Forum emerged to coordinate the campaign to get rid of the communist government. Under severe public pressure, the communists caved in, reforms were introduced and in 1989 **Václav Havel**, a leading playwright and opponent of communism, was elected President. Despite the scale of the demonstrations in Czechoslovakia, there was little violence. Thus, the events in Czechoslovakia were described as **the Velvet Revolution**. Another consequence of the collapse of communism was the separation of the country into the Czech and Slovak republics.

KEY PERSON

Václav Havel (b. 1936)
Czech playwright who became an inspiration for those wishing to oppose the communist regime in Czechoslovakia during the late 1980s. Later became President of the Czech Republic.

KEY TERM

The Velvet Revolution
A term used to describe the collapse of communism in Czechoslovakia in 1989. The communist regime was brought down by widespread demonstrations and protests which involved little violence. The revolution was therefore relatively smooth compared to the violence that marked the overthrow of communism in some of the other eastern European states such as Romania.

The collapse of East Germany

Gorbachev's reforms had important consequences for the very existence of East Germany as a separate country. The DDR was a product of Cold War tensions, which had prevented the unification of Germany after the Second World War. Without these tensions there seemed little reason for Germany to remain divided. Honecker recognised that the DDR could still have a reason to exist if it remained socialist and therefore different from West Germany. In 1989 the DDR was forty years old and the East German leadership prepared to celebrate its anniversary.

At what should have been an event to consolidate the country, the tide was turning against the regime. Honecker was not in favour of any reform but the East German population could not be isolated from events in the rest of Europe. Large numbers of East Germans had traditionally taken their holidays in Hungary but in 1989 the Hungarian government had opened its borders with the West. Thousands of East Germans on holiday in Hungary were now free to travel to the West. On one day alone, 11 September, 125,000 East Germans crossed into Austria and the freedom of the West. The rush to flee to the West was in danger of becoming a severe embarrassment to the East German government. More serious for Honecker was the formation of new political groups such as New Forum who represented those who refused to flee their own country but were prepared to stay and resist the government in order to bring about change. When huge crowds of demonstrators gathered in the city of Leipzig they were shouting 'We are staying'. Honecker seemed paralysed by events. He was seriously ill for much of 1989 and in his absence government decision-making ground to a halt.

In October Gorbachev visited Berlin to attend a parade to mark the fortieth anniversary of the creation of East Germany. The crowds chanted 'Gorbi, Gorbi, Gorbi', to the embarrassment of Honecker, the hard-liner. Avoiding the customary embrace, Gorbachev told Honecker, 'Those who delay are punished by life.' Unmoved, Honecker decided to meet further protest with police action. He was in favour of using the tactics followed by the Chinese government in June 1989, when students protesting in **Tiananmen Square** in Beijing had been massacred by the armed forces. Fortunately, the East German Politburo overruled Honecker and he was sacked as leader to be replaced by **Egon Krenz**.

Krenz was aware of the need for reform but, as a former head of the Stasi, his reputation did not endear him to the public. With popular pressure forcing events to run out of his control, on 9 November 1989 Krenz decided to open the Berlin Wall and allow East Germans to cross freely to the West. Once open, the wall could not be closed. As a symbolic gesture of 'people power' crowds gathered on the wall and tore it down. The government was shocked by the pace of events and revelations of corruption weakened the Communist Party. When free elections were held in 1990 parties in favour of unification with West Germany won a majority of seats. The DDR had voted itself out of existence, a process completed formally on 3 October 1990.

KEY EVENT

Tiananmen Square, 1989
Students protesting against the communist system in China were massacred in Beijing when the government ordered tanks into the Square to crush the unrest. The ruthless action was effective in preventing political reform in China.

KEY PERSON

Egon Krenz (b. 1937)
Became leader of East Germany when Honecker resigned in 1989. Krenz wanted to introduce political reform but, due to the pressure of public demonstrations, events ran out of control. His decision to open the Berlin Wall led quickly to the collapse of East Germany.

An Englishman living in West Berlin witnesses the fall of the Berlin Wall, November 1989

From the late summer of 1989 rumours of the Iron Curtain's demise were rife. On many occasions an entire café or bar would empty to the cries of a passing rumour. So often were these incidents that complacency and disbelief returned. For most Berliners the idea of the Wall's fall was a dream for the future. For the younger Berliners the Wall was something they had grown up with. It had been there all our lives. Its menace, like that of a nuclear holocaust, was part of our lives. It didn't dominate my life but its grey asbestos foundations coloured my views, polarised my opinions and inhibited my freedom.

When the Wall was opened the change was tremendous. The normally spartan border and its corridor, once a lonely place of uniforms, gates and fences, were overflowing with jubilant East Germans. Wave after wave of creaking Trabant cars, themselves a symbol of East Germany's failure, crossed into the West.

The city was transformed into one massive party. All barriers down, all prejudice and fear for the moment forgotten. Crowds of East Berliners bursting across the border bringing the underground system to a standstill. There were fireworks and music, raw energy and emotion surpassing anything I'd seen.

Yet underlying the general jubilation there were minor 'incidents' that suggested bigger problems still to be faced. The most shocking was the graffiti on the holocaust memorial in Wittenbergplatz. A large lime green swastika turned the memorial into a Nazi totem. The neo-nazis' vandalism only served to remind the fragmented and momentarily forgetful Berliners just how they had come to be separated in the first place.

From private letters written by Nicholas Wilmott, November 1989.

Nicolae Ceauşescu, the Romanian leader, panicking on the balcony of the Presidential palace, December 1989.

Romania

Throughout the turbulent events in eastern Europe that took place in 1989, Romania seemed the most immune to calls for change. Ceauşescu was confident enough to leave for a visit to Iran in early December after receiving sixty-seven standing ovations at the Communist Party Congress.

The crisis which brought about the collapse of Ceauşescu started with the seemingly unimportant actions of Laszlo Tokes, a priest from Timişoara in northern Romania. Tokes had broken the law by allowing poetry to be recited in public during his services. The police ordered him to be transferred out of the area. When he refused, crowds demonstrated in support. Being close to the border with Hungary, the people of Timişoara had some awareness of events in the rest of Europe via Hungarian television and radio stations. Ceauşescu sent the army in and opened fire on the demonstrators. Despite attempts to keep knowledge of the massacre of seventy-one people from the Romanian people, rumours spread quickly. When Ceauşescu appeared at a rally in Bucharest, a week later, the crowds booed. The noise of the crowd could be clearly heard above the tape-recorded cheers that were usually played at rallies. This time the army was unwilling to take action against the demonstrators. Ceauşescu and his wife were forced to flee Bucharest by helicopter but were later arrested by the army.

The Securitate remained loyal to Ceauşescu and continued to engage in fierce street fighting until the execution of Ceauşescu and his wife, on Christmas Day. Communism, and the man who had completely discredited the system, had been overthrown in Romania.

CONCLUSIONS

People power played a large part in the dismantling of communism in Poland, Czechoslovakia, East Germany and Romania. In Hungary the hard-line leaders were dislodged by reformers within the ranks of the Communist Party. A similar pattern occurred in Bulgaria where Zhivkov was deposed by his own ministers. Across eastern Europe the forces of communism collapsed. It was a swift and largely peaceful process, with the exceptions of Romania and Yugoslavia. In Yugoslavia the collapse of communism was accompanied by the disintegration of the country and a bloody civil war as Slovenia, Croatia and Bosnia attempted to break away from Serbian dominance.

The role of Gorbachev was vital in changing the context in which the communist regimes of eastern Europe operated. The USSR was not now willing to support unpopular communist governments, which were no longer crucial to its security and were in danger of becoming a political embarrassment and a financial drain.

SUMMARY QUESTIONS

1 Make a list of the factors that led to the collapse of communist regimes in eastern Europe. Which of these factors do you consider to be the most important?

2 In what ways did Gorbachev's policies bring about an end to the Cold War?

AS SECTION: THE COLD WAR IN ASIA AND THE AMERICAS 1949–75

INTRODUCTION

Key questions

- Why, and with what domestic consequences, did many Americans believe they were losing the Cold War in the 1950s?
- Why, and with what success, did the UN intervene in the Korean War?
- Why did the USA intervene in the Vietnam War?
- Why was US involvement in the Vietnam War unsuccessful?
- What were the causes and consequences of the Cuban Missile Crisis?

Until 1949 the Cold War that had developed between the USA and the Soviet Union had been focused on Europe. This changed in 1949, when the Chinese communists secured victory and seized China from the Nationalist forces of the USA's ally, **Chiang Kai Shek**. The focus of Cold War conflict then moved to Asia, where the USA became increasingly concerned about the spread of communism from its newly acquired base on the Chinese mainland. US fears were realised by the outbreak of wars, involving communist aggression, in Korea and Vietnam. These developments convinced many Americans that they were losing the Cold War and the response of successive US governments was to ensure any communist aggression was met with a firm policy and military action where needed. In the wider context of the Cold War, the USA saw itself as the policeman of the free world, standing up to protect democracy and freedom against the spread of communism.

KEY PERSON

Chiang Kai Shek (1887–1975) Leader of the Chinese Nationalists from 1927 until overthrown by the Chinese communists in 1949. He was forced to flee to the island of Taiwan, which he ruled with US protection.

Events between 1950 and 1975 showed mixed success for US foreign policy. The tendency of the US government to concentrate on the ideological conflict between capitalism and communism led them to misjudge the specific circumstances that existed in both Asia and the Americas. This inability to understand fully the situation in Vietnam ended in failure for the USA. Castro's takeover of Cuba brought the communist threat to the doorstep of the USA and raised the stakes in the Cold War. Yet during this period, war was limited in extent, and direct conflict between the two superpowers was avoided. The Cuban Missile Crisis illustrated the potential dangers of direct conflict in an age where nuclear weapons could lead to the world's destruction.

KEY TERM

Secretary of State The head of the department of the US government that conducts foreign policy.

Dates	President	Party	Secretary of State
1945–53	Harry S. Truman	Democratic	Edward Stettinius Jr (1945)
			James Byrnes (1945–7)
			George Marshall (1947–9)
			Dean Acheson (1949–53)
1953–61	Dwight Eisenhower	Republican	John Foster Dulles (1953–9)
			Christian Herter (1959–61)
1961–3	John F. Kennedy	Democratic	Dean Rusk (1961–3)
1963–9	Lyndon B. Johnson	Democratic	Dean Rusk (1963–9)
1969–74	Richard Nixon	Republican	William Rogers (1969–73)
			Henry Kissinger (1973–4)
1974–7	Gerald Ford	Republican	Henry Kissinger (1974–7)

US Presidents and their Secretaries of State, 1945–77.

CHAPTER 5

US foreign policy in the 1950s

In 1949 the USA had dealt effectively with the Soviet Union's blockade of West Berlin by organising an airlift of supplies into the city. When the Soviet Union admitted defeat and lifted the blockade in May, it was a victory for the West. Strengthened by the formation of NATO, a military alliance to defend the West against communist attack, the morale of the USA was high but events elsewhere were to undermine any feeling that the West had the upper hand in the Cold War. The 1950s were a period when many Americans believed they were losing the Cold War. This feeling of vulnerability had a significant impact on attitudes to communism in both domestic and foreign policy.

BACKGROUND

In 1950 President Truman asked the National Security Council to produce a report on US Cold War policy. The result was a document known as **NSC-68**. This report saw the world in **bipolar** terms, highlighting the division of the world into two superpowers in conflict with each other. This situation, according to the report, had been brought about because of the USSR's aim to extend their authority in order to achieve domination over both Europe and Asia. This view saw the Soviet Union under Stalin as aiming for nothing short of world conquest. NSC-68 made recommendations for the direction of US foreign policy: it should do all it could to ensure non-communist regimes were viable as alternatives to communism and it should take military measures to meet the threat of communism. These measures should include the building up of both conventional and nuclear weapons and being prepared to engage in limited wars to prevent the spread of communism and push back communist groups threatening to take over 'free' countries.

These recommendations marked a change from the earlier policy of containment. Containment had accepted the

KEY TERMS

NSC-68 A report of the US National Security Council produced in 1950. It blamed the expansion policies of the Soviet Union for the continuation of the Cold War. The Soviet Union was considered to be aiming to dominate Europe and Asia as part of the spread of world communism. This report recommended much stronger action against communist expansion. It influenced US foreign policy in the 1950s.

Bipolar The idea of the world being divided into two power blocs: that of communism, centred on the USSR, and western capitalism, centred on the USA.

KEY TERM

Roll back The policy of pushing back the frontiers of communism and liberating states where communism had been imposed by force. It was a term which gained currency in the 1950s and marked a more assertive US stance than that of containment, which had dominated US government thinking since 1945.

existence of the Soviet Union and focused on containing communism within its existing borders. The new emphasis was to be on **roll back**, the view that communism needed to be confronted and pushed back to safeguard the free world. This was, therefore, the basis of a more aggressive US foreign policy. This change had been caused by the growing perception in the USA that it was losing the Cold War and firmer action was needed.

WHY DID THE US BELIEVE IT WAS LOSING THE COLD WAR IN THE 1950S?

US satisfaction at the lifting of the Berlin Blockade in May 1949 was soon overshadowed by the communist takeover of China in September. This was the first of a series of events, which seemed to illustrate that the tide was turning in favour of the forces of world communism.

China

KEY PERSON

Mao Zedong (1893–1976) Chinese communist leader since the 1920s. Overthrew the Nationalist government of Chiang Kai Shek in 1949 and established China as a communist state.

China had been in a state of civil war since the 1920s. The Nationalists (Guomindang), led by Chiang Kai Shek, had faced fierce opposition from the Chinese communists organised by **Mao Zedong**. In 1945, at the end of the Second World War, the defeat of Japan had left much of China without any form of control. The communists were successful in quickly gaining a hold over these areas and, by 1949, were strong enough to push the Nationalists out of mainland China. Chiang Kai Shek and the remnants of his party fled to the island of Taiwan. Mao's declaration of a Communist People's Republic of China in September sent shock waves across the USA. But these events were hardly surprising. The Nationalists had been corrupt and out of touch with the needs of the majority of Chinese people. Chiang's reputation was much higher in the USA than among Americans in China who had first-hand knowledge of his limitations as leader. Even the anti-communist US General Stilwell described the Nationalist government as 'corruption, chaos, neglect, taxes, words and no deeds' and acknowledged that in comparison the communists 'raise production and standards of living. Practise what they preach.' Yet back in USA the communist takeover of China was seen as evidence of

Stalin's work in spreading world communism. It was also viewed as the result of the failure of the USA to send enough support to the Nationalists. China had a special place in the hearts of US politicians. Since the nineteenth century the USA had seen itself as the guardian of China against the worst excesses of European imperialism. There was a sense that the guardian had failed in its role and with such a large country under communist rule, the forces of freedom and capitalism seemed, to many Americans, to be under threat.

Korea and Vietnam

With China now in communist hands the US government became more concerned about other possible victims of communist aggression. These concerns were soon realised in Korea. The Korean peninsula had been temporarily divided at the end of the Second World War but attempts to secure unification collapsed when the communist forces of North Korea invaded the capitalist South in 1950. US politicians concluded that this was further evidence of Stalin's attempts to spread communism. Bordering both China and the Soviet Union, North Korea was considered to be under the direction of both Moscow and Beijing.

Vietnam had been part of French Indochina until it was seized by the Japanese during the Second World War. After 1945 the French tried to regain control over its former colonies. The USA was strongly opposed to imperialism and had been very critical of the overseas empires ruled by European powers. But after the Second World War, the countries of Europe no longer had the resources to run vast empires. This posed a serious dilemma for the USA. If France did not regain control over Indochina communism might take its place. In Vietnam the forces of nationalism and communism were combined by the Vietminh, led by the communist Ho Chi Minh (see page 78). Geographically positioned south of China, Vietnam was well placed to receive assistance from Mao's communists after 1949. The US government became concerned about what was termed the **domino effect**; as one country fell to communism it would exert pressure on neighbouring countries to follow the same path.

KEY TERM

Domino effect In 1954 the US President Eisenhower talked of countries falling to communism one by one like dominoes. This view that, if one country fell to communism, neighbouring states would follow became known as the domino effect. Fear of communism spreading in this manner led to US support for anti-communist governments.

The missile gap

Between 1945 and 1949 the USA claimed some superiority in military weaponry as it was the only nuclear power. This security was shattered in August 1949 when the Soviet Union announced it had developed an atomic bomb. This was much quicker than the West had thought possible. In 1952 the USA developed the more powerful hydrogen bomb but the Soviet Union was able to produce its own less than a year later. This led to concerns in the US government that the USSR would match and overtake the West in its nuclear and conventional military capability. Exaggerated intelligence reports about Soviet arms fed these concerns. The result was the so-called 'bomber gap' in 1955–6 and the 'missile gap' of 1957–61. The 'bomber gap' arose because of concerns with Soviet bombing capabilities; the 'missile gap' developed in response to the USSR's launching of its **ICBM** programme in 1957. The fears generated by this perceived gap led the US government to increase its military spending from $15 billion in 1950 to over $50 billion a year. If any gap did exist it was soon closed. In 1957 the USA had the lead in nuclear missiles. It developed its own long-range missiles: both the land-based Minuteman and the submarine-based Polaris. These missiles were superior to the ICBMs of the USSR. American U2 spy-planes were able to confirm the lack of Soviet missiles in comparison with the USA. Nonetheless, the fear of the Soviet Union overtaking the nuclear superiority of the USA remained.

KEY TERM

ICBM Intercontinental Ballistic Missiles. Nuclear missiles for use over a long range of about 8000 miles.

'Sputnik' The first ever space satellite, launched by the Soviet Union in 1957.

Sputnik and the space race

US insecurities about the advance of Soviet technology were increased by the shock announcement in October 1957 that the Soviet Union had launched the first ever space satellite, ***Sputnik***. The 'beep, beep, beep' signal emitted from *Sputnik* caused dismay in the USA. As the historian Harold Evans has stated 'it suggested communism had mastered the universe'. President Eisenhower was more dismissive: 'One small ball in the air is something which does not raise my apprehensions one iota.' In November, the Soviet Union sent Laika, a dog, into space aboard *Sputnik II*, while one month later the first US satellite launch ended in failure. (It was nicknamed *Kaputnik*!) In 1961 the Soviet Union was first to put a man into space. **Yuri Gagarin** orbited the earth in *Vostok I* and returned with much publicity to a hero's welcome. The Soviet Union made the most of what seemed to be tangible signs of its superior technological achievements.

Thus, the 1950s was a period of a loss of US confidence in its ability to prevent Soviet expansion. Asia seemed to be falling to the forces of world communism and the USSR seemed to be overtaking the West in technological terms.

KEY PERSON

Yuri Gagarin (1934–68) Soviet cosmonaut who, in 1961, became the first human in space aboard the spacecraft *Vostok I*.

RESPONSES TO THE LOSS OF CONFIDENCE

The vulnerability felt by many Americans faced with the threat of Soviet world domination produced a fear of communism at home and a hardening of foreign policy.

The Red Scare and McCarthyism

Blame for the USA's failure to match the USSR led some Americans to look for enemy agents at home. The fear of communism within the USA was not new, but in the early 1950s Cold War anxieties led to a wave of hysteria. It was generated by a fear that the USA was being undermined by the enemy within. McCarthyism was to represent this fear.

US Senator, Joseph McCarthy.

KEY TERM

McCarthyism The wave of anti-communist feeling that spread through the USA in the early 1950s. It is sometimes referred to as the Red Scare and was encouraged by sections of the Republican Party, most notably by Joseph McCarthy. The movement aimed to remove communist sympathisers from all sections of US life, including members of Truman's government who were seen as soft on communism.

The Communist Party in the USA was never very large. At its height membership was no more than 100,000. Yet suspicions that there were communist spies within the US government and administration gained momentum during the 1940s:

- Truman had felt pressured enough to set up the Loyalty Review Board in 1947 to check up on government employees and within three years nearly 3000 workers had been sacked. Grounds for dismissal were often vague, with sympathy for communist organisations usually enough to ensure removal from post.
- In addition to this, the US Senate set up its own House Un-American Activities Committee (HUAC) to investigate individuals suspected of unorthodox views. The HUAC put pressure on those called as witnesses to name others they suspected of being communists. The process gathered a momentum of its own.

Those charged – actors, scientists, writers and trade unionists – were 'blacklisted' and many never worked again.

- In 1948 Alger Hiss, a former State Department Official was accused of being a communist. In the trial that followed Hiss was found guilty of perjury and sentenced to five years in jail. A large section of the US public saw the Hiss case as concrete evidence that there was a communist underground working to undermine the US system from within.
- These fears seemed to be confirmed by the uncovering of a spy ring that had passed atomic secrets to the USSR. Julius and Ethel Rosenberg were among those accused. Although probably guilty, they were minor spies who passed on information which was not important. The Rosenbergs were found guilty and executed with little evidence produced in court. Their sentence was a reflection of the anti-communist hysteria gripping the USA at the time.

For Truman, fear of communism was useful in gaining public support for the increased role of the USA in world affairs. For other politicians hoping for an opportunity to revive their careers, whipping up anti-communist fears proved very effective. One such politician was Senator **Joseph McCarthy**. In 1950 McCarthy gave a speech at a Women's Republican Club during which he announced 'The State Department is infested with communists. I have here in my hand a list of 205 – a list of names that were known to the Secretary of State as being members of the Communist Party and who nevertheless are still working and shaping policy.' McCarthy had no evidence: he probably had no list. But thousands of Americans were willing to believe him. Using his position as head of a minor Senate committee, McCarthy targeted individuals and accused them of communist activities. His approach was to humiliate witnesses. According to the journalist William S. White, 'It stank with the odor of fear and the odor of monstrous silliness.' The State Department panicked under this pressure and banned over 400 writers. Yet McCarthy's influence was short-lived. When he turned his attentions to the army in 1954, his accusations were met by Joseph Welch, the elderly Boston lawyer who acted for the army's defence. These proceedings were televised

KEY PERSON

Joseph McCarthy (1908–57) A lawyer by profession who was elected Senator for Wisconsin in 1948. Fiercely anti-communist, he caused a sensation in 1950 when he claimed 205 US government officials were members of the Communist Party. No evidence was produced to support his claims but he was able to tap into fears among US public opinion of a communist conspiracy within the USA. He used the notoriety gained from his accusations to bolster his flagging political career. In 1954 he over-reached himself when he made accusations against the army. When the case went to court it was televised and McCarthy came across as a ridiculous liar. His influence diminished sharply thereafter. Condemned by the Senate and deserted by his colleagues, he died of alcoholism in 1957.

and watched by an audience of 80 million. Welch destroyed McCarthy with his rational and reasoned approach. His rebuke to McCarthy, 'Have you no decency?', struck a cord with the audience. McCarthy had been revealed as a liar and a crook. Anti-communist views remained embedded in US society but the hysteria associated with McCarthy had been broken.

US foreign policy in the 1950s

As in domestic opinion, US foreign policy was to harden against communism during this period. Truman's approach had toughened in response to NSC-68 and this trend developed further during the 1950s. In 1952 the Republican candidate **Dwight Eisenhower** was elected President. The Republicans had long criticised Truman's foreign policy for being soft on communism and it was expected that Eisenhower, the distinguished general of the Second World War, would adopt a firmer line. Eisenhower's new Secretary of State was **John Foster Dulles**, a highly experienced diplomat. Dulles believed that the way to face up to communism abroad was to build up the USA's nuclear weapons so that the enemy would know that the consequences of any aggressive action would be **massive retaliation**. This New Look was to focus on nuclear rather than conventional arms. Backed by superiority in nuclear weapons, the USA could move from merely containing communism to rolling it back. Dulles considered liberating eastern Europe from Soviet domination and sending Chiang Kai Shek back to mainland China to remove the communists. Nuclear weapons would act as a deterrent to the forces of communism. Yet nuclear weapons would be effective as a deterrent only if others thought the USA was prepared to use them. This required a policy of **brinkmanship**, being ready to go to the brink of nuclear war. With both superpowers in possession of the hydrogen bomb by August 1953 the threat of massive retaliation would in reality mean the threat of human extinction. Thus, despite his tough language Dulles was unable to roll back communism. When unrest broke out in eastern Europe against communist rule in 1953 and 1956, the USA failed to intervene.

KEY PEOPLE

Dwight Eisenhower (1890–1969) Elected President of the USA in 1952. 'Ike' Eisenhower had a distinguished military career before entering politics. He had served as Supreme Commander of Allied forces in Europe between 1943 and 1944 before becoming Supreme Commander of NATO forces 1950–2. Eisenhower was a member of the Republican Party and had a strong dislike of communism. Eisenhower had an important influence on the direction of US policy, yet he was prepared to leave the detail of foreign policy to his Secretary of State. Re-elected President in 1956, he retired from politics in 1961.

John Foster Dulles (1888–1959) Served as Secretary of State under President Eisenhower from 1953 until 1959.
A Republican with an experienced career in foreign affairs, Dulles was strongly anti-communist and deeply religious. He believed that international problems could be solved by the application of Christian principles. His term as Secretary of State led to a more assertive attitude to communism in foreign affairs. Despite his tough talking, Dulles's achievements were more limited. A man of amazing energy, Dulles worked at a prodigious rate until ill health forced him to resign in 1959. He died one month later.

KEY TERMS

Brinkmanship The idea, put forward by Dulles, of going to 'the brink of war without being scared'. Set in the context of highly destructive nuclear arsenals on both sides of the Cold War, it would either be a game of bluff or a deadly endgame.

Massive retaliation A strategy put forward by Dulles to be used if the USSR attacked US interests. It involved using all available means, including nuclear weapons, to destroy the enemy. This was typical tough talking by Dulles but it was not universally popular: defence experts saw it as unrealistic; world opinion was worried about the consequences of devastating nuclear strikes. Massive retaliation seemed to imply massive annihilation.

Dwight Eisenhower, US President 1953–60.

CONCLUSIONS

US attitudes at home and abroad were more strident in the 1950s. Both were a consequence of the increasing vulnerability felt in the USA, which had been brought about by the perceived strength of the USSR compared to that of the USA. These reactions were based on exaggerations of reality. The strength of communist support within the USA was never significant; the perceived technological and military superiority of the USSR an illusion. Despite this, the attitudes developed in this period were to have a long-term impact on the USA. The two key symbols of this period of uncertainty were McCarthy and Dulles: both talked tough but in reality they engaged in empty rhetoric. At least Dulles was sincere in his beliefs; the same could hardly be said of McCarthy.

SUMMARY QUESTIONS

1 What impact did the communist takeover of China in 1949 have on US foreign policy?

2 Why did the USA believe that the USSR had gained a technological advantage in the 1950s?

3 What impact did Joseph McCarthy have on domestic politics in the USA?

CHAPTER 6

The Korean War 1950–3

From 1945 to 1949 Europe had been the focus of Cold War conflict. After 1949 attention was to become centred on Asia. The communist takeover of China in 1949 led to US concerns that communism would spread throughout the region. These fears were to be realised in 1950 when communist North Korea invaded capitalist South Korea. The Korean War posed a real danger to international relations. Although in essence a civil war, it was a conflict that the USA, the Soviet Union and China would find difficult not to get embroiled in.

WHAT WERE THE ORIGINS OF THE WAR?

Korea had been annexed by Japan in 1910 but had a long history of independence. When Japan surrendered at the end of the Second World War, Korea was to be occupied by the military forces of the USSR and the USA. The 38th Parallel was set as the dividing line between the Soviet-occupied North and the USA in the South. This arrangement was not intended to be permanent but would oversee the country until elections could be organised by the United Nations. The UN committee to oversee these elections, **UNTCOK**, was dominated by the USA and its allies, therefore North Koreans and the USSR refused to cooperate with its activities. When elections were held in 1948, they were on a restricted franchise and in the South only. The result was a foregone conclusion. The Republic of Korea was formally established in the South under the government of the staunchly anti-communist **Syngman Rhee**, an expatriate who had spent nearly forty years living in the USA. The USA was, however, worried about the viability of his government. At the end of the Second World War much of Korea had been taken over by People's Committees, left-wing groups which had a great deal of popular support for their aim of seizing control of the country and

KEY TERM

UNTCOK The United Nations Temporary Commission on Korea. The United Nations was established in 1945 as a general world peace-keeping organisation. This commission was set up by the UN to oversee the organisation of elections in Korea after 1945. These elections would unify the country under a democratic government. North Korea and the USSR refused to cooperate with the commission. UNTCOK went ahead with the elections in US-occupied South Korea in 1948 and, despite rigging and intimidation, the commission was satisfied with the result; a victory for the US-supported Syngman Rhee.

KEY PERSON

Syngman Rhee (1875–1965) President of South Korea from 1948 to 1960. He lived in the USA for nearly forty years before returning after the defeat of Japan in 1945. He was supported by the USA for the presidency in South Korea. A staunch anti-communist, Rhee's rule involved heavy repression against opponents. Although willing to support him during the Korean War of 1950–3, the US government became increasingly uneasy with his political methods. In 1960 there were mass demonstrations in South Korea against Rhee and he was forced to step down.

KEY PERSON

Kim Il Sung (1912–94)
Leader of North Korea from 1948 to 1994. Kim joined the Korean Communist Party in 1931 and led resistance to the Japanese occupation of Korea. He went to the USSR to receive military training. In Korea he organised guerrilla warfare against the Japanese and his standing among the Korean people was high in 1945. After the Second World War Kim established a communist regime in North Korea. His attempt to unite the country led to the invasion of South Korea and the subsequent war. After the Korean War Kim continued to rule North Korea until his death in 1994.

introducing land reform. The People's Committees were dominated by communists and formed the basis of the government in the North, which became the Democratic People's Republic of Korea led by the popular **Kim Il Sung**. Kim was a hero of the resistance to Japanese rule. In the South, however, the People's Committees were ruthlessly crushed by Rhee's right-wing government. Rhee had a limited base of support, made up largely of middle-class business interests and landowners, and faced several rebellions against his rule by remnants of the People's Committees which had been established in the South. In 1949 the USA and the USSR withdrew their troops from Korea as previously agreed. The government of South Korea was now dangerously exposed.

From early 1949 skirmishes had taken place along the 38th Parallel, 400 soldiers had been killed in May 1949 alone. This fighting was sparked by troops from both sides of the border. It was clear that both North and South were unwilling to accept a permanent division of the country. Rhee talked of using military force to unite Korea but realised the weakness of his position. In January 1950 the USA had implied that it considered Korea to be outside its defence perimeter in the Far East. Therefore when Dulles, a US Special Envoy, visited Seoul in June 1950, Rhee asked for US help. Rhee was to be disappointed: no promises were given. It was in this context that on 25 June 1950 military forces from North Korea attacked the South.

THE US REACTION AND UN INTERVENTION

The war was in origin a civil war over the unification and future direction of Korea but it became an issue of ideological conflict within the context of the superpower rivalry of the Cold War. There has been much speculation on who gave the order to invade the South. Kim had discussed his plans with Stalin who had urged caution and gave no commitment to help the North if an invasion was launched. It seems likely that the decision was Kim's own as an attempt to unite the country. Yet, to the US government, concerned about the spread of communism in China and

Indo-china, this was further evidence of a communist conspiracy directed from Moscow. There was little, if any, evidence of this, but it was what most Americans were ready to believe. Firm action was now needed to prevent the spread of communism.

US intervention followed within two days of the initial attack by the North. Truman, under pressure from anti-communist hysteria at home, authorised the sending of air and naval power to South Korea. US policy in the Far East had changed from one of limited defence to one of total commitment in a matter of days. The UN was then used to ratify US actions. In the words of the official Joint Chiefs of Staff: 'Having resolved upon armed intervention for itself, the US government the next day sought the approval and the assistance of the United Nations.' The UN called on North Korea to withdraw its forces from the South and voted to send assistance to defend South Korea. The USSR, which had the power to veto any decision in the **Security Council** of the UN, was absent at this crucial moment in protest over the failure to admit communist China into the organisation. Thus the USA was able to dominate the UN and, as a result, secured a commitment from sixteen countries to send troops under the UN banner to help South Korea. Among those who sent troops were Britain, Canada, Turkey and the Philippines but the vast majority of the troops sent were American. The USA was using the UN as an instrument of its own foreign policy. It was the USA that paid the bill for most of these soldiers and the UN forces were led by the staunchly anti-communist US General **Douglas MacArthur**. The US government saw UN backing as essential to ensure popular opinion was in favour of a military commitment to Korea which would put American lives at risk. It would also help in the propaganda war against communism throughout the world.

KEY TERM

The UN Security Council
This body is the key decision-making council of the United Nations during crises. It had eleven member states, five of them permanent (Nationalist China, France, Britain, the USA and the USSR) and six elected by all the membership of the UN. Each member of the Security Council had the power to veto any decision and the USSR used this power to thwart US policies. When the Korean War broke out in 1950 the USSR was absent in protest at the refusal to allow communist China into the UN. In its absence the USA introduced the Uniting for Peace Resolution which stated that if a country used its power of veto in the Security Council to block proposals for action, the issue would go to the General Assembly where only a two-thirds majority of all members was needed. Thus, the USA took advantage of Soviet absence to send troops under the UN to help South Korea.

KEY PERSON

General Douglas MacArthur (1880–1964)
A highly competent US general who led the UN forces sent to help South Korea expel the invasion by the North. He had been Commander of the Allied Forces in the Pacific during the Second World War. In 1945 he supervised the occupation of Japan after its surrender. During the Korean War he organised the landings of marines at Inchon which saved South Korea from collapse. Fiercely anti-communist, MacArthur wanted to roll back communism in Korea and China, and use nuclear weapons if necessary. His outspokenness led to his dismissal by President Truman in 1951.

KEY TERM

38th Parallel The line of latitude used as a temporary border between North and South Korea after the Second World War

THE COURSE OF THE WAR

The North's push into the South

Invading North Korean forces pushed southwards with great success, capturing Seoul, the capital of South Korea, and moving towards Pusan (see map on page 73). Despite the arrival of US troops in August, the North Koreans continued to advance. Communist guerrillas in the South attacked South Korean troops as they retreated. As the North took control of areas, People's Committees were re-established and land reforms introduced. This helped clarify the nature of the war: it was a conflict over the future development of the country. By early September South Korean forces had been pushed back to Pusan but the North Korean army was now outnumbered by the arrival of US troops. Under the leadership of MacArthur, US marines landed at Inchon. Two hundred and sixty-one ships landed UN troops almost unopposed. This relieved the pressure on Pusan and within days the South Koreans were able to push North Korea's army back towards the 38th Parallel.

The UN forces push into the North

In the face of superior US forces the army of North Korea started to disintegrate. On 30 September South Korean forces crossed the **38th Parallel** and entered the North. The US government now talked about a 'thrust north'. The 38th Parallel no longer had any validity: it had merely been an instrument to deal with the Japanese surrender in 1945. Right-wing elements wanted a rolling back of communism from the Korean peninsula. The USA went to the UN to win approval for conquering the North and reuniting Korea. As the UN voted its agreement, US forces were already crossing the border. MacArthur began a rapid advance northwards, capturing the capital of the North, Pyongyang, in October. The North Korean army seemed to melt away as many of its soldiers fled into the mountains to regroup. In the areas captured by the UN, the government of the South began to root out communists and collaborators in a wave of violent executions. Over 100,000 were killed by Rhee's officials. Meanwhile, UN forces under MacArthur marched onwards towards the Yalu River, which marked

Korea's border with China. The war was about to take on a different character.

China's entry into the war

As the UN forces moved closer to the Yalu River the Chinese became increasingly concerned about their own security against attack from the USA and its allies. China decided to send troops and supplies into North Korea. China's new communist government was alarmed at the USA's new desire to roll back communism. MacArthur talked openly about the prospects of restoring Chiang Kai Shek's Nationalists to mainland China. Yet Chinese support for North Korea was always likely given the assistance 145,000 Korean volunteers had provided for Mao's communists in the Chinese Civil War. The favour was to be returned when needed. Mao may also have seen the war as an opportunity to replace Soviet influence over North Korea with that of China. In preparation for what seemed an inevitable attack from the Chinese, MacArthur decided to lay waste the area between the frontline and

Directive from the US Joint Chiefs of Staff to General MacArthur, September 1950

Your military objective is the destruction of the North Korean armed forces. In attaining this objective, you are authorised to conduct military operations, including amphibious and airborne landings or ground operations north of the 38th Parallel in Korea, provided that at the time of such operations there has been no entry into North Korea by major Soviet or Chinese Communist Forces, no announcement of intended entry, nor a threat to counter our operations militarily in North Korea. Under no circumstances, however, will your forces cross the Manchurian or USSR borders of Korea and, as a matter of policy, no non-Korean ground forces will be used in the north-east provinces bordering the Soviet Union or the area along the Manchurian border. Furthermore, support of your operations north or south of the 38th Parallel will not include air or naval action against Manchuria or against USSR territory.

Quoted in *The Korean War* by Max Hastings (1987)

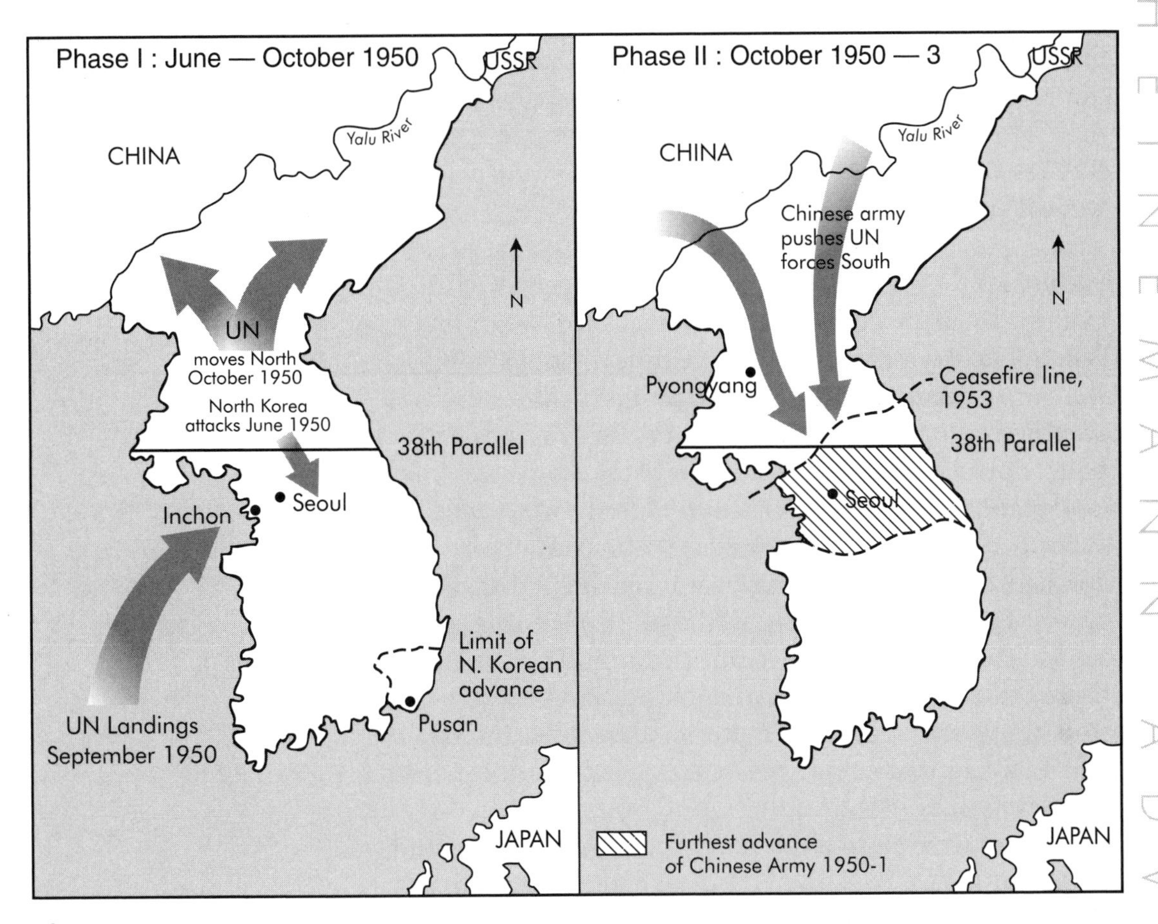

The Korean War.

the Chinese border. **Napalm** bombs were used to turn the area into 'a wilderness of scorched earth'.

On 27 November 1950 Chinese forces poured over the border into North Korea. A force of about 200,000 joined 150,000 North Korean troops and the UN forces were pushed into a rapid retreat. The result was panic in Washington as Truman contemplated the USA's next move. MacArthur recommended using atomic bombs along the border to cut off supplies from China. Truman's refusal to rule out this option caused great concern in Britain and the rest of Europe. Truman stated 'We must meet whatever comes – and we will… We are faced with an all-out situation.' A state of National Emergency was declared in the USA.

The communist advance continued. Pyongyang was recaptured in December and by the end of 1950 North Korea had retaken all land North of the 38th Parallel.

KEY TERM

Napalm Originally a jelly-like substance that spreads when released either by bomb or flame-thrower. It burns everything it sticks to. Napalm was first used against Japan during the Second World War. The USA dropped napalm bombs over large areas of North Korea, causing extensive damage and indiscriminate loss of life. When used later by the USA during the Vietnam War it sparked protests in the USA.

Chinese casualties were high; over 45,000 died fighting during exceptionally cold winter weather of –30°C. But the USSR had now promised to provide supplies should they be needed and the advantage, for the moment, seemed still to lie with the North.

Stalemate

In early 1951 the communist forces pushed South of Seoul. There were now 400,000 Chinese troops in Korea – a vast number that caused logistical difficulties in keeping it supplied adequately. Tens of thousands of porters carried equipment on their backs from the Chinese border to the frontline over two hundred miles away. This could not be sustained indefinitely. The communist forces also had to deal with the superiority of the UN in air power. Extensive bombing raids of the North caused serious damage to bridges, roads and industry. These factors brought about a stalemate at the frontline. Both sides seemed unconvinced that they could win the war. The UN had to contend with widespread guerrilla activity by communists in the South. Up to 30 per cent of UN forces were engaged in rooting out guerrillas behind the frontline. In 1951 the UN launched 'Operation Ratkiller' against guerrilla bandits. The operation was successful but UN troops were starting to become war weary.

To break the stalemate, MacArthur renewed his call for atomic bombs to be used against China. MacArthur's warmongering was beginning to cause tension between himself and Truman. His demands and attitude amounted to insubordination. Truman sacked the general in April 1951 and he was replaced by General Matthew Ridgway. Under Ridgway the stalemate continued as did heavy bombing of the North by air and sea. The bombardment of Wonsan lasted 861 days and reduced the city to ruins. Most of the population of Pyongyang fled to the hills with those who remained living underground in holes and tunnels. Operation Insomnia involved relentless UN bombing to exhaust the population. Heavy fighting at the frontline led US newspapers to raise the issue of US casualties and, in July 1951, both sides were ready to open peace talks at a teahouse at Kaesong.

The peace talks at Kaesong took place while heavy fighting continued and they soon broke down. They resumed later in the year at Panmunjon where agreement was reached over a demarcation line between North and South. Arguments continued over the issue of the return of prisoners of war. Although talks went on, they were to little effect until early 1953.

The end of the war

In 1952 Eisenhower had won the presidential election in the USA on the slogan 'I shall go to Korea.' This was widely interpreted by the US public as a desire to end the war. Thus, when taking office in January 1953, Eisenhower was ready to bring the peace talks to a conclusion. March 1953 saw another significant change of leadership when Stalin died. The new Soviet leadership was willing to see an end to the war. UN casualties reached 23,000 in June 1953 and public opinion in the West was turning against involvement in the war. Rhee's declaration of martial rule in South Korea made the defence of his government a less convincing case for sacrificing young US lives. US soldiers deserted in increasing numbers and many inflicted wounds on themselves to avoid fighting. Ninety per cent of Americans in military hospitals in 1953 had self-inflicted wounds. After visiting Korea, Eisenhower was fully aware of the situation. On 27 July 1953 an armistice was finally agreed. China, North Korea and the USA signed the ceasefire. South Korea refused to do so but had little alternative other than to accept it.

WHAT WERE THE RESULTS OF THE WAR?

The Korean War claimed well over 4 million lives, most of whom were North Koreans. It was a particularly bloody encounter in which both sides could claim partial victory: North Korea had prevented the West from destroying communism in its half of the country; the West had saved South Korea from communism. But neither side was happy with the result. The prospects of uniting the country had disappeared. As historian Bruce Cummings has stated, 'The civil conflict had not been worked through but frozen by outside intervention.'

US troops in the Korean War, mounted on a tank to spearhead a patrol in search of guerrillas, 1951.

For Korea. Both North and South had become pawns in the superpower conflict of the Cold War. In this sense the war was a disaster for the people of Korea. They and their country had been devastated: 5 million had been left homeless. One winner of the conflict was Syngman Rhee, whose regime gained the protection of the USA. Rhee survived as leader of South Korea until 1960 when popular demonstrations against his rigging of elections led to his overthrow. After Rhee's fall, South Korean politics was to be dominated by military rule with brief periods of democracy. North Korea became an isolated communist state under the firm grip of Kim Il Sung until his death in 1994.

For China. The Korean War resulted in many Chinese lives lost and it was a drain on resources. But it had shown its military potential and had emerged as a third superpower alongside the USA and the USSR. China had also gained in standing as the leader of the communist movement in Asia. In contrast, Soviet inaction during the war led to a slump in the USSR's influence over this region.

Losses during the Korean War 1950–3.

	North Korea	China	South Korea	USA	Other UN forces
civilian deaths	2,000,000		1,000,000		
military deaths	500,000	1,000,000	100,000	54,000	3,194

For the UN. The UN had demonstrated the ability to exert its authority against acts of aggression but it had been, as Soviet propaganda was quick to point out, a tool of US policy. Respect for the UN among the developing nations of the Third World declined after the war.

For the USA. The war had a considerable impact on the direction of US foreign policy. It led to the rearming of the USA with a three-fold increase in military spending. The USA would now be ready to meet further examples of communist aggression. The US government saw the need to develop and use a wide range of strategies to help governments facing the threat of communism, from sending military advisers to full-scale use of nuclear weapons. After Korea, the situation in Vietnam provided an opportunity to try out some of these methods.

SUMMARY QUESTIONS

1 Using the maps on page 73 give an outline account of the main events in the Korean War.

2 Why did the UN send troops to the war in Korea?

3 At the end of the Korean War both sides ended up more or less back at the 38th Parallel. What, if anything, did each side gain from the war?

CHAPTER 7

The Vietnam War I: Escalation 1945–68

The US fear that communism would continue to expand in the Far East after the Korean War was soon realised when, in 1954, the French decided to pull out of Indochina. France no longer had the resources or the will to continue fighting in order to keep its empire in Indochina. Its withdrawal, as the USA soon realised, provided the opportunity for communism to extend its influence in the region. The Americans were concerned that, unless action was taken, the whole of Indochina would fall to communism. Thus, the USA was drawn increasingly into the developing civil war in Vietnam. The war escalated into a long and painful conflict for all involved.

THE END OF FRENCH RULE IN INDOCHINA

Indochina had been part of the French Empire since 1887. The Union of French Indochina consisted of Vietnam, Laos and Cambodia, a region of economic and strategic importance. The Japanese recognised this importance and, during the Second World War, they invaded and occupied the area. Resistance to Japanese rule was led by the **Vietminh**. The Vietminh was an organisation of Vietnamese nationalists led by **Ho Chi Minh**. They undertook guerrilla warfare in order to rid their country of foreign rule. When Japan surrendered in 1945 the Vietminh was strong enough to seize Hanoi, the northern capital, and declare independence for Vietnam. The French, however, wished to reassert their control over the region: they were not yet ready to give up their empire. The status and prestige of France was seen to depend on its empire. Thus, after 1945, a civil war of independence was fought between the Vietminh and the colonial forces of the French.

KEY TERM

Vietminh The communist-led nationalist movement that aimed to secure independence for Vietnam. After 1954 the Vietminh formed the government in North Vietnam and established a communist system.

KEY PERSON

Ho Chi Minh (1890–1969) Leader of the Vietminh from the 1930s and leader of North Vietnam from 1954 until his death in 1969. Ho Chi Minh was an alias meaning Bringer of Light; his real name was Nguyen Tat Thanh. Ho spent much of his early life in France where he was one of the founders of the French Communist Party. He was attracted to communism because of its opposition to imperialism. On returning to Vietnam he formed the Vietminh in 1941. He organised resistance to both the Japanese occupation during the Second World War and French rule from 1945 to 1954. A man of integrity and determination, he was admired by both colleagues and enemies.

KEY EVENTS

Dien Bien Phu The site of the key, decisive battle in the war between France and the Vietminh. It was here that the French fortified a small village in the hope of drawing the guerrilla forces of the Vietminh into an open battle. In 1954 the French garrison was attacked by Vietminh forces organised by General Giap. The battle lasted 55 days until the outnumbered French troops surrendered. This defeat led to the French decision to withdraw from Indochina later in the same year.

Geneva Agreements, 1954 These arranged a settlement which brought an end to the French war in Indochina. A ceasefire was signed and France agreed to withdraw its troops from the region. Vietnam was to be temporarily divided along the 17th Parallel until elections could be held to unite the country. These elections were never held. The Vietminh established a communist state in the North. The South was ruled by a right-wing government with US support.

As the civil war dragged on into the 1950s, it became clear to the French that victory was impossible against a guerrilla force that was often difficult to locate. By 1953 the French government was unwilling to continue the war. French voters were also tired of a war thousands of miles away from home which swallowed up vast sums of money and soldiers. General Henri Navarre, the French commander in Indochina, therefore decided to try to inflict a heavy military defeat on the Vietminh in order to force them to the negotiating table and secure a compromise which would allow the French to withdraw with some honour. The Vietminh were coaxed into attacking the heavily fortified French stronghold at **Dien Bien Phu**. The French sat and waited while the Vietminh forces, led by General Giap, poured soldiers and supplies into the surrounding area. When the battle began in March 1954 the French were outnumbered and outgunned. It was a crushing defeat for France and was the decisive event in the French war. 16,000 of its troops were either killed during the battle or captured afterwards. French rule could no longer be sustained. Dien Bien Phu helped commit the French government to the decision to leave Indochina as soon as possible.

In the wake of Dien Bien Phu an international conference was convened in Geneva to try to produce a settlement, which would end the war and allow the French to leave Indochina with some honour. Under the **Geneva Agreements, 1954**, a ceasefire was declared, Laos and Cambodia became independent states, Vietnam was to be temporarily divided at the 17th Parallel until national elections could be held within two years and France would withdraw its forces from the region. The North of Vietnam was to be under the control of the Vietminh, while the South was put under the control of Bao Dai, the Emperor of Vietnam who had collaborated with the French. The French were relieved to be rid of the war but the Geneva Agreements did not end the conflict. Ho Chi Minh resented having to give up the southern half of Vietnam, although he was confident that, if fair elections were held, the country would be united under Vietminh rule. The population of the North, already under his control, outnumbered that of the South. It was the USA that was most unhappy with the Agreements. It was anxious to avoid the Vietminh gaining control of the whole country. The Vietminh was in origin a Vietnamese nationalist movement against foreign rule but it was also heavily influenced by communist ideas. Ho Chi Minh was a communist and, in the North, communist policies were applied. To the US government, which found it difficult to disentangle Vietnamese nationalism from communism, the Vietminh represented the communist threat under orders from Moscow. Thus, the USA did not approve of the Geneva Agreements. The US government had stated that it would not upset the Geneva Agreements but its concerns over South Vietnam's ability to withstand the spread of communism made some form of future involvement likely. The Geneva Agreements did not end the war for Vietnamese independence, it merely delayed it.

SOUTH VIETNAM

Although the division of Vietnam under the Geneva Agreements was supposed to be a temporary arrangement, national elections to unite the country were not held. Communist policies were pursued in the North, but South of the 17th Parallel became a different state. In the south the French forces were replaced by the Republic of Vietnam (South Vietnam) under Emperor Bao Dai. Bao Dai preferred to live the life of an international playboy and was removed in 1955. Real power in the South now rested with **Ngo Dinh Diem**, who had served under the French administration in Vietnam. The regime set up by Diem formed the basis of the USA's campaign against communism in the region. Diem's regime was anti-communist but it was hardly a beacon of freedom.

KEY PERSON

Ngo Dinh Diem (1901–63) Had served in the French administration of Vietnam in the 1930s. Emerged as leader of South Vietnam in 1954 and ruled the country until he was overthrown and murdered in a military coup in 1963. He ruled as a dictator and his government was riddled with corruption. A strict Catholic and strongly anti-communist, his regime was backed by the USA.

What was the nature of Diem's regime?

Dictatorship. Diem ruled South Vietnam as a dictator. His family and cronies were appointed to important positions and often made the most of their new-found power and influence. Diem's brothers acted as advisers and ruled provinces of the country as local dictators. Diem's sister-in-law, Madame Nhu, in particular, enjoyed the trappings of power. Her statement 'Power is wonderful, total power is totally wonderful' did little to endear her to those who saw the corruption of the regime as an undermining influence in its capacity to gain popular support.

Repression of religious sects. Diem was a strict Catholic in a country where non-Catholics were in the majority. The Cao Dai and Hoa Hao sects were crushed and their leaders executed in the 1950s. This action provided a reservoir of supporters for the Vietminh in the South. Buddhists made up the largest religious group and they suffered discrimination at the hands of government policy. The ban on the flying of the Buddhist flag on the Buddha's birthday led to demonstrations in 1963. These protests were ruthlessly dealt with. In June 1963 Quang Duc, a 73-year-old monk, sat in the middle of a Saigon street, dowsed himself in petrol and set himself alight. His very public death in protest at Diem's religious policy was captured on photograph and caused outrage around the world. The response of Diem's government was shockingly insensitive. Madame Nhu said she hoped for more 'barbecues' and her husband commented he would be 'glad to supply the gasoline'. This was too much for some members of Diem's government who resigned and shaved their heads in the style of Buddhists to make their point. US patience was also wearing thin.

Lack of reform. One opportunity Diem had to nurture popular support for his regime was through the implementation of a programme of land reform. The North had ensured land was distributed to the peasants in order to ensure a decent source of income for the majority of its population. In the South, land reform was limited and when it did occur it was undertaken as a device to reward Diem's Catholic supporters and rich government officials. The peasantry made up about 85 per cent of the South's population. They were to be increasingly discontented and alienated from the regime. It was not long before many decided to take a more active stance against the regime.

The growth of opposition. Former members of the Vietminh had continued a campaign of sporadic guerrilla warfare in rural areas of the South since 1954. Discontent with the regime led to an increase in opposition. In 1960 the National Liberation Front had been formed to oppose Diem's regime. The Front was a coalition of twelve different nationalist groups ranging from communists to Buddhists. They called for the removal of the 'colonial regime' in the South, land reform and unification with the North. It was a popular platform, which many were prepared to fight for. Guerrilla activity spread to many areas of the countryside. To Diem all opposition was communist, and the USA, influenced by attitudes generated by the Cold War, was inclined to agree. It was easy to label any opposition as '**Vietcong**', a term of abuse which stamped all opponents as Vietnam communists.

KEY TERM

Vietcong Originally a term of abuse, meaning 'Vietnamese communist', used by Americans to describe the opposition in South Vietnam. Opposition to the South Vietnamese government was much more broadly based than the communists alone; the National Liberation Front was made up of twelve different groups. This was a point the US government failed to understand.

A young Buddhist monk in flames, burning himself in protest at Diem's regime in South Vietnam. This suicide, in Saigon's central market square in October 1963, was the sixth protest suicide in less than four months.

Thus, the regime in South Vietnam was run by a discredited, unpopular government associated with foreign, imperial rule. In 1963 Diem was overthrown by a coup organised by the South Vietnam army but there was no real change in policy. The USA, in its campaign to stop the spread of communism, was drawn into propping up this ramshackle regime as a symbol of the free world. From the beginning of its involvement in the conflict, the USA had misconceptions about the situation it faced, self-imposed by viewing Vietnam within the wider context of the Cold War.

WHY DID THE USA GET INVOLVED IN THE VIETNAM WAR?

The Vietnam War had started as a war of independence that turned into a civil war over the future direction of the country by the intervention of outside forces operating within the context of the Cold War. To the US government the war was less about Vietnamese independence than it was a conflict between communism and the capitalist free world. Despite US hostility to European imperialism the USA had been keen to ensure a power vacuum was avoided after the withdrawal of the French in 1954. The US government had provided the money to finance 80 per cent of the French war effort in Vietnam, although Eisenhower would not commit US forces to help the French. When France withdrew from Indochina the USA transferred its support directly to the government of South Vietnam. According to the US government's belief in the domino effect, if Vietnam was allowed to fall to communism it would lead inevitably to the fall of neighbouring states, such as Laos, Cambodia, Thailand and even the strategically important countries of Malaya and Indonesia. Thus, it was imperative to stop the first 'domino' falling. The USA viewed the Geneva Agreements of 1954 as a failure in the battle against communism. Communism had not been contained; it had been allowed to spread to North Vietnam. Eisenhower was determined to pursue a more hard-line foreign policy against communism than his predecessor Truman, who had seemed unable to prevent the spread of communism to China in 1949 and to Korea during the war of 1950–3.

Thus, South Vietnam's government would be supported as part of the USA's role to uphold those freedoms so cherished in the free world and denied by communism. That South Vietnam's regime was not a good advert for freedom was overlooked by the US government, especially as it soon became clear that South Vietnam could not survive without massive amounts of aid. The dilemma that faced successive US governments was over the form and amount this aid should take, without losing the support of public opinion in the USA for the war.

HOW DID AMERICAN INVOLVEMENT IN THE WAR ESCALATE?

Under Eisenhower's presidency from 1953 to 1961 massive amounts of economic aid were supplied to South Vietnam despite Eisenhower's reluctance to send US troops and military supplies. In 1962 John F. Kennedy, the new President, shared this reluctance but felt another victory for communism would be intolerable. He decided to send military advisers to South Vietnam to help the government tackle the growing guerrilla warfare organised by the Vietcong. Over 16,000 advisers were sent during Kennedy's presidency, including the Army Special Forces, or **Green Berets**. This unit of specially trained troops would train the South Vietnamese army in counter-insurgency tactics to prevent guerrilla groups taking over areas of the country. Unfortunately, the Green Berets had been trained in Texas and their skills were not always applicable to jungle warfare. More importantly, this tactic missed the main point of guerrilla warfare: that success depends on winning over the local population. The Vietcong were able to use 'hit and run' tactics, whereby they struck at their target and then melted into the background, sheltered by sympathetic local peasants. In these conditions it was difficult for the South Vietnamese army to differentiate between guerrillas and civilians.

In 1962, in an attempt to provide security in the countryside, the USA developed a policy of creating **Strategic Hamlets**. This involved moving peasants into fortified villages, guarded by troops. Nearly 3000 Strategic

KEY TERMS

Green Berets Named after their distinctive caps, they were a unit of specially trained US troops, officially called the Army Special Forces. They were trained in the methods of guerrilla warfare but these were not always easy to adapt to jungle conditions in Vietnam. They were used by President Kennedy to support the government of South Vietnam.

Strategic Hamlets The policy of creating fortified villages in the countryside to protect peasants against guerrilla attacks by the Vietcong. It was organised in 1962 by the South Vietnamese troops under US direction. By 1963, two-thirds of the Strategic Hamlets had been destroyed by the Vietcong.

KEY TERMS

Joint Chiefs of Staff
A body made up of the heads of the different armed forces of the USA: army, navy and air force.

Ho Chi Minh Trail The supply route from the North of Vietnam to the Vietcong in the South. It ran through Laos and Cambodia in an attempt to avoid US bombing raids. The journey lasted between two and six months. Losses to disease and attack were high but the route was kept open and ensured losses of troops and equipment by the Vietcong were replaced.

KEY PERSON

Lyndon Baynes Johnson (1908–73) US President 1963–9. As Vice-President LBJ automatically became President on the assassination of Kennedy; he was elected President in his own right in 1964. He had visions of creating a 'Great Society' where social problems would be eliminated, but he sacrificed this to pay for US involvement in Vietnam. After hesitating to send US troops to the Vietnam War, he used the Gulf of Tonkin Incident to persuade Congress to give him a free hand. Troops were then sent in increasing numbers. After 1968 public opinion in the USA turned on Johnson. He was blamed for the increase in US casualties.

Hamlets were established but the forcible moving of peasants from their land and family burial sites caused much resentment and won many over to the Vietcong cause. As the situation deteriorated, Kennedy agreed to send more military support. Aircraft, intelligence equipment and more advisers were sent, coordinated by the Military Assistance Command, Vietnam (MACV). Yet despite the **Joint Chiefs of Staff**'s call to send six US divisions (about 200,000 troops) to Vietnam, Kennedy would not commit the USA to anything more than an advisory role.

When Kennedy was assassinated in 1963, his successor **Lyndon Johnson** inherited a limited but growing US commitment to a war that was not going well for the USA. The year had seen the overthrow of Diem and the start of a succession of military governments, none of which lasted long. This created a power vacuum in the South that the Vietcong took advantage of. By early 1965 there were 60,000 communist guerrillas operating in the South. These guerrillas were supplied by the so-called **Ho Chi Minh Trail**, a supply line running from North Vietnam, through Laos and Cambodia and along the border with South Vietnam. By 1964, 35 per cent of South Vietnam was in Vietcong hands. As the situation got progressively worse, Johnson, like Kennedy, hesitated to make a commitment to send armed US troops to fight in the South. He preferred to expand the advisory role so far taken. Polls indicated that the US public wanted a victory in Vietnam but was against committing large amounts of troops and resources to secure it. In order for the US President to increase the commitment of the USA to the war, some form of convincing justification was needed to carry the support of US public opinion and the backing of Congress.

The Gulf of Tonkin Incident

On 2 August 1964 the US destroyer *Maddox* was fired at by North Vietnamese patrol boats in the Gulf of Tonkin. The *Maddox* was gathering intelligence information at the time. Two days later it was alleged that a further attack took place against the *Maddox* and another US destroyer *Turner Joy*. Evidence later revealed indicates this second attack did not happen. A few months later Johnson

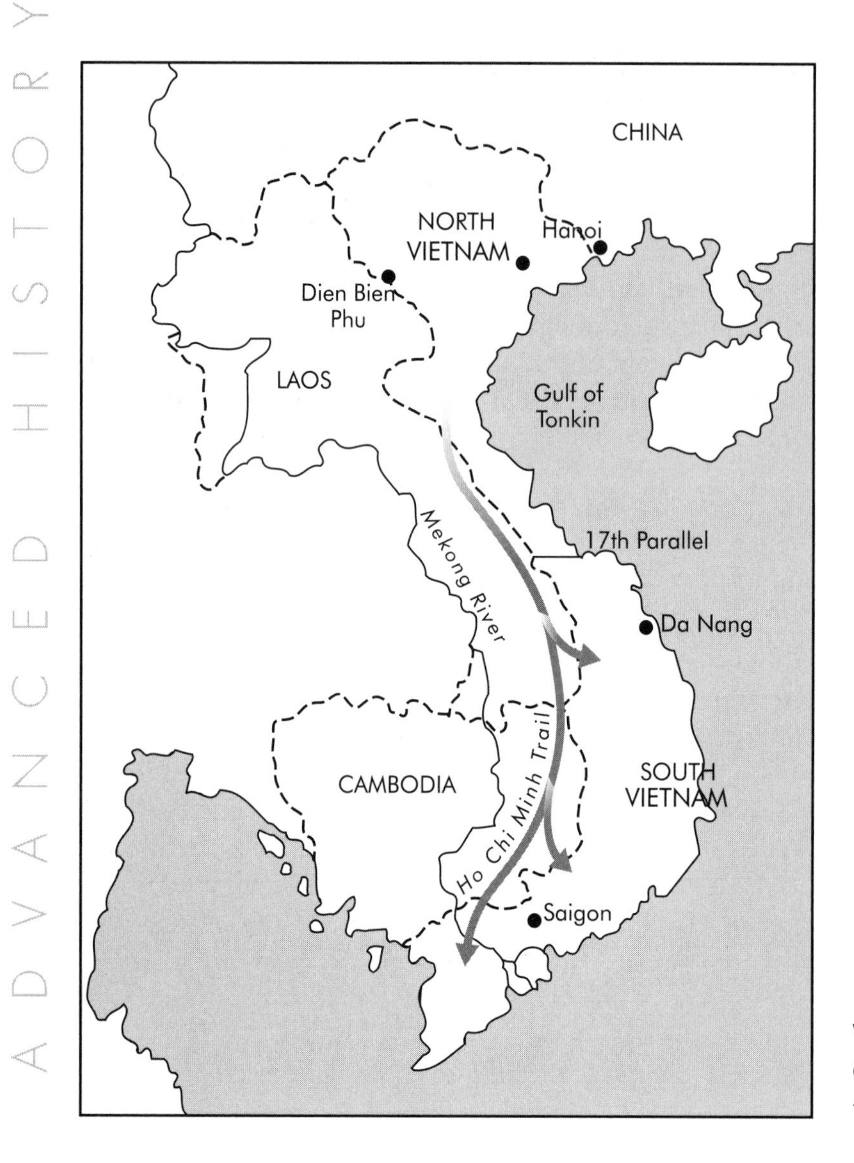

Vietnam after the Geneva Agreement, 1954.

commented 'For all I know, our navy was shooting at whales out there.' Nonetheless, he was to use these attacks as a justification to increase US commitment to the war. The US Congress passed the **Gulf of Tonkin Resolution**, which effectively gave Johnson a 'blank cheque' to send all the support he felt necessary to help South Vietnam. Only two senators voted against the Resolution. Although Johnson was now free to send US soldiers to Vietnam, he still favoured a limited commitment. 'We are not going to send American boys nine or ten thousand miles away from home', he made clear. Nonetheless, Johnson could now enter the war without a formal declaration of war.

KEY TERM

Gulf of Tonkin Resolution
A measure passed by the US Congress in 1964, which allowed President Johnson a free hand to send military supplies, including troops, to Vietnam. It was passed in response to the attacks launched by North Vietnam against American ships in the Gulf of Tonkin. The Resolution led to an escalation of US involvement in the war.

Operation Rolling Thunder

In the presidential election of November 1964 Johnson won an overwhelming victory against his Republican opponent. His position was now much stronger, he had been elected president in his own right and **Congress** was safely under the control of his own party, the Democrats. So when the Vietcong launched a series of attacks against US installations in early 1965, Johnson was confident enough to take decisive action. At Pleiku, nine Americans were killed. Johnson decided to launch bombing raids of North Vietnam. **Operation Rolling Thunder** involved the selection of strategic targets in North Vietnam to be bombed in order to put pressure on the North to stop supplying the Vietcong, end the war and start negotiations. It was hoped that this would bring the conflict to an end at a low cost. Rolling Thunder became more and more extensive but failed to have any impact on the war. Strategic bombing was ineffective against North Vietnam because, as a largely agricultural country, it lacked specific military and industrial targets. The USSR and China were quick to offer replacements for supplies damaged. Soviet MiG fighters and anti-aircraft guns enabled the North to shoot down over 700 US planes. During Rolling Thunder, supplies to the Vietcong by the North actually increased. Hanoi had nearly 90,000 troops in the South by the end of 1966.

KEY TERMS

Congress The US parliament, divided into two houses: the Senate and the House of Representatives. All proposals have to pass through Congress before becoming law.

Operation Rolling Thunder The code name for the US bombing of strategic targets in North Vietnam in 1965. President Johnson and his advisers selected targets every Tuesday over breakfast.

US economic and military aid to South Vietnam.

Year	US economic aid (millions of $)	US military aid (millions of $)
1953–7	823.3	277.8
1958	188.7	53.2
1959	207.1	41.9
1960	180.3	70.9
1961	144.1	65.0
1962	142.9	144.0
1963	186.0	190.0
1964	216.1	186.0
1965	268.2	274.7
1966	729.2	170.8

The start of Rolling Thunder saw the first arrival of US combat troops in Vietnam. Johnson feared communist reprisals for the bombing campaign and sent troops to protect US air bases. Two battalions of US marines arrived at Danang in March 1965. Within nine weeks 99,000 US soldiers were in South Vietnam. Between 1965 and 1968 US soldiers gradually took over from the South Vietnamese army in the role of fighting the war. With their morale and confidence low, South Vietnamese forces were relegated to a supporting role.

The ground war

As the USA took over the running of the war in the South, the number of troops increased rapidly, reaching 385,000 in 1966 and 535,000 in 1968. These troops were under the command of US **General William Westmoreland**. His first move was to secure the coastal areas and build up a base from which the Vietcong could be attacked in the countryside and mountain areas. He was to employ a range of strategies in order to root out the enemy:

- **Search and Destroy** missions were organised to find communist bases in the jungle and eliminate them. This tactic was used against villages suspected of harbouring Vietcong guerrillas. Sometimes it was difficult to be sure civilians were not among the casualties.
- **Air attacks** provided support for ground troops. They were used to destroy enemy supply routes and bases. Large areas of South Vietnam were designed 'free bombing zones' where large numbers of bombs, rockets and napalm were dropped with little regard for the possible target. The large B-52 bombers, which flew too high to be seen or heard, were particularly devastating.
- **Helicopters** were used to provide mobility for US troops in the unfamiliar jungle environment. Unfortunately, this method of transport detached the US forces from the people they were supposed to be fighting for.
- **Operation Ranch Hand** involved the use of chemical warfare to strip the Vietcong of their jungle cover. Defoliants, such as Agent Orange, killed over three million acres of vegetation in the South. It was used despite known links to health problems.

KEY PERSON

General William Westmoreland (b. 1914)
Commander of US military forces in Vietnam 1964–8; Army Chief of Staff 1968–72. Westmoreland was a conventional army man who felt more at ease with conventional warfare than the guerrilla tactics needed in Vietnam. He oversaw the escalation of US involvement in the Vietnam War. He believed that the USA would win the war if the government provided adequate military supplies.

Thus, in the ground war the Americans relied on the use of their superior military technology rather than make attempts to win the hearts and minds of the population. This was in marked contrast to the Vietcong who adopted **Mao's army code** and, when areas were in their control, land reform was organised to illustrate the benefits of throwing off the US-supported regime of the South. When the Americans tried to improve the conditions of Vietnamese citizens in the South it was to little effect. A pacification policy was attempted, involving setting up schools and introducing land reform but this was undermined by its Search and Destroy missions and bombing of large areas of the countryside. There was also a widespread belief among the US military leadership that the war would be won by military means alone: with superior military resources, the US would defeat the Vietcong. It was a view that led to a further, gradual escalation of US involvement. It was also misguided to think that conventional warfare would win so unconventional a war. As the North Vietnam leader Pham Van Dong recognised 'Americans do not like long, inconclusive wars... thus we are sure to win in the end.'

KEY TERM

Mao's army code During the civil war in China during the 1920s and 1930s, Mao Zedong, the communist leader, had developed an eight-point code for use by the Red Army. Its aim was to ensure that the army acted as an advert for the benefits of communism by treating the local population with respect. The code included the following:

- Speak politely.
- Pay fairly for what you buy.
- Return everything you borrow.
- Pay for what you damage.
- Do not hit or swear at people.
- Do not damage crops.
- Do not abuse women.
- Do not ill-treat prisoners.

The code was an attempt to win the hearts and minds of the local people, an essential tool of guerrilla warfare. It was adopted by the Vietcong and contrasted with the lack of respect shown by both South Vietnamese and US forces.

CONCLUSION

A determination to contain the spread of communism had drawn the USA into the conflict in Vietnam. US involvement

US soldiers running underneath an incoming helicopter in the middle of a rice paddy field near Bong Son, South Vietnam, 1966.

A US veteran's impression of the conflict

'In Vietnam, the only measure of victory was one of the most hideous, morally corrupting ideas ever conceived by the military mind – the body count,' Philip Caputo, author of *A Rumour of War*, a memoir of his tour in Vietnam, wrote in an article in *Playboy* magazine. 'We fought over the same ground again and again, month after month, our only object to kill more of them than they did of us.' Commanders liked good body counts, even when they were fudged, which was not uncommon. They liked high kill ratios; it meant they were doing something right.

From B. Edelman, *Dear America: Letters Home from Vietnam* (1985)

Year	Number of US troops
1962	9,000
1963	15,000
1964	16,000
1965	60,000
1966	268,000
1967	449,000
1968	535,000
1969	539,000

US troops in Vietnam.

in the war had escalated from a supporting advisory role under Eisenhower and Kennedy to a large-scale commitment of resources and troops under Lyndon Johnson. The US government had finally committed itself to a policy, which relied on making use of its superior military technology: the belief that by throwing enough resources at the problem it would be solved. It was to be an expression of capitalism's apparent supremacy over communism. It was also doomed to failure.

SUMMARY QUESTIONS

1 Why did the USA intervene in the Vietnam War between 1954 and 1968?

2 How did US involvement in the Vietnam War escalate between 1960 and 1968?

3 What was the significance of the Gulf of Tonkin Incident?

4 Explain the military tactics (both air and ground) used by the USA in Vietnam. How successful were they in the period 1965–8?

CHAPTER 8

The Vietnam War II: US failure and withdrawal 1968–75

The year 1968 was a turning point in the Vietnam War. Under Lyndon Johnson the USA had increased its commitment to South Vietnam in the hope of preventing the spread of communism. The government of South Vietnam had been saved but over 15,000 Americans had already died in the conflict. In 1968 the Vietcong launched the Tet Offensive against the South and its ally, the USA. The consequences of the offensive were to lead the USA to re-evaluate its commitment to Vietnam. Events within the USA were, at the same time, pushing the government to consider whether the human and financial costs of the war were worth the gain, especially as victory over the communists was beginning to look unobtainable.

WHY WAS US INVOLVEMENT IN THE VIETNAM WAR UNSUCCESSFUL?

What was the significance of the Tet Offensive?

In February 1968 the National Liberation Front and Vietcong, supported by elements of the North Vietnamese Army, chose Tet, the Vietnamese New Year, to launch a surprise attack against the forces of South Vietnam and its US ally. It was a simultaneous attack on over 35 towns and cities in the South. Among the targets was Saigon, the capital of the South, and most US bases. The aim of the offensive was to put pressure on the Americans to negotiate a settlement to leave Vietnam. The communists hoped the offensive would encourage the people living under the rule of the South to overthrow its government and thus end the war. The communists launched a force of over 80,000 troops against the South but, after three days of heavy losses, they were driven back. With over half of their soldiers killed, the Tet Offensive was a severe military defeat for the communists. Yet its wider impact was to swing the situation heavily in their favour.

Public opinion in the USA became more disenchanted with the war as a result of the Tet Offensive. The Vietcong's attack on the US Embassy in Saigon was seen to indicate that nowhere was safe from communism in South Vietnam. It was to have a demoralising effect even on those Americans who supported the war. As a leading US general commented at the time 'the average citizen perceived that we didn't know what the hell we were doing'. Thus, the Tet Offensive elevated the Vietnam War to a key issue in US politics during what was an election year.

The 1968 Presidential Election

Lyndon Johnson was entitled to stand for re-election as US President in 1968 but his pledge of 1964, that he would build a Great Society in the USA, had been undermined by both the growth of racial tension at home and the Vietnam War. Some of Johnson's advisers argued for a withdrawal from Vietnam; Robert McNamara, the Defense Secretary, had resigned because of his disillusionment with the war. In March, one month after the Tet Offensive, Johnson announced that he would not seek re-election. His decision came as a shock to many Americans, including those in his own party, but it left the field open to those who wished to stand against US involvement in the war. After the assassination of Robert Kennedy in June 1968, Senator Eugene McCarthy was the leading anti-war voice in the Democratic Party. His main rival for the Democratic candidacy was the Vice-President, Hubert Humphrey, who seemed to offer continuity with Johnson's policy of commitment to the war. The Democratic Party convention in Chicago, where their candidate for President would be chosen, descended into chaos. Outside the convention anti-war protesters were violently attacked by armed policemen while, inside, McCarthy was prevented from delivering his speech at a time when the convention was televised. Humphrey won the Democratic candidacy, but the chaos of the events was a gift to the Republican candidate **Richard Nixon**, who was elected President in November.

KEY PERSON

Richard Nixon (1913–94) US President from 1969 to 1974. A member of the Republican Party, Nixon was elected President in 1968. Nixon introduced a policy of 'Vietnamisation', which allowed US troops to return home. His presidency was marked by anti-war protests, which seemed to have little impact on Nixon. He acted according to his own perceptions and often ignored advice. He opened secret talks with North Vietnam in 1969 but a settlement was not reached until after securing re-election in 1972. His attempts to monitor his opponents at home by bugging the headquarters of the Democratic Party led to the Watergate scandal. Nixon was forced to resign in 1974. His reputation as a manipulative and untrustworthy politician, sometimes referred to as 'Tricky Dicky', was seemingly well deserved.

Richard Nixon, US President (1969–74).

KEY TERMS

SEATO The South East Asia Treaty Organisation. Formed in 1954, it was a defensive organisation set up by the USA to prevent the spread of communism. In addition to the USA, the Treaty was signed by Australia, Britain, France, New Zealand, Pakistan, the Philippines and Thailand. The response of SEATO countries to US involvement in Vietnam was very disappointing for the USA. The failure of SEATO to fully support the USA's role in the war led to a rift in relations between the USA and its allies.

Vietnamisation The policy, introduced by Nixon in 1969, of handing over the fighting of the communists in the Vietnam War to the army of South Vietnam.

Nixon and 'Vietnamisation'

During the election campaign Nixon had pledged to 'end the war and win the peace', by which he implied the USA would win the war. As President, Nixon faced the same dilemma as Johnson. He did not want to lose the war in Vietnam but he did not know how to win it. He also faced an increasingly vocal and violent anti-war movement within the USA. Even those Americans who supported the war were unwilling to contemplate greater involvement. One opinion poll showed that by 1968 a majority of Americans thought the war was a mistake, although a majority was still against withdrawing from Vietnam. Support from US allies for its involvement in the war was also limited. **SEATO** should have ensured support from allies, but only South Korea, Australia, New Zealand, the Philippines and Thailand provided troops for the war. Britain refused to send soldiers and was often critical of US bombing. After their own experience in Vietnam, the French knew better than to get involved. De Gaulle, the French leader, was heavily critical of US policy. Taiwan, one of the USA's staunchest allies, sent less than 30 soldiers to Vietnam. The Australian government, under pressure from protests by anti-war groups, started withdrawing its own troops in early 1970. Thus, the USA's involvement in Vietnam was under severe pressure.

Nixon's solution to this problem was '**Vietnamisation**'. This policy involved training and supplying arms to the government of South Vietnam so that US troops could be withdrawn. Thus, the objectives remained the same but the methods were changed. South Vietnam was to be supplied with superior US military technology. By the end of 1970 South Vietnam had over a million men under arms with rifles, artillery and helicopters. The USA would still supply air cover. Vietnamisation made South Vietnam one of the most militarised nations in the world, yet it still failed.

The policy of Vietnamisation showed that Nixon, like his predecessors, had failed to understand the nature of the war. South Vietnam had become, more than ever, an army without a country. Vietnamisation had little to offer the people of South Vietnam, other than those who dominated the country through their army status. To provide the government of South Vietnam with military hardware reinforced the fact that its people were ruled by a military dictatorship. All opponents could be labelled as communists and arrested, tortured or killed. Between 1968 and 1971, the government of South Vietnam, according to its own figures, killed over 40,000 political opponents. Resentment increased to the point where even the regime could be infiltrated by Vietcong supporters.

To support the regime in South Vietnam Nixon decided to extend the war into Cambodia. In 1970 US troops invaded Vietnam's neighbour to root out Vietcong bases operating in the area. Cambodia's leader, Prince Sihanouk, had tried to keep his country out of the conflict. As a result of US intervention Sihanouk was deposed later in the year in favour of army leaders more favourable to the USA. A civil war then began in Cambodia, involving the communist Khmer Rouge. The US government, dominated by its Cold War perceptions, had again exported war through its Cold War attitude. The consequences were to be devastating for Cambodia. Victory for the communists under Pol Pot led to the genocide of over 3 million people.

THE ANTI-WAR MOVEMENT

Nixon's policy of Vietnamisation was partly designed to appease those who were disillusioned with the war. Yet the anti-war movement in the USA continued to gain support, especially after the US invasion of Cambodia in 1970. The movement led to a wave of protests and demonstrations, many of which ended in violence.

Why did some Americans oppose the war in Vietnam?

It was convenient for those in the government to label all anti-war protestors as rebellious young students who had embraced the flower-power culture of the 1960s and dropped out of mainstream society. There was some truth in this, yet this description does not adequately convey the range of support for the movement. Those disillusioned with the war included students (often referred to by the government as 'campus bums'), intellectuals, liberal-minded politicians and, as the war progressed, returning US troops. Not all were united in their views: liberals tended to attack US policy in the war, radicals used the war to make denunciations of the entire US system. There were several aspects of the war that caused concern and led to opposition:

- From a military point of view the events of the Tet Offensive seemed to indicate that the war was not being won. This led a section of public opinion to believe that the USA could never win a guerrilla war against a revolutionary group by using military methods alone.
- Intellectuals started to query the reasoning behind US involvement. The US government presented the war as a battle for democracy and freedom. Yet the regime of South Vietnam was not a democracy and the freedom of its people was severely limited; it was a corrupt, military dictatorship.
- The methods of warfare used by the USA caused concern. Chemical warfare angered environmentalists; bombing from the air was seen by US public opinion as brutal and unnecessary. The indiscriminate killing that resulted from Search and Destroy missions was criticised. The massacre of women and children at **My Lai** in 1968 caused public outrage. The implication, given by the government, that life was cheap in Asia was not accepted by those who joined the anti-war movement.
- Television and photography played a significant role in influencing public opinion. The war in Vietnam was the first to be televised extensively. What Americans saw on their screens did little to convince them they were winning the war. US photographers had been present in Vietnam before the escalation of the conflict and, because US involvement had grown gradually, it was very difficult for the US government to suddenly limit their activities. Many of the images that found their way into US newspapers and magazines showed the brutality of the conflict. The appalling injuries caused by the use of napalm on civilians, including children, horrified a large section of the US public.
- Opposition to the war grew with the number of US casualties. Less than 2000 Americans had been killed in

KEY EVENT

My Lai The village in South Vietnam where US soldiers massacred between 200 and 500 people, including women and children, in 1968. US soldiers, frustrated at being unable to locate the enemy, suspected the village was sheltering Vietcong guerrillas. Even though no evidence could be found of Vietcong activity, the soldiers went berserk, slaughtering the villagers. The soldiers were new recruits whose average age was nineteen. One spoke of how he 'lost his mind' and obeyed orders to kill, cutting throats and scalping over 25 people. The officer giving the orders was Lieutenant William Calley. The incident was reported by one of the helicopter pilots but the army attempted to cover up the affair. They announced there had been a battle at My Lai and awarded the soldiers involved medals. When a true account of the events was leaked, including photos of the victims, it caused widespread revulsion in the USA. Calley was found guilty and served three years in prison. The My Lai massacre was only one example of the atrocities committed by both sides during the war.

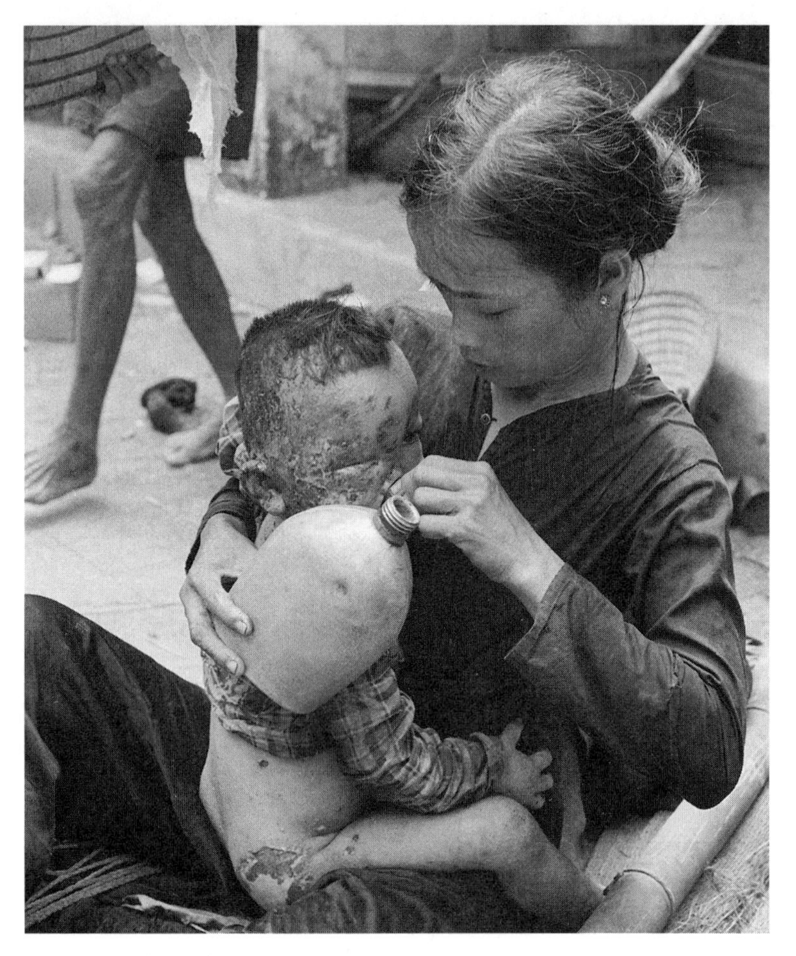

A mother and child with napalm burns during the Vietnam War.

1965; in 1968 the figure had grown to 14,000. As early as 1967 Vietnam Veterans Against the War had been formed by disillusioned soldiers. As coffins and wounded soldiers returned home, many previous supporters of the war started to wonder whether such a sacrifice was worthwhile.

In addition to these aspects relating directly to the nature of the war in Vietnam, there were other factors, stemming from the broader context of the time, which led to support for the anti-war movement:

- The Vietnam War had diverted economic resources away from social and economic policies at home. The war was costing the USA $2000 million per month in 1968. Lyndon Johnson's vision of a '**Great Society**' lacked the resources needed to implement it.

KEY TERMS

Great Society Lyndon Johnson's vision of creating a society in the USA where social problems were eradicated. It was his election slogan in 1964 and received an enthusiastic response from US voters. The resources needed to put the Great Society into practice were instead diverted to the Vietnam War.

KEY TERMS

Pentagon Papers
A collection of government documents relating to the Vietnam War. They were named after the building where government administration is based in Washington. The way in which the Gulf of Tonkin Incident of 1964 was used to hoodwink Congress was revealed. The papers added greatly to a growing feeling of cynicism towards the government on the part of the US public.

- The 1960s had seen the growth of the Civil Rights Movement in the USA, determined to press for equality and fair treatment for the black population of the USA that had been denied the freedoms at home which the USA was fighting to uphold abroad. The Civil Rights Movement had developed a whole range of methods of protest and provided an example that the anti-war movement could follow. There was some merging of the two movements. The proportion of blacks conscripted into the Vietnam War was higher than that of the white population. In this respect the war could be seen as further evidence of a white, racist government oppressing other ethnic groups.
- Young Americans were dissatisfied with the older generation which they viewed as out of touch with the issues of the day. The anti-war movement was part of this growing scepticism with the US system. The movement received additional support and momentum when evidence was revealed of corruption at the heart of the US government. The so-called **Pentagon Papers** were a collection of government documents relating to the Vietnam War. They were leaked to the media and caused a sensation when the *New York Times* published extracts in 1971. The Pentagon Papers revealed government confusion over the war and a deliberate policy of lying to the US public. Nixon attempted to ban publication, but was unsuccessful. Public cynicism about the government's Vietnam policy increased.

The growth of the anti-war movement was therefore caused by the combination of a range of factors. There was growing disenchantment with the war and the nature of the fighting as well as the increasing cost to the USA in human and economic terms. All of this was brought home to the US public by television coverage. The unease it generated added to a growing disillusionment with the entire US system as it existed at the time. It was a powerful combination.

The anti-war movement had shown its presence under Lyndon Johnson. Students had organised sit-ins to protest over the war. Their lecturers arranged 'teach-ins', whereby anti-government perspectives on the war were conveyed.

Marches and demonstrations were held with protestors using slogans such as 'Hey, Hey, LBJ! How many kids did you kill today?!' As armed police faced the demonstrators, the result was often violence. Anti-war protestors launched a campaign against the conscription of young men into the army. Conscription, known in the USA as the draft, had existed since the Second World War. The growth of the US population meant not all young men were needed, so an elaborate system of exemptions was established, which included those at college. Most of these exemptions favoured the wealthy middle class and explains the higher proportion of black and working-class Americans who were conscripted. This fuelled criticism that the draft was not only a method of providing cannon fodder for the war in Vietnam but that it was unfair. The **Draft Resistance Movement** was formed to provide advice on how to avoid being conscripted. Other protestors simply burnt their draft papers or left the country. A quarter of a million young men avoided conscription. As protests grew, matters came to a head under Nixon.

KEY TERM

Draft Resistance Movement An anti-war organisation that tried to disrupt conscription (the draft) in the USA. It encouraged young people, who had been called up, not to join the army and gave help to those who wished to find a method of exemption. Members of the movement were involved in the public burning of draft cards. Many right-wing US politicians condemned them as traitors, yet ensured their own sons were exempted so as not to risk their lives in Vietnam.

In the autumn of 1969 there were large demonstrations of over 250,000 people against the war, organised by the Vietnam Moratorium Movement. Nixon appeared unmoved. He preferred to watch football on the television. When he ordered the invasion of Cambodia in 1970 college students organised another round of protests. On 4 May, at Kent State University, Ohio, National Guardsmen panicked when faced with student protestors. Four students were killed, including two women who were walking to classes. University campuses throughout the USA exploded into violence. Nixon, although troubled in private, remained unmoved in public.

Despite being vocal, support for the anti-war movement in the USA was always limited:

- Protesters were easy to label as communists and 'campus bums'. To the majority of the US public they were cowards and traitors.
- In 1964, 85 per cent of Americans supported government policy in the war. This level of support declined, but remained surprisingly resistant to the

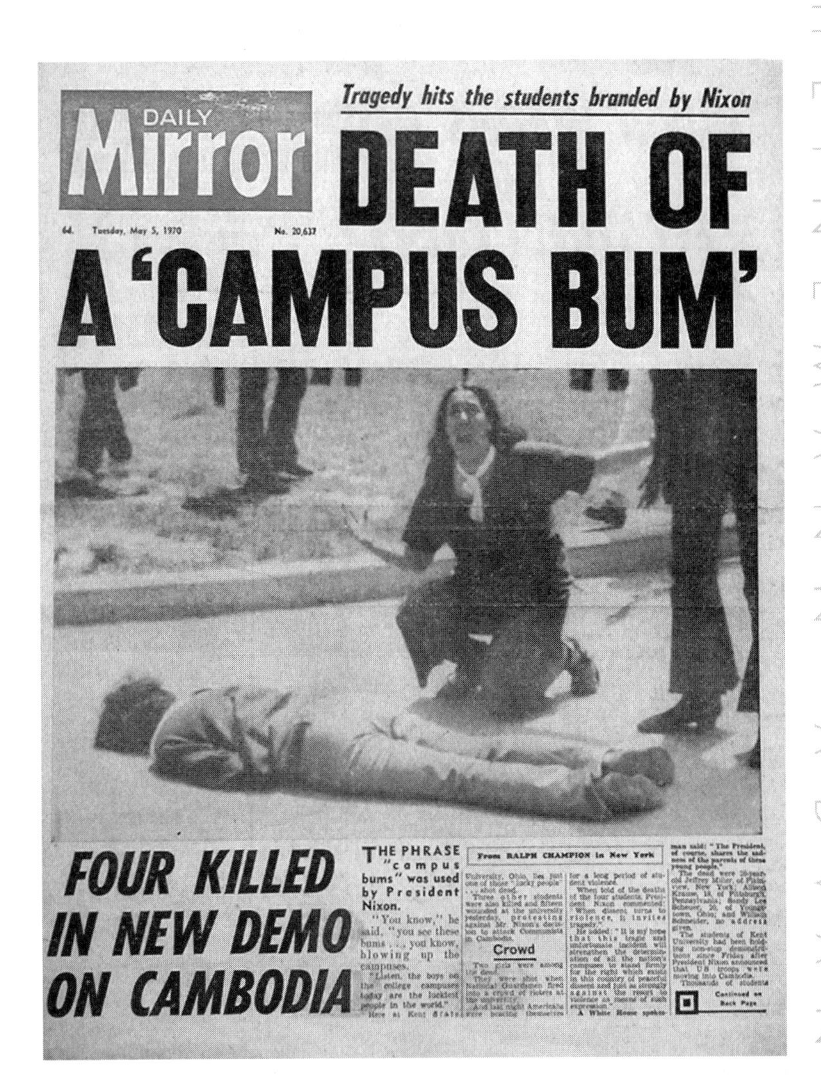

Tragedy hits the students branded by Nixon

DAILY Mirror

6d. Tuesday, May 5, 1970 No. 20,637

DEATH OF A 'CAMPUS BUM'

FOUR KILLED IN NEW DEMO ON CAMBODIA

THE PHRASE "campus bums" was used by President Nixon.

"You know," he said, "you see these bums . . ., you know, blowing up the campuses.

"Listen, the boys on the college campuses today are the luckiest people in the world."

Here at Kent State University, Ohio, lies just one of those "lucky people" . . . shot dead.

From RALPH CHAMPION in New York

Three other students were also killed and fifteen wounded at the university yesterday, protesting against Mr. Nixon's decision to attack Communists in Cambodia.

Crowd

Two girls were among the dead.

They were shot when National Guardsmen fired into a crowd of rioters at the university.

And last night Americans were bracing themselves for a long period of student violence.

When told of the deaths of the four students, President Nixon commented: "When dissent turns to violence, it invites tragedy."

He added: "It is my hope that this tragic and unfortunate incident will strengthen the determination of all the nation's campuses to stand firmly for the right which exists in this country of peaceful dissent and just as strongly against the resort to violence as means of such expression."

A White House spokesman said: "The President, of course, shares the sadness of the parents of these young people."

The dead were 20-year-old Jeffrey Miller, of Plainview, New York; Allison Krause, 19, of Pittsburgh, Pennsylvania; Sandy Lee Scheuer, 20, of Youngstown, Ohio; and William Schneider, no address given.

The students of Kent University had been holding non-stop demonstrations since Friday after President Nixon announced that US troops were moving into Cambodia.

Thousands of students

Continued on Back Page

The front page of the 'Daily Mirror', 5 May 1970, showing one of the students killed at Kent State University. The headline reads 'Death of a campus bum'.

anti-war movement. Even the invasion of Cambodia in 1970 was, according to a Gallup poll, supported by over 50 per cent of Americans; only 35 per cent disapproved.

- Although a belief in victory in Vietnam was fading, much of the US public remained concerned about the status and prestige of the USA abroad. Thus on 8 May 1970, when over 200 hard-hat construction workers attacked a peaceful crowd of anti-war protestors, they were cheered. The protestors had gathered to commemorate the students killed at Kent State University. Nixon later accepted a hard hat as a symbol of 'freedom and patriotism'.

The anti-war movement, while not winning over the majority of public opinion, had deeply divided US society.

The impact of the anti-war movement on political decision-making is difficult to measure but appears to have been limited. After the deaths at Kent State University, Congress was pressurised into passing laws which limited the President's ability to use US troops without its agreement. Later, in 1973, Congress forced Nixon to suspend the bombing of North Vietnam. But the movement had little impact on general policy. What it was able to do was to bring the war to the attention of the US public. The result was that many Americans, including the President, had then to struggle with their own consciences.

THE WAR CONTINUES

Nixon's policy of Vietnamisation enabled US soldiers to be withdrawn as responsibility for fighting was handed over to the South Vietnamese. There were 415,000 US troops in Vietnam in 1970, this dropped to 239,000 in 1971 and only 47,000 in 1972. The morale and discipline of those troops that remained in Vietnam declined as they came to realise that the war was increasingly unpopular at home and that their own government seemed to believe the war could not be won. Desertions became commonplace, increasing by 400 per cent between 1969 and 1971. More concerned with their own survival, soldiers sometimes killed their officers rather than obey orders to fight. 'Fragging', as it was known, involved the murder of officers by using fragmentation bombs. Drugs provided a form of escape from the stress of fighting in the war; in 1971 15 per cent of US troops in Vietnam were addicted to hard drugs and four times as many soldiers were being treated for drug-related problems as they were for combat wounds. Sexually transmitted diseases also did much to seriously undermine the morale of the US soldiers.

In 1972 the communists launched their Easter Offensive against the South. This offensive contained large numbers of North Vietnamese forces supplied with Soviet weaponry. To support South Vietnam's army the

Americans used a heavy bombing campaign against North Vietnam to put pressure on them to negotiate. Despite some early successes, the Easter Offensive ended in stalemate. The realisation that there would be no quick end to the war led both sides to engage in peace talks while continuing to fight.

PARIS PEACE TALKS

Attempts to reach a negotiated settlement to end the war had been started in 1968 by Lyndon Johnson. These talks had achieved nothing. Both sides failed to agree on the shape of the negotiating table! When Nixon became President in 1969 he reopened secret talks in Paris with representatives of North Vietnam. In 1969 the US government was still hopeful of a successful conclusion through military methods. Hopes of an all-out military success faded but the government believed that, if they could not win the war, they could still inflict enough damage on North Vietnam to bring them to the negotiating table in the future. By 1972 this situation seemed to have been reached. By October **Henry Kissinger**, Nixon's National Security Advisor, had reached agreement with Le Duc Tho, leader of the North Vietnamese delegation at Paris. He was able to announce that the North Vietnamese were willing to agree to a ceasefire. Under this ceasefire the forces of North and South Vietnam would retain the areas under their control when the fighting stopped. This was to the advantage of the North because large areas of the South were already in their hands. In return, the North would recognise the existence of the government of South Vietnam. This was a substantial concession by the North as they seemed to accept the division of the country they wished to unite. In addition, all foreign troops and installations would be withdrawn from Indochina.

KEY PERSON

Henry Kissinger (b.1923)
Served as Nixon's National Security Advisor from 1969 to 1973, before becoming Secretary of State. Kissinger was used by Nixon to engage the North Vietnamese in peace talks from 1969 until a final agreement in 1973. He was an expert in international relations and a skilful negotiator. Kissinger combined charm with energy and had a clear grasp of both broad issues and fine detail. He was able to limit Nixon's interventions, which were not always helpful, by the use of outrageous flattery. He was awarded the Nobel Peace Prize in 1973, for his efforts in bringing about an agreed ceasefire in Vietnam.

Why did it prove very difficult to get final agreement for this ceasefire arrangement?

Various obstacles stood in the way of a final agreement:

- President Thieu, the leader of South Vietnam, refused to agree to the settlement. He viewed it as an abandonment of his regime to the forces of communism.
- 1972 was an election year in the USA and Nixon was desperate to get re-elected. He did not want any agreement to look like a failure for the USA. Thus, delays and amendments were used to ensure no embarrassment occurred during the election campaign.
- The North Vietnamese government was suspicious of US intentions and also used delay tactics.
- Nixon used diplomacy to try to isolate Vietnam from its communist allies. He visited Moscow and Beijing and did much to improve US relations with the two communist superpowers. He hoped to isolate North Vietnam and weaken its bargaining position at the talks. This added to the complexity of the negotiating process.
- In December 1972 North Vietnam walked out of the talks. Nixon ordered a resumption of the bombing of North Vietnam, causing severe damage to the cities of Hanoi and Haiphong. North Vietnam returned to the talks and a ceasefire was agreed for 28 January 1973.

Nixon was to present the ceasefire agreement as 'peace with honour'. The USA was able to withdraw all of its forces from Vietnam with the government of South Vietnam accepted by the North. In addition, US prisoners of war, held by the North, were returned. Any optimism that this ceasefire would hold was misplaced. The North was determined to unite the country and South Vietnam, now deprived of nearly all US military help was too demoralised to offer much resistance. The ceasefire only delayed the final outcome of the war.

THE FINAL OFFENSIVE, 1975

The communists launched a Spring Offensive against South Vietnam in March 1975. After initial losses the

South Vietnamese army fled in panic. One month later Saigon was captured by the communists. Thieu resigned and fled abroad as the gates of his presidential palace in Saigon were entered by Soviet-built tanks. The speed of South Vietnam's collapse took the North by surprise but without US support the regime in the South, lacking any popular support of its own, had crumbled.

WHAT WERE THE RESULTS OF THE VIETNAM WAR?

For Vietnam and its people the war was devastating. Over 2 million Vietnamese soldiers (North and South) died in the war. Civilian deaths have been estimated at half a million. In addition to loss of lives, many Vietnamese were wounded and millions were turned into refugees. The economy and society of the South suffered the most dislocation. The war in the countryside led to a movement of millions of peasants into the cities for safety. South Vietnam became one of the most urbanised countries in the world. The new urban population was forced to live in shanty towns on the outskirts of cities, such as Saigon, in conditions of poverty. Rice production declined and food shortages became common. The large presence of US troops, whose wages made them relatively rich, had a marked impact on the South. Large sectors of its economy were geared to providing the comforts expected by US soldiers. Inflation posed a serious problem for those unable to get dollars. The black market flourished. Saigon became infamous for its brothels, one method used to relieve US soldiers of their dollars. When the Americans left Vietnam its economy collapsed. North Vietnam suffered immense damage from the heavy bombing by the US airforce. More bombs were dropped in this war than in the Second World War, yet the population of the North proved to be resilient in the face of continued onslaught. The reconstruction of a united Vietnam after the war was to be a long process.

In the context of the Cold War, the Vietnam War was a victory for communism and a failure for US policy. Vietnam was united under the communist government of the Vietminh, based in the North. Laos and Cambodia fell to communism later in 1975. Yet US fears of a domino effect were not to be realised. The spread of communism in the Far East was restricted to Indochina.

For the United States and its Cold War policies, the consequences were more significant. They had misjudged the situation in Vietnam and failed to realise that each country has its own history and a desire to be in control of its own destiny. Vietnamese communists were not part of a larger conspiracy directed from either Moscow or Beijing. By imposing its own values on a foreign people, the USA misunderstood the situation. Lyndon Johnson's comment, 'We're going to turn the Mekong [the main river of South Vietnam] into a Tennessee Valley' is just one example of this lack of understanding. The US government believed that military policy would win the war but, in the end, they realised that superior weapons alone could not win. To win the guerrilla war in Vietnam the USA needed a political victory to win the hearts and minds of the Vietnamese people but the regime established in South Vietnam deprived them of this possibility. The South Vietnamese government never gained the popular support of its own citizens. All the USA could do was to prolong the war rather than win it. It was an approach which cost 58,000 US lives and was waged at great financial expense. As the journalist Henry Brandon commented 'It was to have a sobering effect on the American belief that everything is possible.'

SUMMARY QUESTIONS

1 What was the significance of the Tet Offensive for the Vietnam War?

2 Why did Nixon introduce Vietnamisation?

3 Why did many Americans oppose US involvement in the Vietnam War?

4 Why did it take so long for a peace settlement to be reached?

5 Why did the USA fail to save South Vietnam from communism?

CHAPTER 9

The Cuban Missile Crisis

The potential dangers of superpower conflict in the nuclear age were demonstrated by the Cuban Missile Crisis that developed in 1962. For the first time during the Cold War the USA and the Soviet Union faced each other in direct conflict. US brinkmanship involved the threat to use nuclear weapons in order to safeguard its interests. In the words of Dean Rusk, the US Secretary of State, the superpowers were 'eyeball to eyeball'. The world waited to see who would be the first to back down.

The origins of this crisis lay in the events that had occurred within Cuba since 1959. In the context of general Cold War tension, a national revolution was transformed into a struggle for superpower supremacy.

WHAT WERE THE CAUSES OF THE CRISIS?

The Cuban Revolution, 1959

The Caribbean island of Cuba had been under US influence since the end of Spanish rule in 1898. Its proximity to the USA made it an ideal target for US economic exploitation. By the middle of the twentieth century, Americans owned most of Cuba's industry, railways, electricity production and the entire telephone system. Cuba's economy was based on the production and export of sugar, much of which was grown on US-owned plantations to be sent to the USA. As Cuba was so reliant on the money it received for this one crop (it made up 80 per cent of its export revenue), the country was heavily dependent on US trade and investment. In short, Cuba was treated as an US colony and holiday destination. Since 1933 the government of Cuba had been in the hands of **Fulgencio Batista**, a military dictator. His regime was corrupt, brutal and inefficient, with most Cubans living in poverty. Batista was, himself, little more than a racketeer and gangster. But under Batista, US interests in the

KEY PERSON

Fulgencio Batista (1901–73) Military dictator of Cuba since 1933. His rule was brutal and repressive. He encouraged US investment and was supported by the US government. He was overthrown by an armed revolt led by Castro in 1959. He fled the country and lived in exile until his death in 1973.

country were protected and encouraged. Thus, Batista's regime received support from the US government. As there was no democratic process for Batista's opponents to use, the only way to bring about change was through armed revolution.

Resentment of Batista's government was widespread in both the towns and the countryside. When **Fidel Castro** launched a rebellion in 1956 by landing an army in Cuba there were many among the population who were willing to see it succeed. Batista's army was able to drive Castro's forces into the Sierra Maestro Mountains but was unable to defeat them. From this base in the mountains, Castro, with the help of **Che Guevara**, built up a force of well-trained guerrilla fighters. Opposition to Batista, encouraged by Castro, spread to the towns and cities. By the end of 1958 Castro's forces were strong enough to pose a serious threat to Batista and on 1 January 1959 Batista fled the country as Castro formed a new government.

The growth of hostility between Cuba and the USA

Castro's supporters were a coalition, including representatives of business, the middle class and the urban and rural poor. It was this broad base that ensured success for the revolution. Castro appeared to be a liberal nationalist and, although he called for land reform, he had not generally associated himself with the ideas of communism. In fact, Castro seems to have had no detailed plan of action for when he seized power.

As a nationalist, Castro wished to make Cuba independent of US control. This in itself was viewed by US business as a threat to its Cuban investments. Initially, however, it was only the US-owned telephone system that was taken over by the government. One action that Castro found difficult to avoid was the arrest, imprisonment and execution of those among Batista's supporters who had been responsible for repression. This action caused tension with the USA as some of those executed were close allies of the USA. Many of Batista's supporters fled to the USA and campaigned to get the support of the US government for an anti-Castro invasion of Cuba. This seems to have persuaded Castro that he needed to tighten his hold over the country against

KEY PEOPLE

Fidel Castro (b. 1926)
Cuban leader since the revolution of 1959, which brought him to power. His revolt against Batista began in 1956 when a group of his supporters landed in Cuba. They were forced to retreat to the Sierra Maestro Mountains, from where they built a base to attack Batista. They were able to overthrow Batista in January 1959. Castro had been a liberal nationalist wishing to rid Cuba of foreign control but, as relations with the USA deteriorated, he was forced to accept help from the USSR. Castro became a communist in 1961 and the revolution developed on communist lines.

Che Guevara (1928–67)
Latin American revolutionary. Argentinian by birth, Guevara spent much of life travelling around Latin America encouraging left-wing revolution. He helped Castro's revolt in Cuba by training his rebels in guerrilla warfare. After Castro seized power, Guevara served as Minister of Industry from 1961 to 1965. He disappeared from Cuba in 1965 and re-emerged a year later in Bolivia where he attempted to encourage revolution. He was captured and shot by the Bolivian army in 1967. He became a student icon, a symbol of revolution.

US interests. The Agrarian Reform Law introduced a measure of land reform that limited the size of farm holdings, although it did not nationalise all land. It was not until early 1961 that Castro announced his adoption of communism but the US government had already come to this conclusion.

President Eisenhower had cut off all trade in arms to Cuba after the revolution and considered cutting trade in sugar, a measure which would have had serious consequences for the Cuban economy. Castro decided to take appropriate action and asked the Soviet Union to purchase Cuban sugar. He also appealed for arms. The USSR was willing to take advantage of the situation and agreed. This pattern was to be repeated. Wherever the USA seemed likely to cut supplies, Cuba looked to the USSR to step in and fill the gap. When US-owned oil refineries in Cuba refused to take Soviet oil, they were nationalised. In July 1960 the USA refused to take any more Cuban sugar and in response Castro nationalised most US-owned assets in Cuba.
A US embargo on all trade with Cuba followed. Castro was forced to swap dependency on the USA for reliance on the USSR.

Relations between Castro's government and the USA declined still further when, in 1961, the new US President, **John F. Kennedy**, supported an invasion of Cuba by anti-Castro supporters. **The Bay of Pigs invasion** consisted of fewer than 1500 Cuban exiles, who were supported by the **CIA**. The US government was hopeful that the invasion would lead to a popular uprising against Castro. This was an over-optimistic view: the invasion was a complete disaster and the invaders never got further than the beach. The whole affair was a severe embarrassment for Kennedy. He could not hide the fact that his government had been involved and embarrassment turned to humiliation when the USA was forced to pay $53 million in food and medical supplies to have the captured invaders returned. Kennedy was beginning to look like a president too young and too inexperienced to deal effectively with the threat of communism. To Castro, the invasion was evidence that the USA was working actively to overthrow his government.

KEY PERSON

John F. Kennedy (1917–63) US President 1961–3. A member of the Democratic Party, he was seen as a progressive liberal who represented a young, vibrant generation. Conscious of foreign policy failures over the Berlin Crisis of 1961 and the Bay of Pigs invasion later in the same year, he decided to stand firm during the Cuban Missile Crisis. In public he used the tactics of brinkmanship, but he was more cautious in private. His stand worked and the Soviet missiles were withdrawn from the island. He was assassinated in Dallas in 1963.

KEY EVENT

The Bay of Pigs invasion, 1961 An attempt by supporters of the ex-Cuban dictator Batista to invade Cuba and remove Castro from power. The invading force was backed by the CIA under orders from Kennedy. The fiasco of the invasion damaged Kennedy's reputation in the USA.

KEY TERM

CIA Central Intelligence Agency. The US agency for collecting information on foreign actions that affect US interests. The CIA has trained and equipped foreign groups in order to depose governments seen as acting against US interests.

Fidel Castro (centre) and Che Guevara (left) during the Cuban Revolution, 1962.

Both leaders recognised that the hostility between their two governments would not go away.

THE MISSILE CRISIS, 1962

Tensions between Cuba and the USA were ignited in October 1962 when US spy planes brought back photos of missile bases under construction in Cuba. The bases were for the installation of Soviet medium-range ballistic missiles, which had a nuclear warhead capable of destroying large cities. Soviet ships carrying military supplies were spotted by intelligence services. They were heading for Cuba. When Kennedy was presented with this information he was horrified. Firm action would need to be taken. The executive committee of the US National Security Council, known as 'ExCom', was called to discuss Kennedy's options.

Why was Kennedy determined to stand firm against communism during this crisis?

In order to understand why Kennedy was prepared to risk nuclear war over the Cuban Missile Crisis it is necessary to consider the specific influences on US foreign policy in this region:

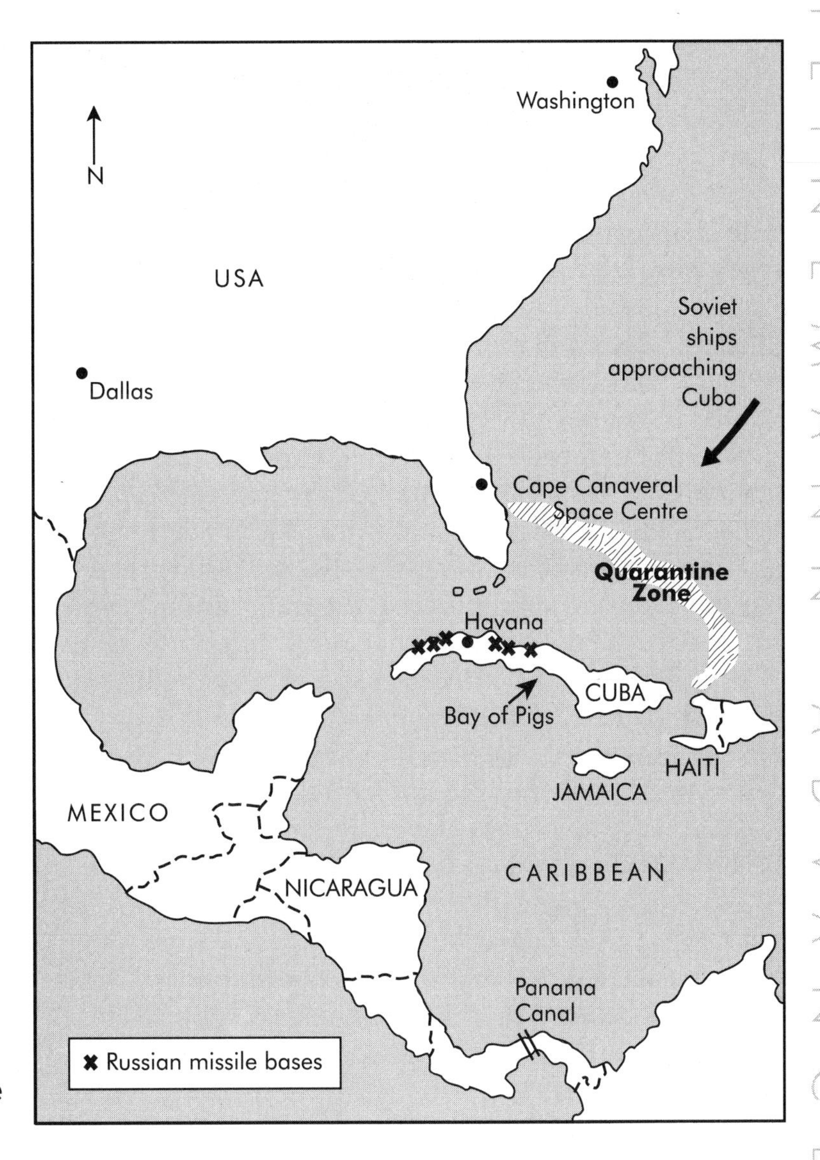

Cuba during the Missile Crisis, 1962.

- The simple matter of geography made the situation dangerous for the USA. Soviet missiles in eastern Europe could not be launched directly against the USA but Cuba was in the USA's 'backyard'. The Soviet missiles based in Cuba could reach most of the large cities of the USA, including New York and Washington, as well as the US space centre at Cape Canaveral. Cuba was only ninety miles from Florida. The most many Americans could expect in the event of a nuclear strike was a three-minute warning.

- Soviet missiles in Cuba would provide a shield to protect the spread of communism in South and Central America. This played on US fears of the domino effect operating in the region. It would pose a serious danger to their economic interests. Situated south of Cuba is the Panama Canal that provides the crucial link for shipping US trade from the Caribbean to the Pacific Ocean. So vital was the Canal that it had been under direct US control since 1903.
- The US government had long considered Latin America (that is, South and Central America) to be within its sphere of influence. The **Monroe Doctrine** had been put forward in 1823 and had formed the basis of US foreign policy towards Latin America. It had asserted the USA's role as the protector of freedom and independence against outside intervention in the affairs of the region's states. In the twentieth century communism was to be classed by the USA as 'outside intervention' and therefore the USA had a duty to step in.
- What gave the crisis its urgency was the belief, by the Americans, that they did not have time on their side. They had to act quickly before the missiles were in place. With Soviet supplies about to arrive in Cuba, a swift response was essential.

These factors meant the missile bases were seen as a direct danger to US interests. In addition, the crisis posed a threat to Kennedy's own position and reputation as President of the USA:

- He had met **Nikita Khrushchev**, the Soviet leader, in Vienna in June 1961. At this meeting the more experienced Khrushchev had gained an impression that Kennedy was a man to give in under pressure.
- Kennedy had been unable to intervene during the Berlin Crisis of 1961. When the Berlin Wall was constructed to prevent East Germans from fleeing communism for the West, Kennedy took no action other than verbal condemnation.
- The fiasco of the Bay of Pigs invasion, also in 1961, had damaged Kennedy's reputation as a leader of the free world against communism.

KEY TERM

Monroe Doctrine A policy developed by James Monroe, US President 1817–25, which asserted the USA's right to intervene in Latin America to protect the independence of its states.

KEY PERSON

Nikita Khrushchev (1894–1971) Leader of the USSR from 1954 until his dismissal in 1964. Khrushchev's approach to the West marked a change from the hard-line aggressive stance of his predecessor, Stalin. Khrushchev developed a policy of 'Peaceful Coexistence', an awareness that the two superpowers had to accept each other rather than slide into mutual destruction. It did not, however, mean the USSR would give up promoting communism throughout the world. He had a tendency to react strongly and display anger in public. He caused a storm in 1960 when he banged his shoe on a table at the United Nations. His decision to back down during the Cuban Missile Crisis, despite the opposition of his own armed forces, averted nuclear war.

- Kennedy was under constant and fierce attacks from Republican Senators for 'doing nothing about Cuba'.

Thus, by 1962 Kennedy was desperate to secure a foreign policy success against the Soviet Union.

On Khrushchev's part there were also reasons why a firm line was needed during the crisis. His own reputation as a Soviet leader able to safeguard the security of the communist bloc was on the line. After the Bay of Pigs incident Kennedy organised Operation Mongoose, a series of CIA activities aimed at undermining Castro's government. Over 10,000 Cuban exiles, supported by 400 Americans were sent in secret to Cuba to blow up railway lines, poison sugar crops and explode bombs in shops and factories. It was in this context that Castro appealed to Khrushchev for military support. In March 1962 Kennedy had written an article where he had made clear his belief that he was entitled to use a nuclear strike. Thus, when the USSR sent arms to help Castro, Khrushchev considered nuclear missiles a necessary part of the package. He also saw Soviet missiles in Cuba as a reasonable counter-measure to the newly installed US missiles in Turkey, a country with a land border with the USSR.

What action did Kennedy take during the crisis?

Kennedy's advisers considered the options. How could they stop the USSR installing missile bases in Cuba? Dean Rusk, the Secretary of State, urged immediate military action. Robert ('Bobby') Kennedy, the President's brother and adviser, preferred an alternative approach put forward by McNamarra, the Defense Secretary. He suggested a blockade of Soviet ships going to Cuba. On 22 October President Kennedy announced a 'quarantine zone' around Cuba. If any Soviet ships entered this zone, action would be taken. US forces were placed on high alert: 54 bombers, each with four nuclear warheads, were on standby; 150 intercontinental missiles aimed at the USSR were armed; and nuclear Polaris submarines were put to sea. Soviet ships with supplies for Cuba were approaching the quarantine zone. The world waited anxiously.

At 10.25 am the Soviet ships stopped and turned away from Cuba. Dean Rusk announced 'We're eyeball to eyeball and I think the other fellow just blinked'. Danger

US President, John F. Kennedy, consulting his advisers during the Cuban Missile Crisis.

still existed. The US Joint Chiefs of Staff called for an immediate invasion of Cuba to destroy the missile bases. While plans for this were being drawn up Kennedy received two messages from Khrushchev. The first message was a long and rambling letter, which took over twelve hours to be transmitted by cable. In the letter Khrushchev agreed to remove all missiles if the USA agreed never to invade Cuba in the future. The next day Radio Moscow broadcast a second and more strident message from Khrushchev that added the demand for the USA to withdraw its missiles from Turkey. Kennedy, on his brother's advice, publicly accepted the first message and ignored the second. It was left to Bobby Kennedy to secretly inform Soviet contacts that missiles would be withdrawn from Turkey. The crisis was over.

WHAT WERE THE CONSEQUENCES OF THE CRISIS?

- **For Cuba.** The crisis had reinforced the trend that had been under way since Castro seized power in 1959. Dependence on the USA had been replaced by a reliance on the USSR. The Soviet Union provided Castro with large amounts of economic aid but restrained him from carrying out his intention of promoting revolution in other Central American states. They had no wish to provoke another conflict with the USA in Central America.

President Kennedy responds to the Cuban Missile Crisis

I, John F. Kennedy, President of the United States of America, … do hereby proclaim that the forces under my command are ordered, beginning at 2.00pm Greenwich time, October 24th 1962, to interdict… the delivery of offensive weapons and associated material to Cuba…

To enforce this order, the Secretary of Defense shall take appropriate measures to prevent the delivery of prohibited material to Cuba, employing the land, sea and air forces of the United States.

The Secretary of Defense may make such regulations and issue such directives as he deems necessary to ensure the effectiveness of this order, including the designation, within a reasonable distance of Cuba, of prohibited or restricted zones and of prescribed routes.

Proclamation issued by President Kennedy, October 1962

- **For Kennedy.** The crisis provided Kennedy with a much-needed foreign policy success. He could claim to have removed the potential danger of Soviet nuclear warheads from America's own 'backyard'. He had, however, given an assurance not to remove Castro from Cuba and, despite at least eight assassination attempts on Castro by the CIA, was left with a communist neighbour for the foreseeable future. The agreement to remove US missiles from Turkey was kept secret from the US public until 1968.

- **For Khrushchev.** Khrushchev could claim credit for securing the American promise not to invade Cuba but it was he who had backed down. Although humiliated, Khrushchev had chosen peace. The Soviet armed forces never forgave Khrushchev and the crisis was a contributing factor in his dismissal from the post of Soviet leader in 1964.

- **For international relations.** Despite the use of brinkmanship both leaders showed restraint during the crisis. Khrushchev took no action when a US spy plane strayed into Soviet air space. Kennedy did not retaliate when one of his spy planes was shot down over Cuba. Both sides recognised the need for improved communication between the two superpowers. A **'hot line' telephone link** was established allowing an immediate exchange of information between the US and Soviet leaders. This would ensure confusion and misunderstanding would not exacerbate a crisis.

In addition to this, the superpowers were prompted into signing other measures which would limit the possibility of nuclear destruction. The **Nuclear Test Ban Treaty** was signed in 1963. This banned the testing of nuclear weapons above ground and under water. This treaty was followed in 1968 by the Nuclear Non-Proliferation Treaty, which was designed to prevent the spread of nuclear weapons to other countries. Both the USA and the USSR signed the treaty. These agreements were encouraged by the changes that occurred in world opinion due to the Cuban Crisis. The crisis had highlighted the danger of world destruction posed by superpower rivalry, over which other countries would have no influence. The 1960s were to see a growth in support for groups campaigning for peace and nuclear disarmament in countries such as the USA and West Germany.

The experience of the Cuban Crisis encouraged both sides to avoid confrontation in the future; thus the paradox of confrontation leading to the establishment of friendlier relations between the superpowers. There had been a 'thaw' in Cold War relations since the death of Stalin in 1953 and, in the aftermath of the crisis, this led to **Détente**, a more permanent relaxation of tensions.

SUMMARY QUESTIONS

1 Why did antagonism occur between the USA and Cuba between 1959 and 1963?

2 Explain the role of Kennedy and Khrushchev during the Cuban Missile Crisis of October 1962.

3 What were the consequences of the Cuban Missile Crisis?

KEY TERMS

'Hot line' telephone link A system of direct communication between the leaders of the USA and USSR. It was set up in 1963 in response to the Cuban Missile Crisis. Its aim was to prevent misunderstanding during a crisis. It was used in 1971 by Nixon and Brezhnev during the war between India and Pakistan.

Nuclear Test Ban Treaty, 1963 A treaty that banned the testing of nuclear weapons above ground and below water. It was signed by the USA, Britain and the Soviet Union and was a measure of the desire to limit nuclear destruction after the Cuban Missile Crisis. It was, however, only a partial ban: testing underground was permitted. France and China, refused to sign the treaty.

Détente A more permanent relaxation in tension. The term was used to describe the improvement in superpower relations that existed after the Cuban Missile Crisis until the Soviet invasion of Afghanistan in 1979 led to a deterioration in relations.

AS ASSESSMENT

ESSAY SKILLS

'Deconstructing' essay questions

As an A-Level History student, you are required to produce extended answers in the form of essays. At AS Level these will be structured essays, often broken down into two parts; at A2 Level you are more likely to face a single question which is broader in scope. Both types of question are designed to test your ability to understand historical issues and use information to support your views in the form of an argument.

When you are asked to write an essay at either AS or A2 Level it is worth remembering that this is the standard way of getting you to show your historical understanding and ability to present an argument. Essay writing is rather like producing a report, in that it is important to organise material into a logical sequence. In order to ensure that this is done effectively, it is important to be aware of the demands of the question. **You ignore the question at your peril!**

If you spend time thinking about the question and planning your answer you will save time later. This will also ensure that time is not wasted writing an inappropriate and irrelevant essay. A useful tool for planning is that of **deconstructing questions.**

How to deconstruct a question

Break the question down into its constituent parts. Look for the following:

- The instruction (I) – e.g. *explain, assess.*
- The topic (T) – e.g. *the Cold War in Europe 1945–50, Soviet influence in Eastern Europe.*
- Keywords (KW) which you need to focus on in your answer.

Example:

Question: Explain how Stalin's foreign policy contributed to the development of the Cold War in Europe.

- I *Explain how . . .*
- T . . . *Stalin's foreign policy and the Cold War . . .*
- KW . . . *contributed . . ., . . . development of . . .*

One of the most common reasons for under-performing in exams is the failure to produce a relevant answer. By using this process you will be able to plan your essays to ensure that the specific question asked is directly addressed.

TYPES OF STRUCTURED ESSAY QUESTIONS

Essay questions can be divided into various categories depending on the instruction given. It is useful to think about the demands of each type of question.

Cause/effect questions

These questions usually start with why or what – for example, **What factors led to the development of the Cold War between 1945 and 1950?** For this type of question a list of factors provides a useful starting point, but there is the danger that each factor is described rather than assessed. Think about assessing the relative importance of each factor. This will help you to develop an argument rather than just describe a list of factors involved.

Discussion questions

These quite often appear as a statement followed by the word discuss or the phrase Do you agree? e.g. **'The end of the Cold War in Europe was brought about by changes within the USSR.' Do you agree with this view?** The best way of dealing with this sort of question is to consider the evidence both for and against the statement given. Evidence against the statement would include a consideration of the role of other factors involved.

Significance/importance questions

These questions often start with phrases such as *assess, how far* or *to what extent*; instructions which require you to weigh up the significance/importance of a given factor. Example: **Assess the success of US attempts to contain communism in Europe between 1945 and 1950.** In order to assess success you would need to weigh up evidence of success against limitations and failures.

Compare/contrast questions

These questions can be notoriously difficult for students. The key point to remember here is to ensure that the instruction is obeyed. If asked to compare the importance of different factors leading to the development of the Cold War, you should ensure that a structure is used which allows you to make direct comparisons. Example: **Compare the importance of Stalin's foreign policy with that of Truman in contributing to the development of the Cold War.** Avoid an answer which describes the actions of each individual in turn with no real comparison until the conclusion. It is much better to think of headings under which they can be directly compared and contrasted – for example, ideology, economic aims, spheres of influence, actions, etc.

PLANNING ESSAYS

After deconstructing a question you are in a better position to draw up a relevant plan for the essay. It is worth spending time thinking about your overall argument and how it will be developed through the essay in a series of paragraphs/sections each looking at a different aspect. There is, of course, no model answer at this level but some general principles can be applied.

A general essay plan

1 INTRODUCTION

State your overall argument; do not leave this to the conclusion. Make it clear what you will be looking at in the essay to develop your argument.

2 MAIN CONTENT

Each section should develop your argument by looking at a particular area or aspect. For each paragraph:

a) make the point(s)

b) explain it in relation to the question

c) support your point with precise evidence – e.g. give figures, dates, factual material concerning relevant events and individuals. Avoid vague statements or generalisations – e.g. people (specify exactly which social groups you mean), some countries (give examples), there were differences of opinion (state exactly what these differences were), there is evidence of… (what evidence?).

3 CONCLUSION

This should sum up your argument and response to the question.

There is an additional section on pages 235–46 that covers tips for further developing your essay skills.

EXAMPLES: QUESTIONS IN THE STYLE OF OCR

Question
The Cold War in Europe

1 The Soviet Union used a variety of methods to gain control over eastern Europe in the years 1945–80. These methods included the following:
– encouraging the communist takeover of governments in eastern Europe
– the setting up of Comecon
– the Warsaw Pact
– the presence of the Red Army in eastern Europe
– the Brezhnev Doctrine
a) Explain how any two of these methods enabled the Soviet Union to gain control in eastern Europe.
b) Compare the importance of the role of at least three of these methods in ensuring Soviet control over eastern Europe.

Examiner's comments
General advice:

- Ensure that you take a direct approach to the question.
- Detailed knowledge will be expected but it should be used to support relevant points.
- Frame your answers with a brief introduction and conclusion.
- Take care with grammar, spelling and punctuation. Make sure your answer is structured clearly and presents material in a logical and coherent manner.

Part (a)
This question requires you to show your knowledge and understanding of two factors that contributed to Soviet control over eastern Europe during the years 1945–80. Weak but adequate answers (Grade E) are likely to show a limited understanding and lack detail. Sound answers (Grades D and C) will show an understanding of the factors and make some relevant links to the focus of the question – i.e. how they helped the USSR gain control. Good answers (Grades B and A) will use detailed knowledge and understanding in a direct and relevant manner to consider the purposes behind each method.

Specific points:
Encouraging the Communist takeover of governments in eastern Europe would require an examination of how this helped extend Soviet influence. The links between communist leaders in eastern Europe and the USSR would be useful to mention. Essential material would include: specific examples of communist takeovers – for

example, in Poland and Hungary; an understanding of 'salami tactics' and how they were used.

The setting up of Comecon should show how this organisation worked to the advantage of the USSR in exploiting the economies of eastern Europe and coordinating economic policy.

The Warsaw Pact can be developed as an example of military coordination under the supervision of the USSR. Soviet dominance over the organisation should be highlighted.

The presence of the Red Army in eastern Europe should be related to the threat of Soviet intervention. The unique situation in 1945 needs to be explained by reference to the power vacuum in Europe. Soviet intervention in Hungary in 1956 is a useful example to develop the point about the ever-present threat of Soviet military action.

The Brezhnev Doctrine would need to be explained and the Czechoslovakian Crisis of 1968 used to demonstrate its application. The threat of the Doctrine being applied during the Solidarity crisis of 1980 would be an effective way of showing your understanding of the policy.

Part (b)
This question is designed to assess your ability to compare the relative importance of different factors. Weak but satisfactory answers (Grade E) will probably go through each factor in turn and present a sequence of unconnected but relevant points. Better answers (Grades D and C) will assess the relative importance of each factor and see links between them. High-quality answers (Grades B and A) will be those that develop an argument based on a thorough assessment of the relative importance and interdependence of the factors involved.

Specific points:
The degree of control that the USSR exercised over the communist governments of eastern Europe would provide a useful point of analysis here. Comecon and the Warsaw Pact both illustrate tensions between Soviet control and eastern European independence. The examples of Yugoslavia and Romania can be contrasted with the greater control over East Germany. The reasons for this difference can then be examined. The role of the Red Army can be assessed by considering whether it was the presence or threat of the Red Army that was important. The limitations of the Brezhnev Doctrine when faced with local hostility to the Russians, as in Poland, can also be related to the theme of a precarious balance between gaining control and not upsetting the governments of eastern Europe and their populations.

Question
The Cold War in Asia and the Americas

1 The USA sent troops to Korea during the war of 1950–3 for a variety of reasons, including the following:
– the war had been started by an act of unprovoked aggression
– the UN authorised intervention in the war to help South Korea
– the US belief in the policy of containment
– domestic pressures within the USA
a) Explain how any two of these reasons contributed to US intervention in the Korean War.
b) Compare the importance of the contribution of at least three of these reasons to the US decision to intervene in the Korean War.

Examiner's comments

Part (a)
This question is designed to assess your knowledge and understanding of factors that led to US intervention in the Korean War. Weak but satisfactory answers (Grade E) will show some understanding but this will be limited. Detail will be thin but show some knowledge of the factors. Better answers (Grades D and C) will show a sound understanding of the material and make some links to the focus of the question – i.e. how the factors help explain US intervention in the Korean War. High-quality responses (Grades B and A) will use detailed knowledge and understanding in a direct and relevant approach to consider US motives and objectives.

Specific points:
The war had been started by an act of unprovoked aggression requires detail on the invasion of South Korea by the North and how the USA viewed this.

The UN authorised intervention in the war to help South Korea would include an examination of the UN resolution that authorised intervention and how the USA viewed the UN as a peace-keeping organisation to prevent acts of aggression.

The US belief in the policy of containment requires an explanation of containment and how the US applied it to Korea. Reference to the spread of communism in China in 1949 would allow you to relate US policy in Korea to the wider context of the Cold War.

Domestic pressures in the US would involve an examination of the Red Scare and the McCarthy witch-hunt against communists. This should be related to the increasing pressure on Truman to take a harder line against the spread of world communism.

Part (b)
This question requires you to show your ability to compare the relative importance of different factors in explaining US intervention in the Korean War. Satisfactory answers (Grades E and D) will be able to make relevant points in relation to each of the factors but will not make links between them. Better answers (Grade C) will attempt to assess the relative importance of each factor and will identify some links between them. Good answers (Grades B and A) will develop an overall argument that includes a thorough assessment of each factor's relative importance and illustrate the way in which they interacted to provide an explanation of US intervention in the war.

Specific points:
An overall argument could be developed around US perceptions of the Korean War within the context of the Cold War. The phrase unprovoked aggression could be challenged by reference to tension in Korea during the period directly before the invasion. The role of the UN as an instrument of US foreign policy could be considered, especially in the light of Soviet absence from the organisation in 1950. US attitudes towards communism that led to containment could be explored and reference made to ideological considerations. The limitations of McCarthyism within the US in terms of its impact on government decision-making could be considered. One useful mechanism for analysis here would be to differentiate between genuine reasons, excuses and methods of justification. This would show an ability to categorise the importance of the factors according to their purpose.

A2 SECTION: COLD WAR TO DÉTENTE 1945–91

INTRODUCTION

The development and course of the Cold War has been the focus of a considerable amount of historical research. Given the enormous impact the Cold War has had on international relations and the domestic politics within countries, this interest is hardly surprising. A lot of attention has been given to the factors responsible for the breakdown in relations between the US and the Soviet Union during the period 1945–50. In addition, there has been an emphasis on examining the influences on superpower relations throughout the duration of the Cold War until its demise in the early 1990s. The following sections concentrate on the main areas of debate.

- **Section 1: What were the causes of the Cold War?** This looks at the relative importance of factors causing the Cold War to develop and differing perspectives on its origins.
- **Section 2: What were Stalin's motives for Soviet expansion?** This examines the specific role of Stalin's foreign policy in the development of the Cold War and considers the issue of whether Stalin's intentions were defensive or expansionist.
- **Section 3: Why did East–West relations change between 1948 and 1962?** This attempts to isolate the factors that influenced the direction of Cold War relations between these years and to assess their relative importance.
- **Section 4: What was the nature of conflict during the Cold War?** This considers the methods of conflict used during the Cold War and their effectiveness. It includes an examination of the role of ideology, economic measures, non-cooperation, propaganda, espionage and the arms race.
- **Section 5: What were the causes and achievements of Détente?** This examines the relative importance of the factors that promoted Détente and assesses the extent to which it brought about change in international relations.
- **Section 6: Why, and how, did superpower rivalry change between 1979 and 1991?** This discusses the factors that led to a breakdown in Détente after 1979 and the development of the Second Cold War. It also considers the reasons why the Cold War came to an end.

SECTION 1

What were the causes of the Cold War?

HISTORICAL INTERPRETATIONS

The study of the origins of the Cold War has produced much historical writing and different schools of thought. The main approaches are as follows:

- **The Orthodox School** sees the Cold War as the product of the aggressive and expansionist foreign policy of Stalin and the USSR. This analysis was adopted by the majority of US and West European politicians and scholars and dominated historical thinking in the West until the 1970s. It has been presented by historians such as W. H. McNeill in *America, Britain and Russia: Their Cooperation and Conflict 1941–46* (1953), H. Feis in *Churchill-Roosevelt-Stalin: The War They Waged and the Peace They Sought* (1957) and A. Schlesinger in his article 'Origins of the Cold War' which appeared in *Foreign Affairs* (1967).
- **The Revisionist School** sees the Cold War as the result of the provocative actions of the USA rather than the USSR. This approach stresses the defensive aspect of Stalin's foreign policy faced with an aggressive USA attempting to gain economic dominance over Europe. Henry A. Wallace, Secretary of Commerce in Truman's administration, argued in favour of greater cooperation with the USSR as the best means of safeguarding US trade abroad. These views were also presented in *The Tragedy of American Diplomacy* (1959) by William A. Williams, and in the 1960s by G. Kolko and G. Alperowitz. They represented the emergence of the 'New Left', writers more critical of the USA and the US system. Their more critical view of the US administration was highly influenced by the growing protest movement against the Vietnam War. The USA had become involved in Vietnam during the 1960s to support the capitalist regime in South Vietnam against the communist North. The failure of the USA to achieve a successful conclusion to the war amid the increasing loss of US lives caused many Americans to challenge the role of the USA as a policeman for freedom in the world. As the war dragged on into the 1970s the USA became more introspective and self-critical. The New Left reflected these concerns in their historical writing.
- **The Post-Revisionist School** has sought to avoid blaming either side for the breakdown in relations and to approach the topic from a more objective standpoint. The generation of writers emerging in the

mid-1970s was more removed from the events of the early Cold War and therefore able to approach the topic in a more detached manner. Instead of trying to decide which side should be blamed for the development of the Cold War, the post-revisionists have attempted to examine in detail the issues involved and bring out the full complexity of decision-making which led to the deterioration in relations. Thus there has been a move away from a mono-causal explanation, involving the identification of a single cause of the Cold War, to examining a wider range of factors. This approach underlies works such as *Shattered Peace: The Origins of the Cold War and the National Security State* (1980) by D. Yergin and *Now We Know* (1997) by J. L. Gaddis. The conclusions reached by Gaddis, however, support, in part, those of the Orthdox School.

WHAT WERE THE LONG-TERM CAUSES OF THE COLD WAR?

Historians have traditionally seen the Cold War as involving a conflict of irreconcilable ideologies: a conflict between, on the one side, capitalism and democracy as represented by the West and, on the other, communism as personified by the Soviet Union and its satellite states. The framework for this ideological conflict was in place by early 1918.

The Bolshevik Revolution 1917

Communism came to the fore as an issue in international relations when the Bolsheviks seized power in Russia in October 1917. The Bolshevik Revolution gave its leader Lenin the opportunity to put communist ideas into practice. The emphasis on state control over the economy, to place the means of production in the hands of 'the people', and on a one-party communist state sent shivers down the backs of the wealthy élites who controlled the governments in the rest of Europe. With one of the largest countries in the world now in communist hands, the leaders of the world's capitalist powers had to take notice. Communist ideology had a divisive influence on foreign policy and international relations. Lenin advocated world communist revolution and believed that in the long term the Bolshevik Revolution would not survive unless communism was spread throughout the world. Thus, communism was a threat to the ruling regimes in the rest of Europe.

Wilsonian Liberalism

In January 1918 the US President, Woodrow Wilson, issued his Fourteen Points. This was a statement of the USA's war aims, those values in international affairs that the USA was prepared to join the First World War and fight for. Although the Fourteen Points were a list of specific aims, they also presented an ideological framework for international relations. Wilson promoted the principles of self-determination, open markets and collective security.

- **Self-determination** was taken to mean the right of all national groups to decide their own form of government according to the democratic wishes of its people. What Wilson did not want was government imposed on national groups without their consent. This was a criticism of European imperialism but was also an attack on the seizure of power by small, armed groups, such as the Bolsheviks, who then imposed their rule on the rest of the population.
- **Open markets** would require the dismantling of trade barriers and spheres of influence that limited the freedom of capitalism throughout the world. Communism and its hostility to capitalist economic development (or, in Marxist terms, exploitation) posed a threat to the greater freedom of world capitalism.
- **Collective security** was a principle close to Wilson's heart. He had a grand vision of a world peace-keeping organisation that would guarantee the safety of any country under attack. This arrangement would make the traditional method of ensuring peace through an elaborate and often unstable system of alliances between individual countries unnecessary. Thus, it was a tool which could be used against injustice in the world. It was also an instrument of the status quo in international relations and therefore, according to the Bolsheviks, a mechanism of world capitalism.

Wilson's ideas were not original and, with the exception of the principle of collective security, were based on traditional US values of personal and economic freedom (i.e. democracy and capitalism). What was different, however, was the vision of these ideas on a world scale.

Thus, Lenin's concept of world revolution and Wilsonian Liberalism represented two widely differing models for the conduct of international relations. The origins of the Cold War lay in the hostility generated between these two competing views. But the Cold War can hardly be said to have started in 1917–18.

WHY DID THE COLD WAR NOT DEVELOP BEFORE 1945?

Despite the seeds of ideological conflict being in place by 1918, the Cold War did not develop after the end of the First World War because neither the USA nor the USSR took on a world role. The reasons for this were different for each country.

The USA after 1918 certainly had the capability to play a dominant role in world affairs. It had emerged from the First World War as a major economic power that had suffered little due to the fighting in the war when compared to Europe. Yet despite the capability of the USA to take on a world role, there was no will on the part of the US establishment or public to do so. Wilson's position as US President was undermined by a senate majority against him and his international programme. The effort of touring the USA to promote his vision left Wilson a nervous wreck. Partially paralysed by a stroke, he was in no position to prevent the USA rejecting membership of the League of Nations, Wilson's world peace-keeping organisation, and returning to a policy of isolationism. In the absence of a clear and pressing source of danger, the USA kept itself detached from European political affairs.

Bolshevik Russia after 1918 was not yet in a position to play a world role. Russia had seen large areas devastated by the First World War. Although the Bolsheviks withdrew Russia from the war in early 1918, they then faced a civil war against their opponents within Russia, who were aided by foreign intervention. The Bolsheviks were able to secure victory in the civil war but it made the recovery from the devastation of the First World War a much slower process. In the 1920s the Bolshevik government was more concerned with ensuring its own survival than spreading world revolution. In the 1930s, under Stalin, the Soviet Union concentrated on the rapid industrialisation of the country in order to defend itself against foreign attack, but the results of Stalin's domestic policies would give the Soviet Union the ability to play a world role in the future. Thus, like the USA, the USSR withdrew from wider European affairs. What brought both countries back into the world arena was the Second World War.

The Second World War provided a danger to the security of both countries. In June 1941 the German invasion of the Soviet Union gave Stalin no choice but to look for allies. In December of the same year the Japanese bombing of Pearl Harbor brought the USA into the war against the fascist powers of Germany, Italy and Japan. Thus, any conflict between the USA and the USSR was submerged beneath the necessity of wartime cooperation. It was the defeat of Germany, Italy and Japan in 1945 that led to the re-emergence of tensions and open hostility between East and West. The USA and the USSR were now in a position of power from which they could both play more assertive roles in the international arena.

WHAT WAS THE LEGACY OF THE SECOND WORLD WAR FOR EUROPE?

The most important consequence of the defeat of Nazi Germany in 1945 was **the creation of a power vacuum in Europe**. This legacy of the Second World War was to provide the situation within which the Cold War developed. At its height Nazi Germany had conquered most of the continent of Europe. Its defeat, therefore, left large areas of Europe without any meaningful government or administration. Much of Europe was economically devastated and in desperate need of reconstruction. The traditional forms of government in Europe had been discredited, especially in eastern Europe, where resistance to Nazi conquest had been particularly ineffective.

The USA and the USSR were each determined not to let the other fill this vacuum completely. Both countries had emerged from the war as dominant powers and were now in a position to fulfil a major role in the post-war world. The USA had emerged from the war as a world superpower: it produced over 50 per cent of the world's manufacturing output, owned a navy as big as the rest of the world's put together and was in sole possession of the atomic bomb. The USSR was in a state of severe economic hardship in 1945, but its Red Army of over 11 million troops occupied most of eastern Europe: it was in a position to enforce its will on large parts of the continent. The result was a division of Europe into spheres of influence, and tensions developed over the relative limits and extent of these different spheres. Thus, the power vacuum caused by the defeat of Nazi Germany was a short-term cause of the Cold War. In the words of the historian John Lewis Gaddis, they were unlikely to fill this vacuum 'without bumping up against and bruising each other's interests'. This would have happened even if both countries were liberal democracies or communist one-party states.

It was ideological differences that gave attempts to fill the power vacuum in Europe an additional edge. The USA was willing to use its influence to ensure peace was based on the principles of Wilsonian Liberalism. Roosevelt wished to promote international cooperation and spread democracy as the basis of world peace. The United Nations, it was hoped, would be a world organisation of free, independent democratic nations. The opening of economic markets was seen as essential to protect US trading interests after the dislocation of the war. The USSR was now in a better position to pursue its foreign policy aims of securing its borders and spreading communism by a process of territorial acquisition. As the Cold War developed the difference, in terms of the realities of each approach, became more obvious. In Europe, US influence was achieved with a large measure of consent: Soviet influence was to be imposed. Stalin had made his view on this clear in 1945, 'whoever occupies a territory imposes his own social system... It cannot be otherwise'.

Another legacy of the war was the deep distrust and suspicion that had developed between the wartime allies. Cooperation between the USA and the USSR had focused on the practical issue of ensuring the defeat of Nazi Germany but, alongside this, was a growing mutual suspicion. The US government was uneasy with Stalin's ruthless policies, especially the purges of the late 1930s. His harsh methods to keep the Soviet people in line were one of many features of Stalin's regime that caused concern in the USA, which had seen the Second World War as a fight to preserve freedom in the world. On Stalin's side, he was deeply suspicious of the USA and of Britain. Their support for the Whites in the Russian civil war led him to question the motives of the West. Fears that they might take another opportunity to undermine the USSR were raised when delays occurred over opening up a second front against Nazi Germany during the war.

Distrust and suspicion were to be heightened by another legacy of the war, the development of the atomic bomb. The power of destruction shown by the impact of the nuclear bombs dropped on Hiroshima and Nagasaki in 1945 sent a clear message to Stalin about the military superiority of the USA. Although the decision to drop the bombs was made in relation to the war with Japan, the failure of Truman to inform Stalin of his decision added to Soviet suspicions of US motives. Stalin determined to develop Soviet nuclear capability as soon as possible. The end of the Second World War had ushered in the nuclear age.

The circumstances produced by the Second World War in 1945 were not conducive to reaching agreement. Even before issues arose concerning the post-war settlement, there was a degree of mistrust which was to taint the superpower relationship.

WHAT WERE THE ISSUES THAT LED TO THE DEVELOPMENT OF THE COLD WAR?

Clashes between the two competing visions of the post-war world occurred when the former wartime allies were in a position to decide the detail of the post-war settlement. The main issues were:

- **The form of government to be encouraged in the newly liberated countries of Europe.** At the wartime conferences of Yalta and Potsdam in 1945 the main source of conflict was over the borders and system of government for Poland. Stalin had agreed at Yalta to the principle of free elections but events were soon to show his interpretation of 'free' was at variance with that of the West. This difference over the nature of elections and government system was to be repeated in connection with all of the countries in eastern Europe. The West tried to insist on western-style liberal democracy guaranteeing freedom of speech and freedom to vote for the party of one's choice. To Stalin, no government in eastern Europe could be tolerated unless it was one friendly towards the Soviet Union. This, he argued, was the only guarantee of Soviet security against future attack.

- **The position of Germany in the post-war world.** The division of Germany into zones of occupation had been agreed at Yalta and Potsdam but this was to be only a temporary measure. The long-term future of Germany became a source of considerable tension. The West soon saw the economic reconstruction of Germany as an important prerequisite of general European recovery, as well as an important market for US goods. For Stalin, Germany was viewed as a future threat to the security of the USSR and therefore its economic recovery and political unification were not considered desirable. This issue was to produce the most serious crisis of the early Cold War, the Berlin Blockade of 1948–9.
- **Economic reconstruction.** The economy of war-torn Europe needed urgent reconstruction in 1945 in order to prevent disease and hunger. It would also be a useful preventive to social disorder. To the USA this required the reassertion of capitalism, which would not only rectify Europe's economy but also aid US industry. In addition it would have a political impact by providing the material benefits needed to stave off communism. To the Soviet Union, the post-war situation provided an opportunity to introduce a communist economic system to meet the needs of the people. State ownership of economic resources would act as a vehicle for the modernisation of the less developed economies of eastern Europe. In 1944 the International Monetary Fund (IMF) and the World Bank had been to set up to aid economic recovery but the tough conditions placed on applications for loans caused disputes between the USA and the USSR. After 1945, economic assistance from the USA became dependent on conditions that favoured free-market capitalism. The tension over this issue, which was highlighted by the arguments over Marshall aid, played an important role in the development of the Cold War.

These issues illustrated the different visions that the USA and the Soviet Union had for post-war Europe. The events, as they unfolded, indicated that the leaders of both superpowers were unwilling to compromise.

HOW IMPORTANT WAS THE ROLE OF PERSONALITY IN THE DEVELOPMENT OF THE COLD WAR?

During the Second World War relations between the Allies were dominated by the 'Big Three': Stalin, Roosevelt and Churchill. All three were dominant personalities who exercised considerable power within their own countries. The power accorded Roosevelt and Churchill was, however, subject to the ballot box. Churchill had played an important role during the war and was able to get Stalin's agreement to recognise spheres of influence by the **'percentages' deal** of 1944. This was to prove effective in limiting Stalin's actions after the war. When Churchill lost the

KEY TERM

Percentages deal, 1944 This was an informal agreement between Churchill and Stalin when they met in Moscow, 1944. Both leaders agreed to recognise spheres of influence in eastern Europe after Germany was defeated. Churchill allowed Stalin the upper hand in Romania and Bulgaria; while Britain could exercise control in Greece. In Yugoslavia and Hungary influence would be shared equally between Britain and the USSR.

British general election in July 1945, there was no change in Britain's foreign policy towards the USSR. Attlee, like Churchill, was deeply suspicious of Stalin.

Roosevelt held a commanding position in US politics in 1945. He had been President since 1933 and as a politician he had great authority. Although he detested all that Stalin stood for, Roosevelt was willing to work with the Soviet leader in order to secure victory against Nazi Germany. His relationship with Stalin was effective during the war but Roosevelt's approach was to come under attack in 1945. As an optimist Roosevelt was ready to give Stalin the benefit of the doubt and refused to believe it was inevitable that Stalin would not keep any promises he made. Historians, such as D. Donnelly, have highlighted Roosevelt's failure to stand firm against Stalin at Yalta as a crucial mistake that allowed Stalin to play 'on the gullibility of the West'. Yet this ignores the point that Roosevelt had been able to establish a reasonable working relationship with Stalin, one where anti-Soviet attitudes had been kept in check within the US government and Stalin had not been provoked into a reactive policy. The death of Roosevelt in April 1945 and his replacement by the more stridently anti-communist Truman has, therefore, been seen by revisionist historians as an important contributory factor in the development of the Cold War. Although Truman tried initially to sustain Roosevelt's policy of accommodation with the USSR, he quickly became suspicious of Stalin's intentions. Inexperienced and insecure, Truman's adoption of an 'Iron Fist' approach caused a rift between the superpowers.

The personality who has received most attention in the study of the early Cold War is Stalin. By the end of 1945 most members of the US and British governments had come to the conclusion that Stalin was untrustworthy and that his personality disposed him to be paranoid and suspicious. Thus, a meaningful agreement with Stalin was impossible. Within the USSR, Stalin operated in a situation of fear and suspicion. This was his preferred method of functioning. This approach, where violence was respected and agreement seen as weakness, was, it has been argued, transferred to foreign policy. Thus, the development of the Cold War can be seen as the result of Stalin's personality operating within the particular and unique circumstances in Europe after the Second World War.

The personalities of both Truman and Stalin had an impact on the course of events. Yet, in terms of attitudes and policies, the two leaders were representatives of the systems they presided over.

HOW FAR WAS THE COLD WAR A PRODUCT OF STALIN'S FOREIGN POLICY?

Historians of the Orthodox School in the West have attributed much of the blame for the development of the Cold War to Soviet foreign policy directed by Stalin. Soviet actions after 1945 were seen in the West as part of a concerted attempt to expand the communist world. The collapse of Nazi Germany in 1945 had left a power vacuum in a large part of central and eastern Europe which Stalin, using the presence of the Red Army, took advantage of in order to strengthen the position of the USSR and spread communism. When looking at the events of the early years of the Cold War there would seem to be much evidence to support this.

At the two important Allied conferences at the end of the Second World War suspicions were raised about the motives of Stalin. At the Yalta Conference of February 1945 Stalin had demanded parts of eastern Poland be given to the USSR and it was clear that Stalin was also trying to establish a communist government in Poland, a move which the West feared would give the USSR permanent control over Polish institutions. By the time of the Potsdam Conference of July 1945 the West were troubled still further by the Soviet expulsion of over 5 million Germans living in areas which were to be part of Poland. To the West this looked like Soviet consolidation in eastern Europe and the Potsdam Conference marked a cooling in relations between the two sides.

Between 1945 and 1948 communist regimes were established throughout eastern Europe and, although the details of this process varied from country to country, the result was the same. The usual pattern was for a 'popular front' government to be formed which the communists quickly came to dominate, purging members of other parties until a communist one-party state, dependent on the Soviet Union, was in operation. The Red Army retained a presence in much of eastern Europe during and after this process. Albania, Bulgaria, Hungary, Romania and Poland followed this pattern. Yugoslavia, although in the hands of a communist regime, retained its independence because, at the end of the Second World War, the country had been liberated from Nazi rule by its own communist partisans before the arrival of the Red Army. Czechoslovakia followed the pattern of Soviet-dominated communism later, in 1948, when Czechoslovak communists launched a coup. The only democratic government in eastern Europe was removed.

Although the Soviet Union had extended its sphere of influence in eastern Europe, the position of Berlin remained a problem. Under the arrangements agreed at Yalta and Potsdam both Germany and its capital Berlin were divided into zones of occupation until a permanent settlement could be agreed upon. The western sectors of both Germany

A cartoon of Stalin choking on Truman's pipe.

and Berlin retained a capitalist economic system and prospered from US financial aid organised under the Marshall Plan. West Berlin lay within the Soviet-occupied eastern zone of Germany, an island of capitalism within the communist zone. When the USSR cut off all road, rail and canal links to West Berlin the West interpreted this as an attempt to starve the West out of the city as a prelude to a possible attack on West Germany. The Berlin Blockade of 1948–9 was thus seen as yet another example of Stalin's expansionist foreign policy. It was defeated only by the West's airlift of all supplies into the western sector of the city.

By the end of 1949 the Soviet Union seemed to have a firm grip over eastern Europe. Not only had communist governments been installed, but Soviet domination was exercised through two Soviet-controlled organisations: Cominform, a replacement for Comintern, which coordinated communist parties throughout Europe to ensure Soviet-style communism prevailed; and Comecon, which coordinated the economies of eastern Europe. After 1949 the focus of the Cold War turned to the Far East, where the communist victory in the Chinese Civil War (1949) and the invasion of South Korea by the communist North, which started the Korean War (1950–3), seemed to provide further evidence of the growth of Soviet power. In the view of many in the West, Stalin's expansionist policy had secured the spread of communism.

HOW FAR WAS THE USA RESPONSIBLE FOR THE COLD WAR?

Although the USA was traditionally seen as the protector of the free world during the Cold War, some of the actions of the West played an important role in its development. Truman lacked confidence in dealing with the USSR and, worried that previous US policy had been too 'soft' on Stalin, resorted to a more hard-line approach. Truman's advisers, growing suspicious of Soviet intentions in eastern Europe, urged him to adopt a firmer stance. 'Unless Russia is faced with an iron fist and strong language, another war is in the making,' Truman observed in 1946. This change in approach to the USSR was an important factor in the development of the Cold War.

Within US diplomatic and government circles, 1945 saw the growth in influence of those who felt a hard-line approach towards the USSR was necessary. The historian Daniel Yergin has highlighted the influence of the so-called 'Riga Axioms', the views and attitudes developed within the US Division of Russian Affairs. These 'Axioms' were based on the reports from a research centre in Riga, the capital of Latvia, part of the old Russian Empire, but an independent state between the wars. Riga was a base for many upper-class Russian exiles who predictably loathed the Bolsheviks. They had a profound influence on the reports sent back to the USA. These emphasised the world revolutionary goals of the new communist government in the USSR and the need to meet any sign of Soviet expansion with a firm hand. These views were reinforced by George Kennan's analysis of Soviet policy in the *Long Telegram* (1946). According to Kennan the USSR as a communist state was fundamentally hostile to the capitalist world and therefore a policy of containment was needed to ensure that its influence did not spread.

The role of economic pressures on the US government has long been debated by historians of the Cold War. Writers from the political left have been keen to highlight the power of big business and the military-industrial sector in pushing the US government towards Cold War confrontation as a way of protecting the economic interests of capitalism at a time when post-war disruption threatened an economic crisis. This view has been put forward in *America's Half-Century* (1989) by T. J. McCormick.

Thus, both political and economic pressures were steering Truman's foreign policy away from the direction taken by Roosevelt. Negotiation and compromise were no longer seen as productive methods of dealing with the USSR. Ignoring the USSR's security needs, Truman's actions were aimed at limiting Soviet power and influence. Yet Truman's actions were unnecessarily provocative. His failure to tell Stalin about the decision to drop the atomic bomb on Hiroshima just a few days after the two leaders had met at Potsdam was viewed with suspicion by the USSR. Churchill's famous 'Iron Curtain' speech at Missouri in 1946, was also considered provocative. It was the situation in Greece in 1947 which helped define Truman's foreign policy against the USSR. In response to the communist threat in Greece, the Truman Doctrine pledged support to those facing communist aggression. This policy was to be applied again in the future whenever communist groups were threatening to remove capitalist governments. The Marshall Plan of the same year represented the economic arm of the USA's attack on the spread of communism in a war-torn Europe. To the Soviet government this was little more than 'capitalist interference'. Cominform and Comecon were, it was argued, merely responses to these actions. Even the Berlin Blockade was presented by the USSR as a response to the provocative policy of the West in introducing a new currency in Berlin, and the formation of the North Atlantic Treaty Organisation (NATO) in 1949 was further evidence of US intentions towards the USSR. This showed there would be no return to US isolationism. Thus, it could be argued, Soviet foreign policy was driven by defensive considerations in response to US actions.

CONCLUSIONS

Who was responsible for the Cold War?

An examination of the development of the Cold War reveals the complexity of the situation within which the Cold War developed. The traditional approaches of historians attempting to apportion blame, often according to their own background, has tended to simplify a complex development. It is, perhaps, better to think about 'what' rather than 'who' carries responsibility.

Both the USSR and the USA were struggling with the new world that was emerging after the end of the Second World War. The exceptional circumstances of 1945, which saw a power vacuum in much of central and eastern Europe, provided greater opportunities and much higher stakes for both the USSR and the West to not only pursue their foreign policy aims but to come into conflict with each other. A lack of understanding of each other's needs led to a cycle of action and reaction, which further increased tension. Thus, attempts by the USA and the USSR to safeguard their security interests resulted in less security for both sides.

When did the Cold War start?

Historians' answers to this particular question depend very much on their answer to the previous one: what caused the Cold War?

- For those historians, such as Arthur Schlesinger, who see the Cold War as an ideological conflict between communism and capitalism, the answer is the Bolshevik Revolution of 1917 when, for the first time, there were states representing both ideologies.
- If the view is taken that the Cold War developed when both the USA and the USSR played a major world role and came into conflict with each other, then the answer would be 1945. This marks the end of the wartime cooperation as the Second World War drew to an end and the issue of the post-war settlement for Europe became impossible to avoid. Revisionist historians, such as William A. Williams in *The Tragedy of American Diplomacy* (1959), emphasise the importance of the decision of the USA to play a major world role after the Second World War as a key factor in the emergence of Cold War conflict.
- For those historians who see the possibility of compromise and negotiation as still possible during the years immediately following the end of the Second World War, the start of the Cold War is placed in 1947. This approach has found favour with post-revisionist historians, such as J. R. Starobin, who focus on the breakdown of the mechanics of diplomacy. Contemporaries, such as General Lucius Clay, argued that an accommodation with the USSR was possible in 1945. But by the end of 1947 the Truman Doctrine and the Marshall Plan, and the tightening of Soviet control over eastern Europe, had made any chance of a post-war settlement through negotiation and compromise between the superpowers impossible. Thus, the Cold War can be argued to have begun properly in 1947, the point of no return.

SECTION 2

What were Stalin's motives for Soviet expansion in Europe?

> 'Taking advantage of exceptionally favourable circumstances, the Soviet Union made full use of the combined strength of the Red Army and world Communism to conduct an expansionist policy which was seen to threaten peace and collective security.'
>
> (NATO Handbook, 1971)

This statement presents the standard view in the West during the period of the Cold War of who was to blame for its development. The provocative and expansionist nature of Stalin's foreign policy after 1945 was singled out as the prime cause of the Cold War and, as the Soviet Union sought to expand world communism, the West was forced into taking action to safeguard the free world. Yet an examination of Soviet foreign policy during this period shows a more complicated picture where mistrust as well as a lack of understanding led to a misrepresentation of Stalin's motives for expanding Soviet influence in eastern Europe.

Two aims can be identified in Soviet foreign policy since 1917:

1. To spread world revolution.
2. To ensure the survival of the new communist state against hostile neighbours.

On coming to power in 1917 the Bolsheviks envisaged a wave of revolution in the rest of the world, which would lead to the collapse of the imperialist, capitalist nations. These hopes were quickly dashed. Attempted communist revolutions in countries which included Germany and Hungary failed, and the old capitalist order reasserted itself across Europe. By 1920 the Bolshevik government found itself in a very weak position. It had been under attack from opponents at home, who were aided by Britain, France and the USA, and an invasion by Poland. Soviet Russia had to come to terms with its own vulnerability in a hostile world. The result was a more traditional foreign policy aimed at protecting national interests rather than stirring up world revolution. In other words, Soviet foreign policy was to become defensive rather than aggressive. Yet the West refused to believe that the Soviet Union had abandoned the aim of spreading world revolution and this was to colour its view of Stalin's motives.

WHY DID THE WEST BELIEVE STALIN'S AIM WAS TO SPREAD WORLD COMMUNISM?

- As leader of the Soviet Union, Stalin was committed to the ideals of communist revolution. These ideals had included the principle of world revolution. Trotsky had been the leading advocate of 'Permanent Revolution'. This was the belief that, without world revolution, the Bolshevik revolution in Russia would not survive, because conflict between capitalism and communism was inevitable. It was a belief strongly held by many within the Communist Party in the USSR. Stalin had not seen this as a priority in the 1930s; he preferred to concentrate on 'Socialism in One Country', the policy of building up the industrial base of the USSR before spreading communism to the rest of the world. Although world revolution was not Stalin's priority, he was unlikely to have abandoned it as a future aim.
- The Comintern was seen in the West as tangible evidence of the USSR's continuing desire to spread revolution. Comintern, or the Third International, was an organisation to facilitate contacts between communist groups throughout the world. The Soviet government controlled its activities and from 1919 to 1926 its chairman was Zinoviev, a leading member of the Communist Party. Comintern encouraged communist groups to stir up unrest across Europe, including Britain and Germany. These actions were not forgotten, even though the organisation was dissolved in 1943.
- The defeat of Nazi Germany in 1945 gave Stalin the opportunity to spread communism throughout eastern Europe. The Red Army controlled large areas of eastern Europe at the end of the Second World War and was in a position to enforce Soviet policy. To the West, the imposition of communist governments on eastern Europe; the civil war in Greece, where communist guerrillas were attempting to remove the monarchists; the communist takeover of Czechoslovakia in 1948; and the Soviet blockade of Berlin in 1948–9 were all seen as evidence of Stalin's intention to spread communism.
- An expansionist and aggressive Soviet foreign policy was viewed as the product of the totalitarian nature of the USSR. George Kennan was to develop this view in his *Long Telegram* of 1946 and subsequent articles such as 'The Sources of Soviet Conduct' (1947). He presented an analysis of Soviet foreign policy driven by notions of class struggle on a world scale and the need of the Soviet government to present its people with a perceived foreign threat which would mobilise the population in order to secure its own position. The concept of **totalitarianism** gained popularity in the West after 1945 and dominated attitudes towards the USSR.

KEY CONCEPT

Totalitarianism
This was a concept used to explain the nature of the dictatorships that had emerged in the 1930s. It focused on a political system by which total control was gained over the economic, social and political life of a nation. It highlighted the use of propaganda and terror as methods of social control. The concept was developed by political scientists in the USA and was used to describe Nazi Germany, Fascist Italy and Stalinist Russia.

The West's interpretation of Stalin's actions was based on the belief that he was driven by the desire to spread communism. This interpretation

A Soviet cartoon critical of US involvement in Greece in 1947.

was, however, based on assumptions about, rather than an understanding of, motives. It was a misleading interpretation, for it failed to understand the reality of the Soviet position in 1945 and it was on this position that Stalin conducted foreign policy.

WHY DID STALIN TAKE CONTROL OF EASTERN EUROPE?

Although some western historians, such as Samuel Sharp and F. Schuman, have seen Stalin's foreign policy as driven by a more traditional Russian expansionism similar to that of the Tsars rather than aiming primarily to spread communism, the view of Stalin as an expansionist for whatever motives needs to be challenged. Rather than seeking to expand, the underlying motive of Stalin's foreign policy would appear to have been more defensive. Soviet foreign policy must be seen within the context of western hostility to the USSR, which had existed since its inception.

The extension of Soviet control to eastern Europe can be seen as a defensive measure; the creation of a buffer zone to protect the Soviet Union from invasion from the West. Thus, a degree of aggression was deemed necessary by the Soviet government in order to secure the defence of the USSR. The Soviet government was under no illusions; it knew that Britain and the USA would be happy to see communism destroyed. The intervention of the West against the Reds during the Russian Civil War had not been forgotten. Even during the Second World War Stalin remained suspicious of the USA and Britain, particularly over their refusal to open a second front until 1944. The USSR had to bear the brunt of the fighting against Nazi Germany enduring severe losses in the process and the suspicion arose that Churchill and Roosevelt were quite happy to see Hitler destroy the USSR. Although there is no evidence to show that either leader considered this, the suspicions remained. Soviet weakness in 1945, caused by exhaustion due to the war effort, made the USSR concerned to protect its borders.

The sheer scale of Soviet losses in the war, which are almost impossible to comprehend, added to a sense of insecurity. The war had resulted in the deaths of over 20 million Soviet citizens, the highest of any of the countries involved in the war. The human cost was also to be measured in the numbers of widows, orphans and invalids. In addition, there was an enormous economic cost, with over 25 million people left homeless and losses in factories and farms amounting to one-third of the country's wealth. Molotov, Stalin's foreign minister, was to itemise the destruction of 1710 towns, 70,000 villages, 31,000 industrial complexes and 98,000 collective farms. The USSR was not only economically weak but also concerned about its military weakness given the development of the atomic bomb by the USA. The USSR did not gain this technology until 1949. The Americans, who saw no fighting on their own soil, failed to understand this Soviet obsession with security. To the USSR a buffer zone of satellite states in eastern Europe was essential and US foreign policy moves after 1945 seemed to confirm the West's determination to undermine communism.

To Stalin, the security of the USSR could be safeguarded only by a ring of buffer states in eastern Europe. Thus, after 1945 Stalin needed to ensure the countries of eastern Europe were friendly to the Soviet Union. This would not be an easy task. Poland was traditionally hostile towards Russia and had spurned Soviet efforts to offer help against Nazi Germany in 1939. The refusal of the Red Army to help the Warsaw Rising of 1944 and the revelation of the Soviet massacre of Poles in the Katyn Forest intensified this hostility between the neighbouring states. Hungary, Romania and Bulgaria had all sided with Nazi Germany during the Second World War. It is within this context that Stalin took firm and direct measures to ensure friendly governments in eastern Europe. In early 1945 Stalin seems to have been prepared to make some accommodation to the West's demands for broad-based coalition governments to be established in eastern Europe. It was only later in 1947 that Stalin insisted on communist regimes on the Stalinist model as a response to a more hard-line US policy towards the USSR. This seemed to be the only way to guarantee pro-Soviet governments. The free elections Stalin had agreed to at Yalta would not guarantee the USSR the security it needed. Greece could be left to the West but eastern Europe was not negotiable: the sacrifices of the Second World War meant the Soviet government felt the USSR deserved the right to impose control over the region to secure its defensive needs. In this sense the spread of communism to eastern Europe was the result rather than the motive behind Stalin's policy to guarantee Soviet security. Stalin actually questioned the suitability of a communist system for East Germany, commenting 'Communism fits Germany like a saddle fits a cow'.

Soviet actions in eastern Europe after 1945 can therefore be seen as attempts to strengthen their hold over the region. Cominform and Comecon were responses to the Truman Doctrine and Marshall Aid. The Berlin Blockade was a defensive measure to prevent the West uniting Germany under capitalism and to safeguard the eastern zone when the West introduced a new currency in West Berlin. Stalin feared a united Germany able to recover its economic and military strength and attack the USSR in the future: 'Give them twelve to fifteen years and they'll be on their feet again.' This also explains Soviet demands for heavy reparations from Germany after the war.

The concern with defence rather than aggression was also a reflection of Stalin's cautious approach to the conduct of foreign policy. In the 1930s his caution was a reflection of the weak economic and military strength of the Soviet Union. Stalin's experiences had taught him to trust no one and proceed with vigilance: an approach he was to use in domestic politics as well as international relations. The Nazi–Soviet Pact of 1939 was an acknowledgement of the weakness of the USSR. Stalin's inability to direct events forced him into signing what was a non-aggression pact with Nazi Germany, a country based on a hatred of communism. After 1945 Stalin recognised that the Soviet Union was in no position to involve itself in another war. The USSR was economically exhausted and lacked the atomic bomb; therefore war must be avoided. Some of Stalin's actions illustrate his unwillingness to provoke the USA into a war. During the Greek crisis Stalin kept his word to Churchill that the USSR did not consider Greece part of its sphere of influence and refused to send help to the communists fighting to remove the Greek monarchy. Tito, the communist leader of Yugoslavia, did send help, to the embarrassment of Stalin. The USSR may have been pleased to see the communist coup in Czechoslovakia but played no active role in the events. The Soviet blockade of West Berlin in 1948 was more provocative but again revealed Stalin's wariness. No action was taken against US and British planes that airlifted supplies into the city during the blockade. Stalin recognised that if war was provoked the superior military might and nuclear monopoly of the USA would decide the outcome.

Soviet foreign policy under Stalin was dominated by the cautious implementation of a defensive strategy to secure the interests of the

USSR. The US government, clouded by notions of world communist revolution, failed to understand this and misread all the signs: Stalin's lack of diplomacy and negotiating skills, coupled with hard-line rhetoric, did little to disabuse the USA of their misconceptions.

HISTORICAL INTERPRETATIONS

When examining Soviet foreign policy, historical writing in the West was caught up in the fear of world domination by the Soviet Union and the spread of communism. Also, after 1949, when both sides possessed nuclear weapons, the fear that the Cold War could develop into the madness of nuclear annihilation gave the debate over Stalin's motives an added weight. There has been a range of historical perspectives that have reflected on Soviet foreign policy which are discussed below.

The Liberal School

Although writers in the West were willing to acknowledge the impressive war record of Soviet forces and the debt owed to them in the defeat of Hitler, most commentators took a hostile view of Soviet foreign policy. The Soviet government was seen as fundamentally hostile to the West, cooperating with the West only when it was necessary. Much stress was laid on the Soviet aim of spreading world revolution. After 1945 the Soviet Union now had the military power to pursue its expansionist objectives with more success. This orthodox view, as it became known, was outlined by George Kennan in his highly influential *Long Telegram* (1946). President Truman used it to justify the need for an 'Iron Fist' approach in dealing with the USSR. This was, in itself, a criticism of the more moderate line taken by Roosevelt in dealing with Stalin.

The Liberal School developed the orthodox view and it dominated historical thinking in the West until the 1970s. It was presented by historians such as W. H. McNeill, H. Feis and A. Schlesinger. In his article 'Origins of the Cold War' (1967), Schlesinger wrote, 'The intransigence of Leninist ideology, the sinister dynamics of a totalitarian society, and the madness of Stalin... made it hard for the West to accept the thesis that Russia was moved only by a desire to protect its security and would be satisfied by the control of Eastern Europe.' The language used in this statement clearly shows the influence of the totalitarian view of the Stalinist regime which was so dominant in the West after 1945. To the Liberal School, the aggressive and expansionist nature of Soviet foreign policy was to be expected, given that it was the product of a totalitarian regime and, as M. Karpovich argued in *The New Leader* (1951), Soviet aggression was therefore different and more dangerous than traditional Russian imperialism.

The views of the Liberal School were clearly a product of the attitudes in the West at the time of the development of the Cold War. It provided a useful justification for US foreign policy and its stand against Soviet actions, particularly when US policy was criticised at home by sections of society who called for a return to the isolationism of the interwar years. The orthodox view has been criticised for ignoring or failing to understand the legitimate defensive needs of the Soviet Union in its rush to lay the blame for the Cold War at Stalin's feet. Despite this limitation the orthodox view still has value in drawing attention to Soviet behaviour and, although this view was challenged in the 1960s, later Soviet actions, such as the invasion of Afghanistan in 1979, often led to renewed support for this perspective.

The Revisionist School – the New Left

The Liberal School was criticised by William A. Williams in *The Tragedy of American Diplomacy* (1959). He was scathing of Kennan's analysis which, he argued, reduced Stalin to little more than a madman.

Williams' argument was to benefit from the emergence of the New Left in the 1960s. The New Left was a group of more radical commentators, often with socialist sympathies, who were more critical of the conservative right in the USA. From this group, writers such as G. Kolko, an ex-student of Williams, and G. Alperowitz paid more attention to the security needs of the USSR in a hostile world, which after 1945 was faced by a more prosperous USA. The New Left also provided economic interpretations of the Cold War as a development promoted by the needs of US capitalism in search of markets.

The Post-Revisionist School

The post-revisionists have attempted to examine in detail the complexity of Soviet decision-making and the USSR's security needs. J. R. Starobin emphasises the destabilising impact of the Second World War 'which had outmoded earlier ideological and political premises'. This theme was developed further by J. L. Gaddis in *Russia, the Soviet Union and the United States* (1990).

The increase in the availability of sources on domestic politics in the USSR has encouraged an examination of foreign policy within the context of internal affairs, with some commentators seeing foreign policy as driven by domestic concerns. In *A History of Twentieth Century Russia* (1997), R. Service stresses the importance of 'dynamic internal processes' in explaining Soviet foreign policy. After 1945 the threat of capitalism to the USSR was used to justify the power of the Communist Party and its leadership. T. Dunmore, in *Soviet Politics 1945–53* (1984), has shown how the rivalry between Zhdanov and Malenkov in the Soviet leadership resulted in a more hard-line approach to the West.

Soviet historiography

Soviet historiography was based on the standard Marxist line that conflict was inevitable, given the hostility of capitalism towards the USSR, which was seen as the bastion of communism. Soviet writers highlighted the actions of Soviet foreign policy as attempts to safeguard the Revolution against the aggressive capitalist powers in the West. In Molotov's own account, *Problems of Foreign Policy* (1949), the USA was accused of attempting to economically enslave Europe 'to the rule and arbitrary will of strong and enriched foreign firms, banks and industrial companies'. In the *Official History of the USSR* (1959), B. Ponomaryov described the Truman Doctrine as a smokescreen for US expansion and Marshall Aid as a tool of US power and influence. It was not until Gorbachev's refusal to support unpopular communist regimes in eastern Europe at the end of the 1980s that Soviet writers could be critical of Soviet dominance over the eastern bloc.

Russian writers since 1991

The collapse of the Soviet Union has produced some interesting reassessment of Stalin's foreign policy. In *The Rise and Fall of the Soviet Empire* (1998) D. Volkogonov has emphasised the role of Comintern as a puppet organisation of the Soviet government to spread revolution. To Volkogonov, Stalin's foreign policy aims were 'based on the twin pillars of Communist internationalism and Soviet great-power status'. This challenges the view that Soviet foreign policy was merely defensive. Volkogonov's work is valuable because of his inside knowledge of decision-making in the USSR. His career within the Soviet army made him highly conscious of foreign policy issues. Yet, as a disillusioned communist caught up in the collapse of the USSR, Volkogonov represents a strand of thinking which is highly critical of the communist past.

Historical writing on Stalin's foreign policy between 1945 and 1953 has come a long way since the early views presented during the initial period of the Cold War. There is now a much more diverse range of viewpoints. Many official sources relating to the foreign policy of the USSR continue to be undisclosed 'in the interests of national security'. The debate over Stalin's motives is certain to remain an area of interest.

SUMMARY OF INTERPRETATIONS OF THE ORIGINS OF THE COLD WAR

The Liberal School

View

- Sees the Cold War as the result of Stalin's foreign policy.
- Stalin's foreign policy was expansionist with the aim of spreading world revolution.
- Stalin's policy was the result of a totalitarian regime trying to keep control over its own people by using the threat of capitalist invasion.

Why

- Used to justify the hard-line approach of the West, especially Truman, in dealing with the USSR.
- Put forward by western historians who saw communism as a threat to the system of liberal democracy that prevailed in the West.

Value

- Draws attention to Soviet behaviour in eastern Europe and Korea.
- But ignores the legitimate defensive needs of the USSR.

The Revisionist School

View

- Blames the hard-line foreign policy of Truman for causing the Cold War.
- Truman's policy was unnecessarily provocative.
- Sees Truman's policy as a product of US economic interests.
- Highlights the defensive needs of the USSR.

Why

- Related to criticisms of Truman's foreign policy.
- Put forward by historians of the 'New Left' who were more sympathetic towards communism.
- Related to the more introspective and self-critical attitudes in the USA caused by US failure in the Vietnam War.

Value

- Emphasises the defensive needs of the USSR.
- Provides a more critical examination of US motives.
- But tends to ignore the provocative actions of Soviet policy.

The Post-Revisionist School

View

- Does not seek to apportion blame for the Cold War.

- Sees the Cold War as the result of a complex set of specific circumstances rather than a single cause.

Why
- Dissatisfaction with both the liberal and revisionist views as inadequate mono-causal explanations.
- Greater availability of sources allowing more detailed study of the structures involved in decision-making.

Value
- Highlights the exceptional circumstances which existed after 1945.
- Based on a wider range of sources.

The Soviet School before 1991
View
- Sees the Cold War as the result of US economic imperialism.

Why
- Based on the standard Marxist view promoted by the Communist Party.

Value
- Highlights the way in which US actions were seen as provocative in the USSR.
- But uncritical of Soviet foreign policy.

Russian views since 1991
View
- Sees Stalin's foreign policy as driven partly by the desire to spread communism.

Why
- Related to the more critical approach to the study of the Soviet Union since its collapse.
- A greater range of official Soviet sources was available.

Value
- Emphasises Stalin's foreign policy aims as being more than merely defensive.
- Utilises newly available Soviet sources.
- But tends to be overly critical of Soviet actions.

SECTION 3

Why did East–West relations change between 1948 and 1962?

In 1948 Cold War positions in Europe had been consolidated. The Soviet blockade of Berlin had reinforced the division of Europe. The setting up of separate West and East German states in the following year marked a securing of the boundaries between the eastern and western blocs. The two sides took measures to turn Europe into two armed camps. In response to the Berlin Blockade, the West established the North Atlantic Treaty Organisation. NATO was to be the vehicle by which the USA would ensure any attack by the communist bloc against western Europe would be met by military means and defeated. The years 1948–55 saw further proposals to reach agreement over Germany in order to prevent the division of Europe becoming permanent, but without success. Both sides seemed to be resigned to the continued division of Europe. The setting up of the Warsaw Pact by the USSR indicated its recognition that there would be two Europes and that defensive measures were needed to secure the eastern bloc. Thus, by 1955 the military division of Europe into two armed camps was complete. On this evidence, relations between the superpowers had changed little between 1948 and 1955, yet alongside this process of consolidation of hostility in Europe there were significant developments, which marked a change in the methods and the arena of Cold War conflict. This change was highlighted by a series of crises in years 1955–62.

WHAT CHANGES TOOK PLACE IN SUPERPOWER RELATIONS BETWEEN 1948 AND 1955?

Before 1950 the Cold War had developed out of the circumstances arising from the Second World War and had been focused on Europe. After 1950, this changed:

- **The development of globalism.** In the 1950s the conflict between the superpowers extended beyond the confines of Europe to other parts of the world. The communist takeover of China in 1949 turned attention to the Far East. The Korean War of 1950–3 and events in Vietnam in 1954 drew in the superpowers, turning civil war into part of the global chess game between capitalism and communism. The process of European decolonisation produced a range of opportunities for both the USA and the USSR to gain influence in the so-called Third World. The need of the newly independent states of Africa and the Middle East for financial assistance provided the superpowers with a motive for extending their influence. The fear that the other superpower would fill the gap if they did not step in led to Cold War conflict on a global scale.

- **The nuclear arms race.** US monopoly in nuclear weapons was ended in 1949 when the USSR successfully tested its own atomic bomb. The speed with which the USSR had developed its nuclear capability shook US confidence. Alongside the considerable increase in conventional weapons that occurred during the Korean War, the USA extended its nuclear strength by developing the more powerful thermonuclear bomb in 1952 and the hydrogen bomb was ready for use in 1954. The USSR announced that their own H-bomb had been developed less than a year later. As both sides attempted to harness nuclear weaponry to missiles, the arms race took on an increasingly destructive and dangerous dimension.
- **The 'thaw'.** After 1953 there was an awareness that some form of East–West dialogue was needed. The leadership of both the USA and the USSR started to recognise the importance of avoiding, or at least limiting, conflict where possible. Attempts to establish a dialogue between the superpowers led to what has been termed a 'thaw' in Cold War relations.

Thus, there was the paradox that, alongside the spread of conflict and a growth in the weaponry available to both sides, superpower relations were experiencing a softening of hostility as the bitter antagonism of the early Cold War gave way to the 'thaw'.

WHAT ISSUES CAUSED TENSION BETWEEN THE SUPERPOWERS IN THE PERIOD 1948–55?

Tensions between East and West remained strong during the period 1948–55. Those issues that had caused division during the early years of the Cold War were still present and still had the potential to provoke a crisis. Yet the situation was also changing:

- **The 'German problem'.** The status of Germany in the post-war world continued to be an issue that generated tension. The Soviet blockade of Berlin in 1948–9 was one attempt to solve the problem. The result of the crisis was a failure for Stalin and an end to the hope for German reunification in the immediate future. Both the USA and the USSR were unhappy with this outcome, yet disputes continued over the status required of a reunited Germany.
- **The rise of communism in the Far East.** The communist takeover of China in 1949 raised US fears over the spread of communism to the Far East. The Korean War of 1950–3 reinforced US perceptions of the aggressive and expansionist tendencies of the Soviet Union. Stalin was

considered to be behind the attack by communist North Korea on the South. The rise of communism in Vietnam in the early 1950s seemed to confirm US suspicions about Stalin's aims.

- **European decolonisation.** World affairs were being transformed by a failure of will and resources on the part of European countries to retain their large overseas empires. The power vacuum in Europe caused by the defeat of Nazi Germany in 1945 had been filled by the end of 1948. The process of European decolonisation was to lead to another power vacuum in large parts of the Third World. Both superpowers were eager to ensure the other did not fill this gap. An area of strategic importance for its oil supplies, the Middle East posed a particular problem. Much of the Middle East was under the control of Britain and France but both powers were exhausted by the Second World War and decided to relinquish their hold over the region. Israel was established as an independent country in 1948 when the British left Palestine. British troops were withdrawn from Egypt in 1955 despite continued Anglo-French ownership of the Suez Canal. The hostility between the Arab states and Israel threatened to suck in the superpowers eager to exert influence over the region. In Indochina, French control had been broken by their bloody defeat at Dien Bien Phu in 1954. As the French pulled out their forces, the USA became concerned about the spread of communism into this region of the Far East.
- **Soviet actions in limiting destalinisation.** When Stalin died in 1953, Georgy Malenkov, the new Soviet Prime Minister, introduced a 'New Course'. This policy instigated a degree of limited liberalisation within the Soviet Union. Terror and repression were partially relaxed. Khrushchev was to develop this process of destalinisation further after 1956 but already in 1953 there were groups within the communist states of eastern Europe who were calling for a similar liberalisation within their own regime. Demonstrations and riots broke out in Czechoslovakia, East Germany and Poland against governments that refused to move away from strict Stalinist policies. When this unrest was crushed by armed troops, the West was appalled at the lack of freedom and at the brutality shown by the communist regimes of eastern Europe, and condemned their actions. The West did not intervene directly, but the level of tension was again raised. Later in 1956 the use of Soviet troops to crush an uprising in Hungary rekindled this issue.
- **The arms race.** With the increase in military expenditure and the development of nuclear weapons, both sides took action to ensure they did not fall behind in their capacity to wage war. The arms race that developed was both a result and a cause of tension between the superpowers. By the end of 1955 both the USA and the USSR possessed the hydrogen bomb: the USA had 560 strategic bombers to the USSR's 60. The race by the Soviet Union to catch up and overtake

the USA raised fears in the USA that they would fall behind unless they continued to increase their arms.

Although these issues led to a continuation of Cold War tension, there were also factors that started to promote the need for some form of dialogue, however limited, between East and West.

WHAT FACTORS PROMOTED A 'THAW' IN SUPERPOWER RELATIONS BETWEEN 1948 AND 1955?

The precarious, hostile stand-off between the superpowers, which had been symbolised by the harsh words and hard-line approach of both Stalin and Truman, changed after 1953. There was a move, albeit rather hesitant, towards establishing a dialogue between the superpowers. This trend was encouraged by a change in leadership in both the USA and the USSR. Yet the 'thaw' in Cold War relations was not merely the result of a change of personnel. There were factors relating to the wider context within which international relations were operating that pushed both sides towards seeking some degree of accommodation with the other.

The consolidation of positions

The fact that, by 1949, the division of Europe into two armed camps had been established and consolidated gave relations between the East and West a degree of stability. The Iron Curtain was now a defined line marking the border between the different spheres of influence. The insecurity of the second half of the 1940s had been caused by both sides attempting to mark out their areas of dominance. By 1949 the division of Europe had become entrenched. The US military commitment to NATO was an indication of the strength of their attitude towards defending Europe from the spread of communism. The Warsaw Pact of 1955 symbolised what had been evident for some time: the willingness on the part of the USSR to protect the eastern bloc from the perceived evils of US imperialism. The USA and the USSR were forced to accept the resulting division of Europe and to eye each other across an established dividing line. With their positions in Europe more secure, the superpowers were more willing to attempt negotiation.

The death of Stalin

Stalin's death was met with great relief in the West where he was seen as the dominant factor in the development of the Cold War. With Stalin now gone the dynamics of Cold War relations were likely to be different. Liberal historians of the Cold War, who have emphasised the role of personality, have seen Stalin's death as a determining factor in the development of the 'thaw'. Yet it was unlikely that Stalin was the only influence on the direction of Soviet foreign policy in the early 1950s.

Historians have argued over the extent of Stalin's ability to retain control over Soviet foreign policy during his final years. Revisionist studies have drawn attention to the loss of Stalin's power and examined his position within the structures of the Communist Party leadership. W. McCagg's *Stalin Embattled 1943–48* (1978) presents an image of Stalin as only one player in a complex political game, and one whose power had been undermined by the growth in power of groups both inside and, in the case of the army, outside of the party. This structuralist view has been supported by W. Hahn in *Post-war Soviet Politics 1945–53: The Fall of Zhdanov and the Defeat of Moderation* (1982) and T. Dunmore's *Soviet Politics 1945–53* (1984). These studies examine the political manoeuvring among the leadership to show the conflict which existed, thus challenging the view that Stalin was able to dominate affairs. It is a view which finds support in comments by Stalin's daughter, Svetlana Allilyeva, in *Twenty Letters to a Friend* (1967): 'All-powerful as he was, he was impotent in the face of the frightful system that had grown up around him like a huge honeycomb and he was helpless either to destroy it or bring it under control.'

Whether it was Stalin who controlled Soviet foreign policy in his final years or not, the initiative was running away from the Soviet Union in 1948–9. The failure of the Soviet blockade of Berlin, the formation of NATO and the defection of Yugoslavia from Cominform were all failures for Stalin's foreign policy. Thus, his death in 1953 provided an opportunity for the new soviet leadership to change its approach to the West.

Beria

The death of Stalin in 1953, probably hastened by medical neglect on the part of his associates in the Politburo, provided the opportunity for his successors to try a different approach to dealing with the West. In the immediate aftermath of Stalin's death it was unclear to the West who was in charge of Soviet foreign policy. Within the Soviet Politburo Laventii Beria, the long-serving head of the secret police, took the initiative and offered the West a proposal for a reunified, neutral Germany, arguing that 'All we want is a peaceful Germany and it makes no difference to us whether or not it is socialist.' Beria's motives may have been to distance himself from Stalin's policies or to merely impress his colleagues in the Politburo, but on both of these counts he failed. Beria's association with the less pleasant aspects of Stalin's policies was too much for the other members of the Politburo and he was arrested within months. Absurdly accused of being a British agent, he was later executed. An opportunity to end the division of Germany was therefore lost.

Malenkov's 'New Course'

With the removal of Beria, Soviet foreign policy fell into the control of

The Soviet leaders Georgi Malenkov (left) and Nikita Khrushchev during the mid-1950s.

Georgi Malenkov who, with Khrushchev and Bulganin, formed a Collective Leadership. Malenkov was able and intelligent and recognised the limitations of a hard-line approach of confrontation towards the West. He decided to embark on a 'New Course'. Malenkov believed that war between capitalism and communism was no longer inevitable and therefore resources could be directed away from arms and heavy industry and towards consumer goods and raising living standards in the USSR. This approach did not mark an end of conflict between capitalism and communism, merely a belief that, as the collapse of capitalism was inevitable, there was no need to engage in war to ensure its demise. The advent of the nuclear age made war a risky strategy; there were other, safer methods that could be used to defend communism while waiting for the inevitable collapse of the world capitalist system. Malenkov's 'New Course' was criticised by Khrushchev during his struggle for power, yet after Malenkov was removed from the position of Prime Minister in 1955 Khrushchev was to adopt and develop the 'New Course'.

KEY TERM

Peaceful Coexistence The policy put forward by Khrushchev in the late 1950s that capitalism and communism should accept the existence of the other, rather than use force to destroy each other. As a communist, Khrushchev believed that capitalism would collapse eventually due to its own weaknesses. Thus, war with its danger of nuclear devastation was not worth the risk.

Khrushchev and Peaceful Coexistence

Building on the 'New Course', Khrushchev articulated a new approach towards the West which became known as **Peaceful Coexistence**. Malenkov had used the term in 1952 but under Khrushchev it was developed into a fully formed policy. As Khrushchev accepted the Marxist belief that the downfall of capitalism was inevitable, Peaceful Coexistence was the best way of conducting relations in the meantime. Thus, the class struggle would continue, but by different means. With nuclear war too dangerous to contemplate, the two systems would have to accept the existence of each other in the short term. As Khrushchev was to make clear, 'There are only two ways – either Peaceful Coexistence or the most destructive war in History. There is no third way.' Khrushchev developed this approach between 1955 and 1957. By June 1957 he was established firmly as leader of the Soviet Union and was able to pursue this policy relatively unhindered.

Eisenhower and Dulles

Change in the Soviet leadership was accompanied by a change in the US presidency. Eisenhower had won the presidential election of 1952. No less hostile to communism than Truman, Eisenhower presented a different style and approach towards the USSR. He was a war hero of the Second World War and had served as Commander-in-Chief of NATO. Eisenhower's credentials in the fight against communism were difficult to fault. He was, therefore, more immune to the constant attacks by Joseph McCarthy, of being 'soft' on communism than Truman had been. Eisenhower had the self-confidence gained from his military career to pursue his own policies and was a firm believer in the benefits of personal face-to-face diplomacy. He was also ably supported by his Secretary of State, John Foster Dulles. During the election of 1952 Dulles had talked of 'rolling back' communism and of the 'liberation' of the states of eastern Europe from the evils of communism. This 'New Look' was a hard-line approach to foreign policy that won much support in the USA. When in office, Dulles continued to call for 'massive retaliation' against communist aggression. This implied the use of nuclear weapons. The policy of brinkmanship seemed also to increase the danger of future war. Dulles explained that 'the ability to get to the verge without getting into war is the necessary art. If you cannot master it, you inevitably get into war. If you try to run away from it, if you are scared to go to the brink, you are lost.' As a military man Eisenhower was aware of the destructive force of nuclear weapons. Like the new Soviet leadership in 1953, he was keen to avoid the prospect of nuclear annihilation.

In private both Eisenhower and Dulles were cautious and their actions were based on a reasoned approach to the situation they faced. Eisenhower was very conscious of the growth of power and influence of the military-industrial complex within the USA. He was also aware that economic resources that could help improve living standards were being diverted into arms production. The huge expansion of the USA's armed forces, which had taken place during the Korean War, was in danger of distorting and unbalancing the US economy. With the growth in expensive nuclear missiles, this problem was unlikely to go away unless some sort of agreement could be reached with the USSR.

Thus, from the early 1950s the governments of the USA and the USSR were facing the same pressures, pushing them towards reaching an accommodation with each other. These were:

- **Economic pressures.** How to reduce military spending to free resources for other sectors of the economy? Domestic reforms and living standards were held back by pouring money into an unproductive military sector. In the USSR approximately one-third of the economy was geared to the military sector. By 1954 over 12 per cent of the

USA's GNP was spent on armaments. Eisenhower's 'New Look' was designed in part to save money on conventional arms by relying on fewer but more powerful nuclear weapons. Neither country could sustain huge military costs indefinitely without long-term damage to its economy.

- **Avoiding nuclear war.** Both superpowers possessed atomic bombs by 1949 and the hydrogen bomb by 1955. The destructive power of the H-bomb, a thousand times more powerful than the bomb dropped on Hiroshima, posed a danger to the existence of life on earth. This was to weigh heavily on the minds of those leaders on whose shoulders responsibility for using these weapons would fall.

These concerns pushed the superpowers towards some accommodation with each other. It was a hesitant and delicate process but the trend was there.

WHAT, IF ANYTHING, WERE THE ACHIEVEMENTS OF THE 'THAW'?

The 'thaw' in superpower relations that developed after 1953 resulted in a series of summits between Eisenhower and Khrushchev. These summits became part of the so-called 'Geneva Spirit'. After the years of mud-slinging, the fact that the two most powerful leaders in the world were talking to each other was a significant step forward, even if what was achieved was rather limited.

The election of Eisenhower and the death of Stalin enabled an armistice to be concluded in 1953 which brought the fighting in the Korean War to an end. The war had produced a stalemate since 1951 and peace talks that had been going on had been protracted. The change in leadership in both the USA and the USSR gave these talks the impetus needed to reach a conclusion. The new Soviet leadership put pressure on North Korea's Kim Il Sung to agree to a ceasefire.

At the Berlin Foreign Ministers' conference of January 1954 Molotov, the Soviet representative, called for the creation of an all-German government out of those in West and East Germany to begin the move towards reunification. The West opposed this proposal, arguing that free elections must be held *before* the creation of a German government not afterwards. Although Molotov's proposal came to nothing it was viewed in the West as rather more constructive than previous Soviet proposals which appeared to be aimed at merely provoking the West. The Berlin conference also provided a useful preparation for a conference at Geveva in April.

At the Geneva Conference the Korean Armistice was confirmed and a settlement was reached which allowed the French to withdraw its forces from Indochina. Despite reservations on the part of Dulles over the wisdom of the settlement, the agreement was endorsed by all involved. Dulles was concerned that the agreement confirmed communism in North Vietnam and he walked out of the conference before it had finished. His verbal endorsement was given reluctantly. Despite these difficulties, the communists had not proved as obstructive at Geneva as the West had feared. Further evidence of this new approach came in early 1955 when the USSR agreed to the reunification of Austria, which, like Germany, had been divided into zones of occupation in 1945. The USSR was prepared to accept a united Austria providing it remained neutral.

In this atmosphere of increasing cooperation much was expected by the West when the first summit meeting of Soviet and US leaders since Potsdam in 1945 was held in July 1955. The Geneva Summit was attended by Eisenhower, Khrushchev, Eden (Great Britain) and Faure (France). Hopes were high that the new 'Geneva Spirit' of cooperation would produce results. The issue of German reunification was raised again. Khrushchev was prepared to allow a united Germany providing it was neutral. This issue was now complicated by the admission of West Germany into NATO in May. The USA saw West Germany, due to its geographical position, as central to the defence of western Europe. Khrushchev replied to this with a suggestion that both NATO and the Warsaw Pact be dismantled and replaced by a new system of collective security. The West was not prepared to agree to this but was willing to look at proposals for a limit on arms. Eisenhower surprised Khrushchev by calling for an 'Open Skies' agreement whereby spy planes would be allowed to fly over each other's territory in order to verify arms agreements. Khrushchev did not accept this offer.

The Geneva Summit therefore achieved very little. Eisenhower was personally very disappointed at 'Soviet duplicity', which he blamed for the summit's failure. The only agreement to come out of the summit was one on cultural exchanges of scientists, musicians and artists between the USA and the USSR. Yet the summit marked an improvement in relations which should not be overlooked. As Eisenhower acknowledged in his memoirs, 'It had been held in a cordial atmosphere, which represented a sharp departure from the vitriolic recriminations which characterised so many meetings in the past.' The expectations for the summit on both sides had been high. Although they had been dashed, even the frustrated Eisenhower recognised there was still hope for future agreement, 'People had been given a glowing picture of hope and, though it was badly blurred by the Soviets, at least the outlines of the picture remained.'

Khrushchev also had little to show for his efforts. For the USSR, the

Geneva Summit had seen their new approach of Peaceful Coexistence fail to secure any concessions from the West.

Peaceful Coexistence also had an effect on relations within the communist bloc. One success for Khrushchev was an improvement in relations with communist Yugoslavia but, perhaps more serious for communist unity, was the split with China. Mao, the Chinese communist leader, had not been consulted about destalinisation and was pursuing Stalinist policies within China. Mao's resentment led to a breach in relations with the USSR that was to complicate the Cold War.

Overall, the 'thaw' was a cautious and limited move towards establishing a meaningful dialogue between the USA and the USSR. Yet by 1955 the level of trust and understanding between the superpowers had not improved in substantive matters: the essential dynamics of the Cold War remained unchanged.

WHAT DO THE CRISES BETWEEN 1956 AND 1962 TELL US ABOUT THE NATURE OF COLD WAR CONFLICT?

Despite the fact that the superpowers had made steps towards an improvement in relations, the period 1956–62 saw a series of important crises develop, which revealed the superficial nature of the thaw. These crises were also important in highlighting the need for some form of rules by which conflict should take place and therefore be limited. These themes can be illustrated by an examination of three examples of Cold War crises during this period.

The Hungarian Rising, 1956

The events in Hungary in 1956 showed the vulnerability of the Soviet sphere of influence, which had been built up after the Second World War. The calls for liberalisation within Hungary were encouraged by Khrushchev's policy of destalinisation and demonstrated the impact that changes within the Soviet Union could have on its satellite states. The result was the appointment of the moderate Nagy as head of the Hungarian government in 1953. Despite a degree of liberalisation within the USSR, the subsequent actions of the USSR in Hungary indicated that there were limits to the independence of the eastern bloc countries. The Soviet response to calls for reform was to invade Hungary and restore a government of its own liking. Nagy was replaced by the more conservative Kádár. These actions showed a willingness on the part of the USSR to maintain a tight hold over its sphere of influence in eastern Europe. The Warsaw Pact, which had been created the previous year, helped Soviet dominance and the organisation ensured other eastern bloc countries contributed to the Soviet straitjacket over the region. The reaction of the West was important in establishing some of the rules of the Cold War. The USA and Britain led the protests against Soviet actions in Hungary. Yet, other than issue statements of condemnation, the West did little to intervene in a crisis that was seen to be within the Soviet sphere of influence. The talk of Eisenhower and Dulles about liberating those living under communism against their will was shown to be empty rhetoric, of which there was much during the period of the Cold War.

Berlin, 1958–62

The unique position of West Berlin as an island of capitalism within the communist zone of Germany ensured continuing tension, especially as there had not been a formal settlement over Germany since 1945. The Berlin Crisis of 1948–9 had not solved the problem; it merely entrenched the division of Germany and the city of Berlin. While West Germany underwent an 'economic miracle', East Germany struggled to present itself as a meaningful independent state. The failure of the East German government to win over its own people was shown by the growing exodus across the 'Iron Curtain' into the increasingly prosperous, and capitalist, West Berlin. By 1958 Khrushchev had decided that firmer action was needed to shore up the eastern bloc and issued an ultimatum to the West that called for the removal of all occupying forces from Berlin. Khrushchev wanted Berlin to become a free city with the existence of East Germany recognised formally by the West. The West was unwilling to give up West Berlin because of its immense propaganda value in undermining the Socialist Bloc. Thus, Khrushchev's ultimatum resulted in another crisis over Berlin. It was only after Eisenhower invited Khrushchev to visit the USA that he dropped the ultimatum. This highlighted the role of personal diplomacy between the individual leaders of the two superpowers in reducing international tension. The ultimatum was renewed in June 1961, when Khrushchev met Eisenhower's successor, Kennedy, at the Vienna Summit. When Kennedy made clear his intention not to relinquish West Berlin, Khrushchev finally gave his approval to the East German government's request to build the Berlin Wall. The wall prevented the loss of young and skilled East Germans which had become so severe that the survival of the country was under threat. More than anything else, the wall was a symbol of the economic and political bankruptcy of the eastern bloc. It also achieved its aim: East Germany was stabilised and the threat posed by West Berlin to the Soviet sphere of influence was successfully contained. The USA, once again, issued statements of condemnation but did nothing to directly prevent measures taken within the Soviet orbit. During the crisis, the USSR and East Germany had been careful not to interfere with the rights of the West within the city. Thus, despite the rhetoric and tension generated, the Berlin Crisis illustrated the growing entrenchment and stability of the spheres of influence created by the superpowers in Europe.

The Cuban Missile Crisis, 1962

The impact that individual leaders could have on international relations was illustrated by the increasingly erratic foreign policy moves of Khrushchev. He and his policies had played a significant part in the Hungarian Rising and the Berlin Crisis. The Cuban Missile Crisis was also due in part to Khrushchev's policy, specifically in his tendency to push the limits and test his opponents. Yet Khrushchev was under pressure from the USA, which had by 1962 developed a sizeable lead in the arms race. The Cuban Crisis was in two senses the result of the arms race. Firstly, Khrushchev's action to install nuclear bases in Cuba was a response to US bases in Turkey. In addition, it was the development of increasingly large numbers of nuclear missiles that gave the crisis its potential to be so devastating.

For the USA, the Cuban Crisis brought home the dangers of communism spreading to its own backyard. Until 1959 the global chess game of the Cold War had been played at a relatively safe distance from the USA: Europe and Korea. Castro's revolution in Cuba enlarged the arena of conflict to include Latin America, which had been considered part of the USA's sphere of influence since the Monroe Doctrine of 1823. The conversion of Castro to communism would have put severe pressure on any president but this was exacerbated because of the relative youth and inexperience of Kennedy. Thus, factors related to geography and personality combined to produce an especially hard-line policy on the part of the USA at a time when the Soviet leadership was acting in an increasingly unpredictable manner.

Kennedy's threat to use nuclear weapons, if Soviet ships did not return to Russia and the missile bases were not dismantled, was brinkmanship in action. Nonetheless, Kennedy was keen to ensure opportunities for a peaceful compromise were pursued. The difference between hard-line rhetoric in public, and caution and negotiation in private, was a vital part of Kennedy's approach. Although Khrushchev was seen to have backed down during the crisis and gave in to Kennedy's demands, the USSR did gain concessions on the removal of US bases in Turkey.

Both Kennedy and Khrushchev were removed from power, although in different circumstances, not long after the events of 1962, but the impact of the Cuban Crisis on superpower relations was longer lasting. The dangers of nuclear devastation that were exposed by the crisis led to a recognition that relations had to be improved. And if ideological differences remained too deep to heal tension, then at least rules should be established for the conduct of conflict. The 'hot line' telephone link and the Nuclear Test Ban Treaty of 1963 were the first steps towards the cooperation that developed in the 1970s into Détente.

Assessment

Between 1956 and 1962 events in Hungary, Berlin and Cuba revealed both the potential dangers of crisis and confrontation as well as the rules each side was prepared to adopt in order to stabilise relations during the Cold War. One particular issue that emerged during this period was the influence of individual personalities on the direction of international relations. The lurch from crisis to crisis was in many respects a consequence of the erratic policy pursued by Khrushchev. The large degree of power vested in the Soviet leader was a product of the political system established in the USSR by Stalin. Thus, changes in Soviet foreign policy were strongly influenced by the personal preferences of individual leaders. Khrushchev's destalinisation policy had a marked impact on superpower relations as well as the Soviet Union's control over its satellite states. His changing temperament could also help assist the trend towards a 'thaw' in relations, as in his promotion of Peaceful Coexistence; or lead to confrontation, as it did during the Cuban Missile Crisis. It is worth noting that when Khrushchev was dismissed as Soviet leader the Politburo accused him of 'hare-brained scheming'; he had become increasingly unpredictable.

CONCLUSION

The context of superpower conflict was changing after 1948. The growing stability of entrenched positions in Europe gave both sides some security from which to operate, and pressures arising from the nuclear arms race and economic concerns meant different approaches to the conduct of Cold War relations were needed. A change of leadership in both the USA and the USSR promoted a different approach to their foreign policies, which led to attempts to establish a framework for improved relations. Although tension was reduced there was little in the way of tangible achievements for either side by 1955. Periodic crises from 1956 to 1962 illustrated how the 'thaw' could easily give way to more dangerous conflict and how much the direction of superpower relations could depend on individual superpower leaders.

SECTION 4

What was the nature of conflict during the Cold War?

The Cold War is the term given to the period of poor relations between East and West, which developed after 1945 and did not come to an end until the collapse of the Soviet Union in 1991. The term 'Cold War' was used by the US columnist Walter Lippmann to describe this state of international affairs and by 1947 it was in common usage. It was a term that related specifically to the nature of the conflict involved. There was an absence of 'hot' or direct, armed combat between the two superpowers, which would have allowed one side victory in the conflict. Cold War involved attacks through a range of methods that included:

- ideological conflict
- economic measures
- non-cooperation
- propaganda
- espionage
- an arms race.

As the Korean and Vietnam wars indicated, war was not avoided, but it was limited and stopped short of direct, armed combat between the two superpowers. When the Cold War ended it was due not to military victory but to the collapse of the Soviet Union, which was brought about by a combination of factors that included the pressure of sustaining the effort required to continue the Cold War. An examination of the role of the different methods of conflict involved illustrates the nature of the Cold War in its many facets.

WHAT ROLE DID IDEOLOGICAL CONFLICT PLAY IN THE COLD WAR?

The Cold War is often portrayed as a conflict between two competing ideologies: capitalism and communism. With the USA and the USSR committed to the belief that their respective systems were superior to the other, the Cold War developed out of a desire to ensure the evils of alternative ideologies were not inflicted on the peoples of Europe after the Second World War. This battle was then extended to other parts of the world.

The ideology of Marxism-Leninism was the cornerstone of the whole

Soviet State. The USSR symbolised communism, involving a political system of the one-party state and an economic system of state ownership. Stalin's foreign policy was couched in ideological terms and, although his successors, Malenkov and Khrushchev, may have moved away from Stalinism, they were both committed communists. Peaceful Coexistence, like Stalin's more hard-line approach, was justified in relation to Marxist notions regarding the inevitability of the downfall of capitalism.

On the US side, there is no doubt that Truman and all the presidents that followed him were convinced of the superiority of capitalism and the benefits to be gained by its adoption in other parts of the world. The USA stood for liberal democracy, with its freedom of political expression, and capitalism with its emphasis on private ownership of the economy. Presidents such as Eisenhower and, later, Reagan seemed to embody US values; for others like Truman and Kennedy the American way of life provided a powerful inspiration.

Any common ground between the two ideologies was merely superficial. Although both the USSR and the West claimed to be upholding democracy and freedom, their views on what these concepts meant in practice illustrated that there were irreconcilable differences of ideology. To the West, democracy and freedom could be guaranteed only by constitutional rules within which political parties could compete for power; to the USSR, democracy as an expression of the people's will and freedom could be gained only by preserving socialism from 'corrupting influences'.

Writers such as Norman Graebner and Hans J. Morgenthau have been critical of the view that Cold War conflict was based primarily on ideological differences. They see the Cold War as a battle for supremacy between two powerful countries pursuing their own self-interests. Ideology was merely a tool with which to attack the opposing side. This **realpolitik** approach is based on the assumption that conflict was highly likely given the size and resources of the two superpowers. In this respect the Cold War can be seen as the result of **geopolitical** factors, with conflict being little different from the great-power rivalry that had dominated world affairs just before the First World War. This approach can be criticised for underestimating the role of ideology but it does draw attention to the methods used by both sides during the period to secure their spheres of influence. The USA and the USSR behaved like two imperialist powers aiming to secure supremacy in a large part of the world.

KEY TERMS

Realpolitik Policies which were practical in the conduct of international relations between two countries. Historians who stress this factor in explaining the Cold War see geopolitics as more important than ideological differences.

Geopolitics The political situation resulting from geographical considerations. In the case of the Cold War, both superpowers were large countries with extensive economic resources whose rivalry was highly likely no matter what their ideologies.

HOW IMPORTANT WERE ECONOMIC MEASURES IN THE COLD WAR?

In order to ensure that spheres of influence were brought firmly under their control, the superpowers used economic measures. Restoring the economies of Europe after the Second World War was a powerful weapon of the USA against the spread of communism, as well as securing its own markets. The introduction of the Marshall Plan in 1947 resulted in large sums of US money being available to the countries of Europe. Aid to France and Italy allowed their governments to deal effectively with the discontent that had led to communist-inspired strikes. The conditions placed on those receiving Marshall aid made it difficult for the countries of eastern Europe, with their state-controlled economies, to accept. The USSR viewed Marshall aid as an instrument of capitalist interference and put pressure on its satellite states to refuse the offer. But the Soviet Union did little to improve the economic prospects of eastern Europe. Much of East Germany's industrial plant was dismantled and sent to the USSR as reparations, even though most of it was left to rust rather than reassembled for use. The establishment of Comecon in 1949 provided the hope that eastern Europe would receive financial assistance from the Soviet Union but, in opening up Soviet access to eastern Europe's economic resources, it tended to work to the advantage of the USSR. It also helped the regimes of eastern Europe to impose Stalinist economic systems on their countries. Thus, both the superpowers were using economic measures to secure capitalism and communism in their spheres of influence.

The difference in approach to economic measures was to be demonstrated by the situation that arose in Berlin in 1948. Marshall aid had been used by the West to ensure economic conditions were improved in West Berlin. By 1948, its prosperity contrasted with the impoverished conditions in communist East Germany to the embarrassment of the USSR. The West's decision to introduce a new currency in the western sector of the city highlighted the recovery of economic confidence in West Berlin and the difference between the two systems in the city. It was the last straw for Stalin who decided to blockade West Berlin. Thus, economic measures played a significant role in the Berlin Blockade of 1948–9.

As the Cold War developed in the 1960s and 1970s offers of financial assistance became an important tool in securing influence in the Third World. Newly independent countries of Africa wished to develop their own economic resources and this seemed to require an end to what was seen as economic exploitation by their former European rulers. The attraction of Soviet aid lay partly in the ideological standpoint of communism. The anti-imperialist credentials of the USSR were much better understood than those of the USA, and the communist policy of nationalisation had an attraction when applied to foreign businesses. Soviet economic aid, often coupled with military supplies, was given to countries such as Egypt, Mozambique, Angola and Ethiopia in Africa and Cuba in Central America. The USA used the same tactics to prop up right-wing, anti-communist governments in Taiwan, Guyana, Thailand and Chile.

Economic measures, therefore, played a significant role in the process of extending influence during the Cold War. In Europe, the USA used economic assistance to gain consent for capitalism; the USSR used economic measures as a form of control in order to impose communism on eastern Europe. Later, both superpowers used similar economic methods to gain influence in the wider world.

HOW WAS NON-COOPERATION USED BY THE SUPERPOWERS DURING THE COLD WAR?

The Yalta and Potsdam conferences of 1945 may have been marked by disagreements between the superpowers, but at least they were still talking to each other at this stage. By 1947 both sides seemed resigned to the fact that superpower cooperation had broken down. The degree of mistrust between the USA and the USSR had caused each side to view the other as employing strategies of deliberate non-cooperation in order to secure their own interests. What was the point of negotiation if the other participant's word could not be trusted? The superpowers came to the conclusion that non-cooperation was a more effective method of safeguarding their interests than negotiation.

The withholding of information was one aspect of non-cooperation and this was used to great effect when in 1945 Truman failed to inform Stalin of the decision to drop the atomic bomb on Hiroshima. The prime motive for dropping the bomb was to bring about a swift end to the war against Japan but, by failing to inform Stalin, the USA had gained a psychological advantage in the growing tension of the Cold War.

The conferences of the Council of Foreign Ministers between 1945 and 1949 illustrate the manner in which tactics of non-cooperation were employed with regard to the post-war settlement for Europe. The Council consisted of the foreign ministers of the USA, USSR, Britain, France and China. When the Council met in London in October 1945, both sides complained about each other's interpretation of previous agreements, especially in connection with the meaning of 'free elections' for eastern Europe. Molotov, the Soviet foreign minister, was viewed by the West as being deliberately obstructive. This conference collapsed.

Meetings of the Council in Moscow and London in 1947 descended into slanging matches over the treatment of Germany and achieved little. By the time the Council met in Paris in 1949 the participants could not even agree on an agenda.

The contention over the status of Germany after 1945 had resulted in a failure to reach an agreement on the conditions for its reunification. With an agreed settlement seemingly impossible both superpowers decided to implement first economic and then political reforms that made cooperation even more difficult. The West's decision to introduce a new currency in West Berlin was reached without consulting the Soviet Union but was in part the result of the failure of the USSR to cooperate on this issue. The subsequent blockade of West Berlin was a stark example of non-cooperation. By cutting off the road, rail and canal links between West Berlin and the western sector of Germany, the USSR illustrated its unwillingness to cooperate with the West. Stalin's tactic was to be used by later Soviet leaders. Khrushchev saw Berlin as 'the testicles of the West. Every time I want to make the West scream, I squeeze on Berlin.' The building of the Berlin Wall in 1961 provided a physical, as well as psychological barrier to cooperation. The Iron Curtain that Churchill had

Soviet military parade on the political stage of the USSR – the Red Square in Moscow, 1962.

warned about in 1946 was now a physical reality. The Berlin Wall was to become symbolic of the non-cooperation between the superpowers over Europe and its demolition in 1989 marked an important stage in the ending of the Cold War.

Tactics of non-cooperation were used elsewhere during the Cold War and played an important part in delaying and obstructing agreements that could have ended conflict at an earlier stage. The process of reaching an agreed ceasefire to end the Korean War was long and protracted. This was due to obstacles being placed in the way of agreement by all sides involved. Similarly the conclusion to the Paris Peace Talks concerning the Vietnam War was delayed by the deliberate use of amendments. The situation was complicated further by Nixon's stalling while he attempted to win the US presidential election in 1972.

Non-cooperation was an effective method of avoiding reaching an agreement that necessitated unpleasant compromises. It was not until after the Cuban Missile Crisis of 1962 had highlighted the dangers of non-cooperation that meaningful cooperation was partly resumed.

HOW WAS PROPAGANDA USED TO REINFORCE COLD WAR DIVISIONS?

Differences in ideology were highlighted by propaganda, which was viewed by both sides as an important tool in ensuring loyalty at home and attacking the enemy abroad. For the USA and the USSR, propaganda was used to consolidate their control over their spheres of influence.

US propaganda

The US government sought to celebrate the benefits of 'Americanism' and to use this as an attack on what were seen as the evils of communism. Deep philosophical exploration of ideology was avoided in favour of simplistic notions. Indeed, it was difficult for some US presidents to handle ideas. Eisenhower may have been the embodiment of US values but his ideological beliefs were rarely articulated. He talked of 'conservativism', 'progressivism' and 'moderation' without saying what he meant by these terms. As one contemporary concluded with regret when asked what Eisenhower stood for, 'he is a golfer'.

US propaganda focused on freedom as the basis of Americanism and attacked communism for the limits it seemed to impose on this. The restriction placed by communism on religion and religious worship was attacked as ungodly. It was hoped that by highlighting these differences the people of eastern Europe and, later, those elsewhere in the world would be encouraged to throw off communism and embrace the freedoms of the West.

In order to get its message across, the US government established the United States Information Agency, an organisation of more than 10,000 staff covering 150 countries. Its message was conveyed in over 70 languages and was supported by over $2 billion a year. Radio stations, such as Voice of America and Radio Free Europe were set up to spread the message. Truman had taken the lead in coordinating propaganda by setting up the Office of International Information and Cultural Affairs and establishing US libraries in foreign countries. Eisenhower increased these activities and provided funding for beaming US radio stations into eastern Europe. The importance the US government attached to propaganda was indicated by the attendance of the head of the US Information Agency at government foreign policy meetings. In official government circles propaganda was referred to as 'public diplomacy', a term that implied it was a direct link to those peoples who were living under communism rather than their leaders.

One means of conveying the American message was through the film industry. At the end of the Second World War Hollywood produced some films that were pro-Russian but in the atmosphere of Cold War tension they quickly fell out of favour. The film *Mission to Moscow* (1943) was soon nicknamed *Submission to Moscow*. Although the majority of films avoided political themes, there was a trend towards films with anti-communist themes. These included *The Red Menace* (1949), *The Iron Curtain* (1949) and *Red Snow* (1952). Communists were portrayed as rude, humourless and cruel to animals, Soviet women were either worryingly unfeminine or nymphomaniacs using their bodies to lever state secrets from American good guys. In *The Red Menace* the Soviet agent seduces her man and then presents him with a copy of Marx's *Das Kapital.* These films were shown in western Europe as well as at home. Overtly political films were rarely box office successes but those that glorified US military success were better received by the European audience. The film *Patton*, which Nixon watched to psyche himself up before ordering the invasion of Cambodia in 1970, was one example.

In the 1980s the development of the video provided an additional means for US attempts to push their message by film. Libraries and information centres located abroad were used to distribute videos, but the results were often disappointing. In Pakistan the most popular video was Jane Fonda's exercise video. The government was often concerned about the representation of American life in films such as *The Texas Chain Saw Massacre.*

Another form of propaganda was the direct appeal of the US President.

Political statements by US leaders at times of crisis were used as vehicles to justify US actions and condemn those of the USSR. When Soviet forces invaded Hungary in 1956 to reverse liberalising measures and restore communism, condemnation through propaganda was the main tactic used by the USA. Their options for intervening in a crisis within the Soviet sphere of influence were otherwise severely limited.

Soviet propaganda

Lenin had stated that, 'Ideas are more dangerous than bombs', and Stalin took measures to ensure that the ideas that the Soviet population was exposed to were restricted. The development of the Cold War was used as evidence of a continued foreign threat against which the Soviet population needed to be vigilant. Any signs of western influence were to be condemned and severely dealt with. This was to have a direct impact on all aspects of Soviet culture and led to the xenophobic campaign of the 'Zhdanovshchina'. Andrei Zhdanov, a member of the Politburo, laid down strict guidelines for literature and other arts in an attempt to purify them of western 'bourgeois' influences. Jazz music was singled out for particular condemnation for its frivolity. Although Zhdanov died suddenly in 1948, his policies continued until 1953. There was, according to Zhdanov, no place in Soviet literature for political neutrality. The Soviet writer Zoshchenko was described as 'the scum of the literary world' for his novel *Adventures of a Monkey* in which a monkey escaped from a zoo only to find himself in Soviet society. As a result of his encounters the monkey rushes back to the safety of his cage in the zoo.

The cinema was also rebuked for showing too many foreign films and giving a distorted view of Soviet life. The film *The Great Life* (1946) showed workers who were barely literate enjoying sex and vodka. This may have been true to life but it was not the image of socialism that the Party wished to present. More in tune with government thinking was *Meeting on the Elbe*, in which Soviet troops were threatened by a seductive but vicious American spy. Music also suffered from excessive interference with leading composers called in to meet Zhdanov who personally demonstrated acceptable tunes on a piano. The heavy restrictions of the Zhdanovshchina were in danger of turning the public off the arts altogether.

In 1948, in order to prevent access to foreign propaganda, the Soviet government began to jam western radio stations to prevent those living in eastern Europe receiving the programmes. By the 1950s there were over 2000 jamming stations in the Soviet Union but the sheer size of the area to be covered limited the effectiveness of the task. Those workers employed to jam radio stations were often found asleep at work: it was a low-paid, tedious job.

As all Soviet media were under state control, the government was able to coordinate the information provided to its own population. *Tass*, the Soviet government's news agency, had offices in 126 countries and was able to supply these countries with information directly from the Soviet leadership. At least 70 per cent of those who worked for *Tass* were secret police agents. News material from *Tass* was often used in the developing countries because it was cheaper than the BBC or US sources. In the propaganda battle with the West, *Tass* scored some successes. The chemical explosion at Bhopal in India, which killed over 2000 people in 1984, was portrayed as a US experiment to collect data on gas poisoning. According to *Tass*, the Americans had released the AIDS virus to kill the black population in Africa. The US government initially had some difficulty in disputing these lies.

Soviet films were rarely successful when exported, even in communist countries. Documentaries on railroad construction, not surprisingly, failed to grab the attention of the public. Often poorly made on a low budget, Soviet films could not compete with the Hollywood blockbuster. One attempt to deal with this was to allow the distribution within the USSR of US films that seemed to confirm the evils of capitalism. *The Grapes of Wrath*, with its depiction of US poverty in the 1930s, was one such example.

The Soviet propaganda machine was disadvantaged by its technological backwardness in comparison with the USA. By the end of the 1980s satellite broadcasts and the development of home computers were starting to pose a serious threat to Soviet control over access to information in the eastern bloc.

In the absence of direct, armed struggle between the two superpowers, propaganda took a central place in the conflict of the Cold War. The significance both superpowers attached to propaganda resulted in large organisations devoted to controlling and distributing information. These organisations could, however, reduce tension during a crisis. In 1962, during the Cuban Missile Crisis, Khrushchev and Kennedy conveyed their messages to each other by means of the radio services they had developed as a method of spreading propaganda. This allowed communication to be quicker than the usual diplomatic channels and played a part in averting the crisis.

HOW SIGNIFICANT WAS THE USE OF ESPIONAGE DURING THE COLD WAR?

The Cold War saw an increase in the resources devoted to espionage by both the USA and the USSR. In the absence of direct conflict the use of spies became a central weapon in the battle for superpower supremacy. Espionage was used to gain information on the enemy as well as to act as a support to the other methods of securing influence in those parts of the world where the battle between capitalism and communism was being fought.

Soviet agents played a vital role in securing the information required to make the atomic bomb. R. Rhodes in *Dark Sun* (1995) has detailed the direct links between what Soviet spies were reporting and the achievements of Soviet scientists. Igor Kurchatov, who was head of the Soviet atomic programme, admitted that the information gained through espionage was 'huge, inestimable, significant for our state and science'. This view is confirmed by Molotov's own recollection that, 'They neatly stole just what we needed.' Some Soviet scientists have taken exception to this and have tried to make it clear that not all their developments were based on the results of espionage. Although this is probably an accurate statement, the Soviet atomic development programme had slowed during the Second World War and the information provided by Americans working as Soviet agents was vital. Spies such as Julius Rosenberg, Harry Gold and their small ring of US communists provided atomic secrets to the USSR. Rosenberg sent over 2200 coded messages by cable to Moscow between 1943 and 1945. The British spies Burgess, Philby and Maclean were recruited by the Soviet authorities while at Cambridge University and later passed important British secrets to the Soviet authorities.

Soviet espionage was organised by the KGB (State Security Committee) which was formed in 1954 from its forerunners the MVD (Ministry of Internal Affairs) and the MGB (Ministry for State Security). The KGB rose to a membership of half a million staff whose role included guarding customs posts, controlling communications networks and coordinating spies abroad. The First Main Directorate gathered intelligence material on western technology and military operations.

On the US side espionage was slower to become a widespread tool of Cold War conflict. The CIA (Central Intelligence Agency) was established in 1947 in order to collect and analyse information on threats to US security as well as to perform 'other functions', which covered undermining the enemy by covert means. Truman had rarely used clandestine methods but Eisenhower was prepared to support a wide range of actions. The CIA expanded its operations greatly under Eisenhower's Presidency. This was helped by the appointment of Allen Dulles as the Director of the CIA in 1953: he was the brother of John Foster Dulles, the Secretary of State. The successes of the CIA included the overthrow of a left-wing government in Guatemala in 1954. The agency also developed successful intelligence gathering using the U2 spy plane and space satellites. The U2 spy planes were able to fly over the

USSR at heights that made it more difficult for the Soviet authorities to detect. When the USSR shot down a U2 plane flying over Soviet air space in 1960, it was an embarrassment for the USA. The pilot, Gary Powers, was put on trial in Moscow. One investigation by the *US News and World Report* suggests that as many as 252 US airmen were shot down in this secret air war. Yet the spy planes were invaluable in providing evidence of the building of Soviet missile bases in Cuba in 1962.

One of the CIA's biggest successes was in helping the overthrow of the left-wing government of Allende in Chile (1973). Allende's government had been democratically elected but Allende was a communist and his policies provoked a backlash by the Chilean business classes and army officers. The CIA provided support for the army coup that seized power and Allende was killed. Perhaps the most serious failure for the CIA was its involvement in the Bay of Pigs invasion of 1961. This attempt to help right-wing opponents of Fidel Castro invade Cuba and remove his communist government from power ended in disaster and was a severe humiliation for President Kennedy.

The very nature of espionage makes a complete assessment of its significance difficult. Many of the underhand actions carried out by both sides remain secret. Nonetheless, it is evident that both superpowers gained valuable information about the other. Espionage provided a form of monitoring that became so well established that it helped stabilise relations. US fears that a missile gap had opened between themselves and the USSR in the period 1957–61 were quelled by the information gathered by its spy systems. Although both sides resented foreign espionage, it became one of the accepted rules of the Cold War 'game'. The regular tit-for-tat expulsions of spies from West and East was an illustration of this.

WHY DID AN ARMS RACE DEVELOP AND WHAT IMPACT DID IT HAVE ON THE NATURE OF THE COLD WAR?

The arms race became an integral part of Cold War conflict. It was a cause of tension and a significant factor responsible for the continuation of hostility between the superpowers. The arms race also became a weapon in itself. The vast resources needed to sustain the arms race posed severe economic strains on both the USA and the USSR. By the 1980s it was used as a deliberate method of bankrupting the enemy.

Causes of the arms race

External factors. The build-up of arms by both sides was a response to external factors: the growing hostility between the superpowers after

1945. As the Cold War developed, arms were viewed as necessary to safeguard the interests of East and West. What gave this particular arms race a unique feature was the development of the atomic bomb. The nuclear age greatly increased the destructive power of the weapons available and therefore increased the feeling of vulnerability of the side that failed to keep pace with the new technology. The USA had a monopoly in nuclear warfare from 1945 until the Soviet Union developed its own atomic bomb in 1949. Soviet secrecy, coupled with Stalin's and Khrushchev's tactic of boasting about their nuclear capability, helped fuel US concerns that they needed to keep ahead of the USSR. Each power viewed the nuclear capacity of the other with anxiety and became convinced that their nuclear superiority was the only way of guaranteeing their defensive needs. The pattern of developing more and more sophisticated and powerful weapons continued until the 1980s when the US government announced its decision to develop the so-called Star Wars initiative. This would result in defence systems located in space to shoot down nuclear missiles. The cost of matching this would have bankrupted the USSR.

Internal factors. Because the arms race provided lucrative orders and resources for those sectors of the economy related to the armaments industry, it can be seen as resulting from the situation within each country rather than external factors. Those groups who benefited from armaments orders gained considerable power and influence. In the USSR the armed forces were able to exert influence within the Soviet government because defence needs were given such a high priority. Any attempt to cut the amount of spending on arms, and therefore threaten the power of the military, was strongly resisted, as Khrushchev, the Soviet leader, found out in 1964. In the USA the arms race provided large sums of money to manufacturers, scientists and the armed forces to the extent that it led to the employment of over 30 million US civilians. This **military-industrial complex** was able to wield enormous control over US politics. President Eisenhower raised concerns about this development but was unable to reduce the power of this sector of the economy. In was in the interests of the military-industrial complex to highlight the danger posed by the Soviet Union. The Soviet army, in turn, emphasised the US threat in order to secure resources. Thus, both fed off each other in perpetuating the arms race, and with it their power and influence within their own country was maintained.

KEY TERMS

Military-industrial complex The term given to the powerful bloc created by links between the armed forces and those sectors of the economy reliant on defence orders. In the US this included firms such as Lockheed and General Dynamics, who lobbied Congress to ensure arms manufacture continued, and the armed forces, who wanted resources and armaments. In the USSR this term is applied to the Ministry of Defence, the armed forces and those industries involved in the manufacture of military products.

The impact of the arms race

Rather than reducing insecurity the arms race increased it. The period of US nuclear monopoly between 1945 and 1949 gave the Soviet Union a disadvantage in the manoeuvring for position in the early years of the Cold War. The vulnerability felt by Stalin stemmed partly from the

Widespread devastation caused by the atomic bomb on Hiroshima, 1945.

KEY TERMS

Hydrogen bomb A bomb which sets off a fusion of hydrogen atoms, releasing enormous energy. It was one thousand times more powerful than the simple atomic bombs dropped on Japan in 1945. The first US H-bomb was tested in the Marshall Islands where it destroyed an island and left a crater one mile across. The effects of radiation are long lasting.

ABM (Anti-Ballistic Missiles) Missile systems used to intercept and destroy nuclear weapons.

suspicion that the atomic bombs had been dropped on Hiroshima and Nagasaki as a warning to the USSR. Stalin ordered his scientists to develop their own atomic bomb as soon as possible. When this was announced in 1949 the US government was surprised at the speed of this development. They then increased their efforts to develop the **hydrogen bomb** which both countries possessed by the end of 1955. By 1957 the USA was concerned that the Soviet Union had pulled ahead in the arms race and a 'missile gap' had developed. The launching of the first ever space satellite, Sputnik, by the USSR seemed to confirm these fears. The US Air Force reported that the USSR would have 100 missiles in place by the end of 1960 compared with only 30 US missiles. The result was a massive build-up of US missiles to put in place over 1000 land-based missiles and over 600 missiles in submarines. The Soviet response to this was to increase their own arsenal of nuclear weapons and develop **ABM** defensive systems that would prevent the USA using nuclear missiles against targets such as Moscow. By the end of the 1960s the USA was so concerned about the effectiveness of their missiles that the

MIRV (Multiple Independently Targetable Re-entry Vehicle) programme was instituted. This increased the chances of nuclear missiles hitting their intended target. The USSR decided to develop its own MIRV programme in 1975 and the arms race reached a new intensity. By 1981 the number of Soviet warheads had increased to 6800: the USA had 7000. As both sides were attaining a rough balance in the number of missiles, the new US President, Ronald Reagan, decided to press ahead with a huge weapons increase in 1981. Part of this programme was the expensive **SDI** (Strategic Defence Initiative) Star Wars programme. By 1985 the Soviet Union had come to the conclusion that it could no longer bear the cost of continuing the arms race. It was an important factor in bringing the USSR to the negotiating table to limit the production of nuclear arms. The constant pressure of matching US military capability had undermined the Soviet economy and was a significant factor in bringing about the collapse of the USSR and therefore ending the Cold War.

During the arms race, the dangers inherent in the use of nuclear missiles became increasingly evident. This had an impact on the nature of military strategy. The danger of initiating nuclear war restrained both the USA and the USSR from direct, armed confrontation. As John Lewis Gaddis has stated, 'This pattern of tacit cooperation among bitter antagonists could hardly have emerged had it not been for the existence of nuclear weapons.' There was, of course, conventional warfare during the Cold War but this was played out on immediate territory and was kept localised. The concept of limited war was used to avoid direct confrontation. This concept first emerged during the Korean War of 1950–3 where there was a real threat of the war escalating. The USSR took no direct role in the war and, despite the calls of General McArthur to use nuclear weapons against China, Truman preferred to use military tactics that ensured the war remained limited in scale. Nuclear weapons forced each side to think twice before taking any measure to escalate war.

By the mid-1950s the US government was concerned to develop a strategy that seemed to avoid the dilemma of how to use nuclear weapons. What was the point of having weapons that you were too scared to use? If the USSR believed the threat to use nuclear bombs was based on bluff their value as a deterrent would be negligible. Under Eisenhower and Dulles the US government developed a strategy of Massive Retaliation. This was based on the threat of using large numbers of US nuclear bombs against communist aggression. As the USA still had nuclear superiority this would, it was hoped, act as a deterrent. The result of this strategy was the tactic of brinkmanship, of being prepared to go to the brink of nuclear war in order to stop enemy aggression. It was a risky business as Kennedy found out during the Cuban Missile Crisis of 1962. It no longer had the same impact by the 1970s, when both superpowers

KEY TERMS

MIRV (Multiple Independently-Targetable Re-entry Vehicle) A device launched by a missile that allows several warheads to be used, each guided to a different target. MIRV systems made Anti-Ballistic Missiles less effective as there were far more warheads to shoot down at any one time.

SDI (Strategic Defence Initiative) Often referred to as Star Wars, it was a programme of placing defensive missile systems in space. It was launched in 1983 by US President Ronald Reagan.

possessed enough nuclear missiles to destroy the other and when systems had been developed to ensure a counter-strike was possible even after being hit first. The result was a situation referred to as MAD (Mutually Assured Destruction). Both sides recognised the limitations of this all-or-nothing approach and decided that a more flexible range of responses was needed. This led to the strategy of Counterforce, which would use smaller, targeted nuclear missiles to provide the option of using more limited action to achieve more specific objectives.

The arms race also had an impact on conventional arms. If the devastation caused by nuclear weapons was too horrific to contemplate except as a last resort, the importance of conventional arms remained central to military strategy. Moves to reduce conventional arms were attempted by Eisenhower and Khrushchev, both of whom saw nuclear weapons as a cheaper alternative. The Korean and Vietnam wars were fought with conventional arms and showed the need to keep a numerical advantage in conventional weaponry. This would allow each side an alternative to the use of nuclear missiles: a strategy Kennedy referred to as Flexible Response.

The fact that nuclear arms were not used during the Cold War does not make them an insignificant part of the conflict: the arms race was one of the chief methods by which conflict took place and it was therefore an integral part of the struggle for supremacy. As nuclear weapons developed and became more devastating they became less usable. Few would disagree with the assessment of Kurchatov, the Soviet nuclear scientist who, after witnessing the damage caused by testing the hydrogen bomb, stated: 'That was such a terrible, monstrous sight! That weapon must not be allowed ever to be used.' The nuclear arms race provided one of the reasons for ending the Cold War and, by bankrupting the Soviet Union to the point at which it could no longer continue the race, it also provided the means.

CONCLUSION

The nature of conflict during the Cold War differed from that of traditional warfare in that 'hot' war between the superpowers was avoided and armed conflict was limited. In this absence a wider range of tactics took on a greater significance. The reasoning behind these methods was that of zero sum, that is, any setback for the enemy is a gain for the other side. In this respect, indirect methods of attack were seen as the difference between success and failure and their contributions were central to the conduct of the Cold War.

SECTION 5

What were the causes and achievements of Détente?

Despite the signs of a 'thaw' in Cold War relations after 1953, the period 1956 to 1962 saw a series of confrontations between the superpowers. The Hungarian Crisis of 1956, the Berlin Crisis of 1961 and the Cuban Missile Crisis of 1962 all indicated the superficial nature of the 'thaw'. Yet, as well as raising the level of tension between East and West, the growing seriousness of these confrontations caused the superpowers to rethink their strategies for conducting the Cold War. The resulting changes in policy were to lead to Détente, a more permanent relaxation of tension in the 1970s. Détente provided a window of opportunity to attempt to reduce international tension, and some of the initiatives taken produced agreements that attempted to limit the nuclear arms race and ensure meaningful links were established across the Iron Curtain. The achievements of Détente proved both fleeting and temporary by 1979. This year saw a resurgence of tension that reached breaking point in December with the Soviet invasion of Afghanistan.

WHAT WERE THE CAUSES OF DÉTENTE?

A move towards a Détente between the superpowers was stimulated by developments within the US and the USSR, as well as involving initiatives taken by European leaders keen to reduce tension in Europe. What made some agreement between the superpowers more necessary was a growing awareness of the potential danger of confrontation leading to nuclear destruction.

The fear of war

The Cuban Missile Crisis of 1962 had highlighted the danger of superpower confrontation resulting in nuclear war. President Kennedy's threat to use US nuclear missiles if Soviet missile bases were not withdrawn from Cuba had caused anxiety across the world. With the nuclear arms race leading to the development of ever more efficient missiles the fear of future war continued to increase. By 1969 the USSR had matched the capability of the USA for mutually assured destruction: each superpower now had enough nuclear missiles to destroy the other in the event of a first strike by the opponent. This situation not only posed a threat to the economic well-being of both superpowers but also provided a balance of power that would, it was hoped, act as a deterrent. The pressure to forge ahead in the arms race did, however, threaten constantly to disrupt this delicate balance. The necessity of reducing the risk of future nuclear war pushed both East and West towards Détente.

The needs of the USSR

The humiliation suffered by the Soviet armed forces due to Khrushchev's back-down during the Cuban crisis was a significant factor in his dismissal. Yet the new Soviet leadership, led by Leonid Brezhnev, made little change to foreign policy. Peaceful Coexistence continued to be pursued. The Soviet Politburo faced mounting economic problems and needed to divert resources away from the military sector of the economy to deal with these. The Soviet population had failed to gain the improvement in living standards they had been led to expect by Khrushchev and Brezhnev. With the continuation of the arms race, the Soviet government found it difficult to transfer production capacity in industry to consumer goods. Détente would provide the international background necessary to make this possible. Improved relations would allow the USSR access to much-needed western technology and grain supplies. All this would be possible if friendly relations could be established with the USA. The USSR hoped to gain recognition from the West for their influence and control over the eastern bloc. This would help stabilise the situation in Europe.

The needs of the USA

The USA had resisted previous attempts to recognise the Soviet sphere of influence because it might seem to give it legitimacy. This acceptance of the status quo would be viewed by the American Right as a betrayal of those people living under communist regimes. The American Right had argued for the need to roll-back communism. It was the US experience in the Vietnam War that changed US public opinion. The failure of the USA to secure victory in Vietnam led to a re-evaluation of US power in the world. In 1969 President Nixon and his National Security Advisor, Henry Kissinger, had to grapple with the impact on the USA of the Vietnam War. Both were right-wing in terms of domestic policy but they were practical politicians. The Vietnam War had caused high inflation, a large budget deficit, and had led to a decline in support for foreign intervention in the wider world. They also recognised the painful reality of the Vietnam War: there were limits to the power of the USA. Détente would offer them an opportunity to uphold the interests of the USA without the need for military intervention that might not succeed. More could be gained by negotiation than confrontation. Détente would, in addition, allow the influence of the powerful industrial-military complex to be reduced. Plans for social reform in the USA had been undermined by a lack of resources due to continued military spending. Kennedy had a vision of a New Frontier, Johnson a New Society: both were sacrificed for increased armaments. The urban riots that broke out across the USA in 1968 provided the evidence that social issues within the USA needed to be tackled as a matter of urgency. Moves to Détente would allow resources to be released from the military budget to improve the lives of the American people.

The position of China

Relations between the USA and the USSR became increasingly affected by the dynamics resulting from the Sino-Soviet dispute, which had developed after 1953. The communist government of China had started to implement Stalinist policies at a time when the USSR was condemning them. Khrushchev had failed to develop an effective relationship with Mao, the Chinese leader. When Khrushchev announced his policy of Peaceful Coexistence with the West, it was done without consulting the Chinese government. Mao, insulted by the actions of Khrushchev, took steps to undermine the USSR as the leader of world communism. By 1964 China had developed its own atomic bomb and had gained superpower status in its own right. The bi-polar world of the early Cold War had become one of multi-polarity. China started to encourage Romania to adopt an independent line in its relations with Moscow, competed with the USSR for influence in the Third World, and engaged in territorial disputes along the border with Russia. A border dispute along the Ussuri River erupted into fighting in 1969. These developments had a considerable impact on relations between the USA and the USSR. By the early 1970s China was worried about its international isolation and saw accommodation with the USA as beneficial to its own interests as well as a snub to the Soviet Union. Thus, Détente was to involve a Chinese dimension that provided a useful opportunity for the USA to reduce the power and influence of the Soviet Union through peaceful diplomacy.

European needs and 'Ostpolitik'

The pressure for Détente did not derive solely from the superpowers. Developments in Europe during the late 1960s also encouraged links across the Iron Curtain. In 1968 events showed substantial instability on both sides of the Iron Curtain in Europe. The Soviet invasion of Czechoslovakia revealed the tension in eastern Europe. In France, large-scale student demonstrations had resulted in a general strike that threatened both President de Gaulle and the French system of government. Political disorder posed a danger to East and West in Europe. The West German politician Willy Brandt took the lead in promoting links across the divide. Brandt served as West German Foreign Minister (1966–9) before taking over as Chancellor (1969–74). He saw a stabilisation of European relations as essential to the interests of the continent as a whole. By reducing tension and establishing links between East and West, the divisions that had scarred Europe since the early Cold War would be gradually eroded. Brandt's response to this situation was to develop his 'Eastern Policy', better known as *Ostpolitik*. By opening up channels between East and West in Europe, *Ostpolitik* greatly aided the impetus towards Détente. Brandt's policy encouraged other European countries to establish links across the East–West divide, such as the French government's policy of establishing friendly relations with Romania.

By 1969 there was a range of factors in existence that provided considerable pressure for a détente to be reached in international relations. Yet Détente did not mark an end, however temporary, to Cold War conflict; it developed out of a recognition that there was more to gain in the struggle between East and West by a degree of cooperation rather than confrontation. Thus, Détente represented a change in the tactics of superpower conflict rather than an end to the Cold War.

WHAT WERE THE ACHIEVEMENTS OF DÉTENTE?

By the early 1970s the superpowers were in a position to accept the compromises necessary to secure agreements on issues of mutual concern. Treaties such as SALT and the Helsinki Agreement have been seen as the central achievement of Détente and their limited success has led some historians to see Détente as superficial. But there was more to Détente than concrete agreements.

US–USSR relations

Deals were reached after long and painstaking attention to detail in the key areas of nuclear weapons and the security of Europe. The main agreements are discussed below.

a) SALT (Strategic Arms Limitation Treaty). Early attempts to negotiate treaties on nuclear weapons, such as the Rapacki Plan of 1957, had failed. The Cuban Missile Crisis had shocked the superpowers into reaching some agreements to limit the use of nuclear arms. The Nuclear Test Ban Treaty (1963) and the Non-Proliferation Treaty of 1968 provided the first move in this direction and this continued under Détente. In 1968 the Soviet Union had been ready to talk about limiting strategic nuclear weapons but the Soviet intervention in Czechoslovakia, to replace a liberalising government with one more in line with Soviet expectations, had caused outrage in the USA and the talks were delayed. When they resumed later in the year the talks proved slow and protracted. It was not until 1972 that both sides were ready to sign a final agreement.

The key issues over which the two superpowers found agreement difficult were how arms should be limited and which types of weapon should be included in the arrangements. The differing weapons systems of each side made comparison difficult. There was also a tendency to focus on setting limits for existing weapons as the USA in particular recognised that the arms race would be won only through the development of newer technologies.

Nixon's visit to China in February 1972 caused concern in the USSR. The Soviet government was anxious to avoid an agreement between its two superpower rivals and this worked to exert pressure on the USSR to sign the SALT I treaty in May. Agreement was reached in three areas: first, on the use of anti-ballistic missile (ABM) systems; second on offensive nuclear weapons and, third, on a code of conduct.

- **The ABM Treaty** reduced the tension caused by the destabilising impact of defensive systems. With ABM systems in place the ability to retaliate if hit by a nuclear missile was uncertain and therefore encouraged each side to strike first. By limiting ABM systems to two sites the deterrence provided by the knowledge that the other side could strike back was maintained. Thus, the USA and the USSR agreed to a limit of two ABM systems each, one for their capital city and one to protect their nuclear missiles.
- **The Interim Treaty** on offensive nuclear missiles was much barer. Both sides could agree only to an interim agreement, which would expire in 1977. Limits were placed on the number of ICBMs (Intercontinental Ballistic Missiles) and SLBMs (Submarine-launched Ballistic Missiles) of 1618 and 740 respectively for the USSR and 1054 and 740 for the USA. The Soviet Union was allowed more of these missiles because in other areas, such as strategic bombers, the USA had a large lead. This was an important step towards limiting nuclear arms but it omitted new technological developments such as the MIRVs, which carried multiple warheads on a single missile. Each side could replace old, obsolete missiles with new ones within these limits and the technological advantage lay with the USA.
- **The Basic Principles Agreement** laid down some important rules for the conduct of nuclear warfare. The Seabed Pact of 1971 had banned the placing of warheads on the seabed. The Basic Principles Agreement extended the guidelines to be used by both sides to minimise the development of nuclear war. The USA and the USSR pledged 'to do their utmost to avoid military confrontations' and to 'exercise restraint' in international relations. Trade was to be encouraged between the two superpowers. This agreement marked a shift from the atmosphere of confrontation even if the Principles were little more than a statement of intent.

A lot remained unsettled in the SALT treaties. The treaty on offensive weapons was, in particular, thin on substance. Each superpower retained enough nuclear weapons to destroy the other several times over. Nonetheless, they indicated a desire to move away from dangerous confrontation. US–Soviet trade increased as a result of the agreements but it tended to be limited to grain supplies for the USSR. In the 1970s the Soviet Union came to rely on US grain to make up shortfalls in domestic production. The US government recognised that trade could be used as a lever to extract further concessions from the Soviets.

Despite its limitations SALT marked the high point in the spirit of cooperation engendered by Détente. Nixon visited Moscow in 1972 and 1974: Brezhnev visited Washington in 1973. These visits were symbolic of the new accord between the superpowers.

b) The Helsinki Agreement, 1975. In 1971 the Warsaw Pact countries had proposed a conference to discuss European security with the countries of NATO. Thirty-three states attended the conference in Helsinki, which began in 1973 and produced an agreement in 1975. At the conference the Warsaw Pact countries wished to secure US recognition of the European borders established after the Second World War. The USA saw this as an opportunity to gain concessions from the Soviet government in return. The result was an agreement covering three 'baskets'. Basket one declared the borders of European countries were 'inviolable'. This meant they could not be altered by force. By signing this agreement all countries accepted the existence of the Soviet bloc in eastern Europe, including East Germany. This received a lot of criticism from the right wing in the USA, but it merely acknowledged the reality of the situation that had existed since the late 1940s. Basket two covered trade and technology exchanges to promote links across the Iron Curtain. Basket three contained the concessions the West had tried to gain from

Jimmy Carter and Leonid Brezhnev at the Vienna Summit, 1979.

the USSR. It included an agreement to respect human rights, such as freedom of speech and freedom of movement across Europe. For the communist states of eastern Europe to accept this was seen by the West as a significant step forward. The West hoped this would undermine the hold of the repressive Soviet regimes in eastern Europe. Organisations were established to monitor governments and their actions against these principles. In practice the Soviet bloc governments ignored or paid lip service to the human rights agreement. Brezhnev was heavily criticical of human rights in the West but did nothing to change Soviet policies at home. When a follow-up conference met in Belgrade (1977–8) the countries involved bickered over whether the previous agreement had been upheld and little was achieved. The Soviet concessions gained at Helsinki were shown to be hollow.

c) **SALT II.** SALT I had been an interim agreement and there had been an intention to negotiate further, but SALT II ran into difficulties. An agreement for SALT II was outlined at the Vladivostok Summit in 1974 between Brezhnev and the new US President, Gerald Ford. It set equal limits for missile launchers and strategic bombers but, importantly, left out cruise missiles where the US had a significant lead. The proposed treaty was too much for right-wing US senators who saw all arms control as a mechanism for allowing the USSR to catch up with superior US weaponry. Led by Senator Henry Jackson, the right was too powerful for Ford to ignore. When Jimmy Carter became President in 1977, he attempted to renegotiate the SALT II treaty in order to reduce the number of Soviet missiles. It was not until 1979 that precise figures could be agreed and the SALT II treaty was signed by Carter and Brezhnev at a summit in Vienna in June. The treaty was highly technical and detailed and, according to the historian Ralph Levering, it was not understood by 'the average senator'. One wonders whether Brezhnev, the now aged and increasingly senile Soviet leader, understood the treaty. In the USA public opinion as well as the opinion of senators was turning against arms control agreements, with a Soviet government considered to be untrustworthy. Increasing conflict in the Third World, especially in Iran, Angola and Afghanistan, led to the Senate's rejection of SALT II in 1980.

US–China relations

Nixon and Kissinger had attempted to improve US relations with communist China in 1969 but the continuation of conflict in Vietnam prevented progress. By 1972 relations were good enough to allow Nixon to visit China as a guest of the government. As symbols of the improvement in relations, Nixon was given two giant pandas, and a US table-tennis team was invited to tour China. The Chinese helped relations by ensuring the Americans won. On a more substantial issue the USA raised only mild objections to the United Nations decision to permit the Chinese Communist Party to take up China's seat in the Security Council and expel

Taiwan from the organisation. US support for Taiwan, which the communists wished to see reunited with China, continued to pose difficulties for US–Chinese relations. Nonetheless, the real value for the USA was the concern that closer US–Chinese relations posed for the USSR.

European Détente

Brandt's policy of *Ostpolitik* abandoned the Hallstein Doctrine, which had been designed to snub East Germany by refusing to recognise its existence as a separate state. Brandt preferred to establish links between East and West in Europe as a method of reducing barriers. The results of this policy included several treaties, which involved a recognition of reality rather than an abandonment of the principle of reunification. Treaties with Poland and the Soviet Union agreed to accept the Oder-Neisse Line as the border between Germany and Poland as well as recognising the border between East and West Germany. An agreement by the USA, USSR, France and Britain in 1971 gave a legal basis to access routes from West Germany to West Berlin and provided some security for the western half of the city. The most significant agreement was, however, the Basic Treaty of 1972, in which West Germany accepted the existence of East Germany as a separate state and agreed to increase trade links between the two countries. *Ostpolitik* played a major role in reducing tension in Europe and contributing to Détente but it was at a cost. West Germany had to accept Soviet control over eastern Europe, and in doing so gave legal recognition and reinforcement to the division of Cold War Europe.

Assessment

After the dangers of potential war and nuclear destruction that had been evident in the confrontations of the late 1950s and early 1960s, Détente was a welcome trend to those who wished to reduce the sources of tension. The achievement of Détente was that superpower relations had been stabilised and risks minimised. Yet on substantial matters little was achieved: armaments had increased during this period and many of the agreements signed were ignored, as in the Helsinki Agreement, or withdrawn later, as in the case of SALT II. In addition, Détente did not reduce tension in all areas of international relations. Europe was more stable, but tension between the USSR and China remained high. Conflict continued and even intensified in the Third World. Events in Iran, Angola and Afghanistan showed that the USSR had extended its influence during the period of Détente. This situation was to produce a lot of the renewed suspicion and mistrust that led to the breakdown of Détente in 1979. The collapse of Détente showed its fragility. It had suited the USA and USSR to use Détente as a method of conducting the Cold War in the 1970s because each thought it would work to its own interests in the ongoing battle for superpower influence. Thus, Détente was not the beginning to an end of the Cold War but rather its continuation through other means. Brezhnev described Détente as 'the way to create more favourable conditions for peaceful socialist and communist construction'. Détente worked to the advantage of the USSR in allowing it to continue to compete in the arms race. It also proved useful to the USA when it was feeling the strains of the Vietnam War. When it no longer served its purpose, Détente fell apart.

HISTORICAL INTERPRETATIONS

In judging the achievements of Détente, historians in the West have been influenced by the debate within US politics. During the period of Détente, politicians on the American left and in the centre of the political spectrum viewed Détente as a positive step in the reduction of tension and highlighted its stabilising effect on international relations. This was the standard view, presented by Nixon and his advisers, during the early and mid-1970s when there was optimism that Détente would limit the arms race and reduce the threat of nuclear war. Not surprisingly, the autobiographies of Nixon and Kissinger, the main architects of Détente on the US side, give a positive view of their own attempts to bring about Détente.

The view that Détente was a beneficial policy for both sides has gained support from some post-revisionist historians, such as Gordon Craig and Alexander George in *Force and Statecraft* (1983). They present a more detached analysis that emphasises Détente as a method pursued by both superpowers in order to create a less dangerous and more useful international relationship.

Yet it has been the disillusionment with Détente on the American right, resulting in a more critical approach, that has tended to dominate historical thinking. Détente was seen as a sign of weakness and of being 'soft' on communism by allowing the Soviet Union to continue the Cold War. This view was developed by many American writers in the 1980s who supported Ronald Reagan's massive rearmament programme. The collapse of the Soviet Union in the late 1980s was viewed as a result of the pressure of matching the USA in the arms race, and therefore Détente can be seen as prolonging the Cold War rather than as a realistic step towards bringing about its end. An evaluation of Détente from the perspective of the right has been presented forcefully by Richard Pipes in *US-Soviet Relations in the Era of Détente* (1981). This view does, however, tend to neglect the advantages Détente held for the USA during a time when US self-confidence was under serious threat.

Assessments of Détente are now influenced by our knowledge of the events of the late 1980s that saw an end to the Cold War. But there is a danger of neglecting to set the motives and achievements of Détente within the context of the period in which it was pursued. Because it deals with the nature of international diplomacy and the methods that can be used in dealing with hostile states, Détente illustrates dilemmas which still face world leaders, even though the antagonists are different. The debate is likely to continue.

US and Soviet leaders during the Cold War

US Presidents

1945–53	Harry S. Truman
1953–61	Dwight Eisenhower
1961–3	John F. Kennedy
1963–9	Lyndon B. Johnson
1969–74	Richard Nixon
1974–7	Gerald Ford
1977–81	Jimmy Carter
1981–9	Ronald Regan
1989–93	George Bush

Soviet leaders[1]

Joseph Stalin	1922*–53
Georgi Malenkov	1953–5
Nikita Khushchev	1955–64
Leonid Brezhnev	1964*–82
Yuri Andropov	1982–4
Konstantin Chernenko	1984–5
Mikhail Gorbachev	1985–91

[1] There was no definitive position as leader of the Soviet Union. From the 1920s onwards the Soviet leader usually held the position of General (or First) Secretary of the Communist Party rather than Prime Minister or President. This situation produced several periods when it was unclear who held real power in the USSR. This includes the periods 1924–9 and 1964–6 (marked with an asterisk in the table above).

SECTION 6

Why, and how, did superpower rivalry change between 1979 and 1991?

As the 1970s drew to a close, the superpower rapprochement of the Détente period broke down. The Soviet invasion of Afghanistan in 1979 marked the start of renewed hostility as the so-called Second or New Cold War occurred. Under Ronald Reagan, the USA embarked on a programme of unprecedented arms expansion in order to meet the perceived threat from the 'evil empire' of the Soviet Union. The Second Cold War was, however, short-lived. When Mikhail Gorbachev became leader of the USSR in 1985 he represented a new generation within the Politburo. His determination to implement a reform of the Soviet system led to a fundamental shift of emphasis, which brought about, not just an end to the Cold War, but also an end to the Soviet Union.

WHY DID THE SECOND COLD WAR DEVELOP?

An explanation of the reasons for the development of the Second Cold War usually takes the Soviet invasion of Afghanistan in 1979 as its starting point. The invasion led to widespread condemnation of the USSR and was perceived in the West as evidence of the continuation of the expansionist tendencies of the USSR. Yet the relaxation in superpower relations that had taken place under Détente in the 1970s had already broken down before Brezhnev ordered Soviet tanks into Afghanistan. The development of renewed superpower hostility can be seen as early as 1976 during the US Presidency of Jimmy Carter.

The foreign policy of Jimmy Carter

The Democrat Jimmy Carter was elected US President in 1976. He hoped to use respect for human rights as the basis of his foreign policy with the USSR in order to reduce tension. Unfortunately, Carter lacked experience in foreign affairs and failed to realise that a constant emphasis on human rights as they were defined in the West was likely to increase rather than reduce tension. Carter has often been portrayed as a 'dove', soft on communism, but this view is misleading. It is more accurate to see Carter's foreign policy as a struggle between two opposing positions: on the one hand the approach advocated by Cyrus Vance, the Secretary of State, of using negotiation to lessen tension; and on the other, a more hard-line approach, as advocated by Zbigniew Brzezinski, Carter's National Security Advisor, of using increased arms and strong language to put pressure on the Soviet leadership to change its policy. Because of his inexperience Carter was heavily reliant on the advice of these two men, and perhaps the central weakness of his foreign policy was his inconsistency in choosing which advice to follow.

Carter reached agreement with Brezhnev on the SALT II Treaty in June 1979 but he was under growing pressure from critics at home. As Soviet influence in the Third World increased, the approach of negotiation recommended by Vance seemed, to many on the American right, to give the USSR the advantage, as they were unlikely to keep to agreements signed with the West. Thus, it was always the West that gave concessions and the USSR that gained. By the late 1970s negotiation with the Soviet Union became increasingly difficult because of Brezhnev's failing health. He had suffered a series of heart attacks since the mid-1970s and by 1979 he could function only with the aid of drugs. Without firm guidance at the top, Soviet decision-making became very slow and painstaking. It was easier for the Americans to adopt the hard-line approach recommended by Brzezinki. A Pole by birth, Brzezinki found it impossible to trust the Soviet Union and believed that only a show of US strength would make the Soviet leadership change its policy. Carter increased supplies of arms to anti-communist groups and governments in the Third World, such as in El Salvador and Nicaragua, to prevent the spread of Soviet influence. In the summer of 1979 Carter and Brezhnev argued over the presence of Soviet troops in Cuba and relations between the superpowers were already difficult when, in December, the Soviet Union invaded Afghanistan. The invasion provided the last straw for Carter, who condemned the Soviet action and withdrew the SALT II Treaty from the Senate.

The Soviet invasion of Afghanistan, 1979

The events in Afghanistan marked the end of any further negotiation between the superpowers. Détente was dead. Lying south of the USSR, Afghanistan was viewed by Moscow as an important buffer state. The situation in this region had been complicated by events in nearby Iran. In January 1979 the US-supported Shah of Iran had been removed by a popular uprising led by the Muslim Fundamentalist, Ayatollah Khomeini. The new government of Iran was violently anti-American and US oil assets were under threat. But the Iranian Revolution also posed a threat to Soviet interests. The spread of Muslim Fundamentalism through the region was a danger to the stability of the Soviet Union. The Central Asian republics of the USSR, which bordered Afghanistan, contained Muslim populations whose integration into the Soviet Union had always been superficial. Thus, the importance of maintaining a pro-Soviet government in Afghanistan was given added significance. In April 1978 the pro-Soviet People's Democratic Party of Afghanistan (PDPA) had seized power without the involvement of the USSR but Moscow was to provide economic assistance for the new Afghan government. The PDPA soon faced severe resistance from those opposed to its social and economic policies, such as Muslim Fundamentalists, as well as factions within its own party. One PDPA faction was led by the radical Hafizullah Amin, who seized control of the government in the summer of 1979. The USSR viewed Amin with alarm. He had initiated contacts with the CIA to bolster his attempts to hold on to power. The prospect of US involvement in Afghanistan was too much for Brezhnev who decided to send in Soviet troops to remove Amin and install a pro-Soviet faction of the PDPA. The Afghan government remained unpopular and the Soviet Union needed to send over 100,000 troops to ensure its survival. Afghanistan was to become a Soviet Vietnam: a war that they could not win against an enemy located in the countryside using guerrilla tactics.

The Soviet Union justified the invasion under the Brezhnev Doctrine but President Carter was unwilling to let the USSR get away with another intervention in the affairs of a foreign country so easily. His language in condemning the Soviet action was more strident than expected. As well as withdrawing the SALT II Treaty from the Senate, he cut off trade contacts between the USA and the USSR and encouraged a western boycott of the Moscow Olympics in 1980. Most of western Europe followed the US lead with the exception of Britain, which participated in the Moscow Olympics much to the annoyance of its new, staunchly anti-communist Prime Minister, Margaret Thatcher. A sign of the developing tension and hostility was Carter's decision to increase arms spending. Presidential Directive 59 authorised an increase in the US nuclear arsenal: the era of arms limitation was at an end.

Ronald Reagan and the Reagan Doctrine

President Ronald Reagan's attacks on the Soviet Union were a major factor in the escalation of the Second Cold War. The Soviet invasion of Afghanistan had been one of the key issues of the US presidential election of 1980. Carter's perceived weakness at dealing with yet another example of Soviet aggression was one of the deciding factors that resulted in defeat for Carter and victory for Ronald Reagan. A staunch right-winger, Reagan's hatred of communism was well known. He saw the USSR and communism in unsophisticated moral terms as the embodiment of evil. As a former B-movie actor, Reagan had difficulty handling complex political ideas but he was highly skilled at articulating a vision of world affairs that was shared by a large section of the US population. Reagan's forthright hostility towards the USSR symbolised the change in US public opinion caused by the growing disillusionment with Détente.

Reagan decided to pursue the Second Cold War with vigour on all fronts. He was able to convince the US Congress to increase military spending on a scale that was unprecedented in US history. Defence spending was increased by 13 per cent in 1982 and over 8 per cent in each of the

Ronald Reagan, in London for an economic summit, shakes hands with Margaret Thatcher at No. 10 Downing Street, June 1984.

following two years. New nuclear missiles were developed, including the Stealth bomber and Trident submarines. Central to this arms build-up was the Strategic Defence Initiative, announced in 1983. The aim of this arms programme was to regain US military supremacy against the Soviet Union to the extent that they would not be able to continue the Cold War. Thus, supremacy in arms would allow the USA to gain more meaningful concessions from the Soviet leadership. In pursuit of this aim, Reagan was supported by Margaret Thatcher. The two leaders shared a view of the USSR as the 'evil empire'. Thatcher's harsh attacks on communism led the Soviet press to dub her the 'Iron Lady'. She established a highly effective working relationship with Reagan and her agreement to have US nuclear missiles based in Britain was of vital importance in putting pressure on the Soviet Union. Without European bases the threat to use nuclear missiles against Soviet territory would have been much diminished.

Reagan took decisive measures to try to halt the growth of Soviet influence in the Third World by developing what became known as the Reagan Doctrine. This term was given to the policy of sending assistance to anti-communist insurgents as well as anti-communist governments. In Nicaragua, the Doctrine was used to supply military aid to the Contras, a right-wing guerrilla group fighting against the communist government of the Sandinistas. In El Salvador, the USA supported an unpopular right-wing government facing a growing popular revolt by the left. In 1983,

US forces invaded the Caribbean island of Grenada and deposed its left-wing government. These actions were not always popular in the wider world and were often counter-productive. Some of the regimes supported by the USA, such as the Marcos government in the Philippines, had a very poor record on human rights. The Reagan Doctrine showed the Soviet Union that the USA was prepared to take forceful action against communist expansion.

Inertia in the Soviet leadership: the Gerontocracy

If US foreign policy was changing in the early 1980s, Soviet policy was grinding to a halt. No new initiative was possible from the Soviet leadership because of the nature of its leaders during this period. A succession of old and infirm leaders resulted in inertia in decision-making. The increasingly aged and confused Brezhnev finally died in 1982. His physical incapacity had prevented any change in the direction of Soviet foreign policy. Brezhnev's successor was Yuri Andropov who aged 69, was only seven years younger than Brezhnev. It seems likely that Andropov would have introduced policy initiatives – he attempted to start domestic reform – but he was an ill man. Wired to a dialysis machine in his Kremlin apartment for most of his time as leader, he succumbed to kidney failure in February 1984. His replacement was Konstantin Chernenko, a conservative who represented the desire of the majority of the Politburo to avoid reform. Chernenko was unable to have an impact on policy. He was dying of emphysema when he became leader and lived less than a year in office.

KEY TERM

Gerontocracy
Rule by geriatrics. The term is used to describe the Soviet leadership in the years 1980–5 – i.e. the last years of Brezhnev, Andropov and Chernenko. At a time when the Soviet Union was in desperate need of reform it was led by a series of men whose physical condition prevented strong, decisive leadership.

An example of the impact inertia had on relations between the superpowers is shown by the response to the shooting down of the Korean airliner KA007 by Soviet fighters in 1983. The incident, which cost the lives of all 269 passengers, caused outrage in the West. The aircraft had been en route from Alaska to Seoul when it strayed into Soviet airspace. The Soviet authorities assumed it was a spy plane and shot it down. The Politburo showed its inflexibility during the furore that followed. Gromyko, the Soviet Foreign Minister, ignored questions from the West, and the Soviet military merely reiterated the standard line that any unidentified aircraft flying over Soviet airspace would be treated in exactly the same way. Old age and illness had rendered the Soviet leadership incapable of action. It was unable to respond to the incident in any meaningful manner. The 1970s had shown that the best method of improving relations was by face-to-face meetings between the US and Soviet leaders. The condition of Andropov had made this impossible during the KA007 affair. The incident marked a low point in the Second Cold War.

Assessment

The Soviet invasion of Afghanistan has been used to apportion blame for the Second Cold War to the USSR. It was viewed by western leaders, such as Carter and Thatcher, as showing the unwillingness of the Soviet leadership to change its policy of expanding the influence of communism in the Third World. Yet the development of the Second Cold War was marked by a change in the USA's foreign policy rather than that of the USSR. The last years of Carter's presidency saw the emergence of the hard-line approach to US policy, recommended by Brzezinki, and led the way for Reagan to implement a vigorous campaign against communism. Soviet inflexibility during the early 1980s did nothing to prevent the level of tension rising to dangerous levels once again.

WHY DID THE COLD WAR COME TO AN END?

If the Second Cold War was generated by a change in US policy, it was a change in Soviet political thinking that brought about the end of the Cold War. In 1985 the Soviet leadership was in the hands of Mikhail Gorbachev, who was from a younger generation than previous Soviet leaders. He recognised the need for urgent reform of the Soviet system and understood that domestic reform required a change in international policy. Gorbachev's new approach took the international community by surprise. Its impact was to have far-reaching consequences for the Soviet Union, its satellite states and ultimately stripped away the preconditions of Cold War conflict.

Gorbachev's new political thinking

As a committed communist Gorbachev's aim on gaining the Soviet leadership in 1985 was to make the Soviet system more productive and responsive. He recognised that in order to achieve this, military spending had to be reduced. This could be done only if arms limitation talks with the USA were reopened. Arms agreements would allow Gorbachev to reduce military spending without leaving the USSR exposed to attack, and therefore avoiding opposition at home from the Soviet armed forces. An indication of Gorbachev's new approach to the West was the replacement of the veteran Foreign Minister Gromyko with Eduard Shevardnadze. Gorbachev and Shevardnadze launched a charm offensive on the West with their new political thinking. Margaret Thatcher had met Gorbachev in 1984 and declared, 'This is a man with whom I can do business.' To the new Soviet leadership, confrontation between the superpowers was viewed as unproductive because it led to an escalation in arms and retaliatory measures that increased insecurity. The Soviet experience in Afghanistan, where the war had dragged on without a decisive result, led to a re-evaluation of Soviet interference in the Third World. The Afghan War highlighted the cost of making a commitment. Over 15,000 Red Army soldiers were killed in the war, which cost $8 billion per annum. Supporting communist regimes in Cuba, Vietnam, Afghanistan, and even in eastern Europe, had become a drain on Soviet resources. The USSR spent approximately $40 billion annually on propping up communist governments throughout the world. This money could be used to promote domestic reform. Instead of seeing foreign policy as an implement of class struggle against the forces of capitalism, Gorbachev focused on universal values of human rights to promote the interests of all peoples. Thus, Soviet foreign policy was 'normalised': it would no longer be an instrument for furthering the interests of world communism.

The impact of the new political thinking was felt quickly. A summit meeting between Reagan and Gorbachev was arranged for Geneva in November 1985. Little was decided at the summit but it was important in establishing a personal rapport between the two leaders. Reagan hated everything the Soviets stood for but liked Gorbachev and the other Soviet representatives he met. Gorbachev soon realised Reagan found detail hard to grasp and ensured discussions focused on general principles. The Geneva Summit was important in laying the foundations for future negotiation in an atmosphere of cordiality. After the summit, Gorbachev proposed phasing out nuclear weapons and offered a series of ever-increasing concessions that took the US leadership by surprise. The price of these concessions was to be the withdrawal of the US SDI (Strategic Defence Initiative) programme. When the two Presidents met at Reykjavik in 1986 Reagan was not prepared to put SDI on the negotiating table and no agreement was reached. But the deadlock did not last long. At Washington, the following year, the INF (Intermediate Nuclear Forces) agreement was signed, leading to the scrapping of all intermediate-range ballistic missiles. It was the first time the superpowers had agreed to arms reduction rather than arms control.

By 1988 Gorbachev had announced his intention to withdraw Soviet troops from Afghanistan and reduce its forces in eastern Europe by half a million. When George Bush replaced Reagan as US President in 1989 Soviet actions had convinced the US government that Gorbachev could be trusted. Relations were now so close that Gorbachev commented that it was in the Soviet interest to support the USA's role in world affairs. At the Bush–Gorbachev summit in Malta in 1989, Shevardnadze was able to announce that the superpowers had 'buried the Cold War at the bottom of the Mediterranean'.

The end of the Brezhnev Doctrine

Gorbachev's policies had an important impact on eastern Europe. His domestic policies of Perestroika, Glasnost and Democratisation encouraged those in eastern Europe who wished to see similar liberalisation in their own countries. In foreign affairs Gorbachev's new political thinking meant it was unnecessary to have eastern Europe as a Soviet sphere of influence. Most importantly, Gorbachev made clear to

Crowds dismantling the Berlin Wall, 1989.

eastern European leaders in 1985 that the Brezhnev Doctrine would no longer be applied. The peoples of eastern Europe could choose their own governments. This posed a particular problem for those leaders who wanted to resist reform. They could not rely on Soviet military intervention to buttress their regimes. Evidence that Gorbachev meant what he said came in 1989 when Hungary adopted a multi-party system and Polish elections returned a non-communist government. The USSR took no action; Gorbachev even offered his encouragement. The end of the Brezhnev Doctrine was of particular concern to the East German regime. The creation of East Germany had been a result of superpower tension and hostility after the Second World War. As an artificial country, East Germany was more reliant on Soviet support than the other regimes of the region. When Gorbachev visited East Berlin in October 1989 he became the focus of those East Germans who wanted to reform the country. Erich Honecker, the East German leader, refused to contemplate reform of any kind and his intransigence led to his removal by other members of the East German Politburo. With mass demonstrations on the streets of East German cities, the pressure for reform became unstoppable. Earlier in the year the Chinese government had responded to demonstrations calling for reform by using force. The massacre of students in Tiananmen Square, Beijing, in June had illustrated one method of dealing with the situation. Egon Krenz, the new East German leader, refused to sanction widespread repression and, amid the growing chaos, decided to open access across the Berlin Wall. On 9 November the Berlin Wall, the symbol of Cold War Europe, was dismantled by 'people power'. The future position of Germany, however, still remained in Gorbachev's hands.

If Germany was to reunify Gorbachev wanted it to be neutral. Helmut Kohl, the West German Chancellor, called for German membership of NATO and, bolstered by the election results in East Germany in April 1990, which saw a victory for parties favouring reunification, Kohl was able to persuade Gorbachev to accept a reunified Germany with NATO membership. The Soviet Union also gave up any claim to occupy German soil. Gorbachev appears to have seen these developments as inevitable, but the close relationship between himself and Kohl certainly helped speed up the process. The importance of the personal role of Gorbachev cannot be overestimated. Many of his decisions were taken without reference to his advisers. Shevardnadze had doubts about the wisdom of Gorbachev's actions and the Soviet military viewed their President's policy as one of capitulation. By the end of 1989 every pro-Soviet communist government in eastern Europe had disintegrated.

The end of the Soviet Union

The forces for change unleashed by Gorbachev's policies ran out of his control. By the summer of 1991 the superpowers had signed the START (Strategic Arms Reduction Talks) Treaty. Nuclear arsenals were to be rapidly reduced. The hostility between East and West was gone. Cold War conflict was a thing of the past but, for those who saw the Cold War as a conflict between the competing ideologies of the superpowers, the fall of the USSR in 1991 was the final conclusion to a conflict which had threatened the world since 1945.

The dismantling of communism within the Soviet Union was opposed by conservative members of the Communist Party and many in the Soviet armed forces. Yet the weakness of their position was revealed by the failure of their attempted coup against Gorbachev in August 1991. When the coup collapsed Gorbachev was back in power but no longer in control of events. The rise of nationalist sentiment in the Soviet republics had led the Baltic States of Lithuania, Latvia and Estonia to declare their independence from Moscow by the end of 1990. In December 1991, the remaining republics dissolved the Soviet Union as a sovereign state. The Cold War was over.

Interpretations

The Cold War came to an end primarily because of a change in Soviet thinking. The Soviet leadership came to the conclusion that the Cold War was no longer worth fighting. Politicians and historians have argued over the reasons for this change of policy.

Politicians from the American right, including supporters of Ronald Reagan, credit the hard-line approach of the USA in the early 1980s as providing the pressure that caused the Soviet Empire to collapse. SDI was the final straw for a Soviet economy on the brink of bankruptcy. Unable to match the increased defence spending of the USA, the USSR had no choice but to call an end to the arms race and the Cold War. This view is also presented by historians such as J. L. Gaddis in *We Now Know* (1997).

The views of the right have been challenged by those who point to the fact that Soviet leaders had already come to the conclusion that superpower rivalry was counterproductive before the arms programme of Reagan. Soviet scientists did not consider SDI to be a realistic policy; rather something in the realm of science fiction. Although there was some alarm within the Soviet leadership at SDI, there is no evidence of an increase in Soviet military spending as a result. Thus, Reagan's arms programme created little additional pressure. According to M. Bowker, in *Russian Foreign Policy and the End of the Cold War* (1997), Reagan's policies may have delayed the end of the Cold War by giving conservative elements within the Soviet leadership a better case for continuing the conflict by highlighting the hostility of the enemy.

Conclusion

The Cold War came to an end when the USSR had lost its will for empire. It could not sustain the resources needed to pursue an empire it no longer felt it needed, to secure itself against its enemies. Cold War conflict had involved the superpowers building empires abroad to secure spheres of influence. As the USA found in Vietnam and the USSR found in Afghanistan, empire building was a painful and costly policy. The Soviet Union had failed to gain from its emphasis on pursuing class struggle with the forces of capitalism. With the collapse of communism the ideological conflict between two competing systems was no longer relevant. Conflict in world affairs continued but the specific nature of the conflict of the Cold War, which had blighted international relations since 1945, was finally over.

A2 SECTION: CONTAINING COMMUNISM – THE USA IN ASIA 1945–73

INTRODUCTION

Cold War conflict between East and West took on a global dimension after 1949. The communist takeover of China directed US concerns about the spread of communism to the Far East. Here the USA pursued a policy of containing communism within its existing frontiers. The withdrawal of European powers after the exertions of the Second World War and the power vacuum that resulted from the defeat of Japan in 1945 did much to add to the instability of the region. When civil wars broke out in Korea and Vietnam the US policy of containment led to an escalation of conflict in an attempt to prevent communism gaining control. The efforts of the USA to act as 'the policeman of the world' were to have a significant impact on the USA and led to a fundamental reassessment of its role in world affairs during the Cold War. US actions also had devastating consequences for the people of the Far East. The painful experiences of Cold War conflict in Asia have made interpretations of these events a source of heated debate, especially as the psychological impact of the Korean War and Vietnam War has proved to be so long lasting. The following sections concentrate on the main areas of debate:

- **Section 7: For what reasons, and with what results, did the USA intervene in the Korean War?** This attempts to assess the relative importance of the factors that led to US involvement in the Korean War and whether this involvement achieved the results the USA desired.
- **Section 8: What was the significance of the French withdrawal from South East Asia for the conflict between capitalism and communism?** This looks at the French experience in Indochina and the legacy of their defeat in 1954.
- **Section 9: By what means, and for what reasons, did the USA participate in the Vietnam War?** This examines the methods by which the USA intervened in the conflict and how they relate to the aims and objectives of US foreign policy.
- **Section 10: What was the response of the American people to the Vietnam War and to what extent did this influence its outcome?** This looks at attitudes to the war among different groups in US society and the impact they had on the outcome of the war. The reasons for US failure in Vietnam are considered.

SECTION 7

For what reasons, and with what results, did the USA intervene in the Korean War?

In January 1950 Dean Acheson, the US Secretary of State, had implied that Korea was not considered to lie within the US defensive perimeter. Yet a few months later the USA committed itself to a land war on the peninsula. The USA sent over 260,000 troops to Korea to help the government of the South repel an invasion by the North. Although in essence a civil war over the nature of unification, the US entry into the Korean conflict was conditioned by attitudes generated by the development of the Cold War between the USA and the USSR after the Second World War. Despite the widespread devastation of Korea caused by the conflict, the consequences of US involvement in the war were viewed by the US government predominantly in terms of its impact on the rivalry between capitalism and communism.

WHY DID THE USA INTERVENE IN THE KOREAN WAR?

The entry of the USA into the Korean War was, on the face of it, a response to the invasion of South Korea by the North. The USA therefore intervened to help a victim of aggression repel a deliberately provocative enemy: the use of the United Nations to send troops to the aid of South Korea was possible because the war was framed in this manner. Yet the prompt and vigorous action of the USA in committing itself to the assistance of South Korea was due less to the general principle of upholding democracy against the threat of an aggressor than to the wider context of the Cold War.

The principle of deterring aggression

The USA used the United Nations to justify US intervention in the Korean War. A UN resolution passed within a month of the war clarified the reasons for UN involvement: 'The armed attack upon the Republic of Korea by forces from North Korea constitutes a breach of the peace.' The resolution also called on member states to 'assist the Republic of Korea in defending itself against armed attack and thus to restore international peace and security in the area'. UN involvement had been important as a mechanism for securing firm support for US military intervention in the war under the aegis of acting in the interests of the wider principles of upholding democracy and peace against aggression. Syngman Rhee's regime in South Korea was hardly a model of freedom and democracy but the US government was willing to overlook this fact because of Rhee's anti-communist credentials. Some members of the UN, notably Egypt, Britain and France, were not convinced that the invasion by the North was unprovoked, due to the many breaches of peace that had occurred in Korea in the previous months. Nonetheless, the US resolution was passed by the UN. With the Soviet Union absent from the UN at this crucial juncture the USA was able to use the organisation to ratify its own decisions and involvement in the conflict. Truman later wrote in his memoirs that the UN was used to ensure its success in upholding peace against acts of aggression: 'I believed in the League of Nations. It failed. Lots of people thought it failed because we (the US) weren't in it to back it up. Now we started the UN. It was our idea, and in its first big test we just couldn't let them down.' By using the UN the US government was able to gain the support of its allies for intervention in a foreign war. The USA would probably have preferred indirect intervention, offering supplies to the South, but the South Korean army was disintegrating rapidly under the assault of the North's People's Army. The urgency of the military situation in Korea required a swift and direct response.

There has been some debate over which side started the war in Korea. The North claimed it had been attacked by the forces of South Korea, who had begun by shelling an area on the Ongjin Peninsula on 23 June and had invaded the town of Haeju. This view was counter to that accepted by the West that the North had sent its army across the 38th Parallel on the Ongjin Peninsula in order to seize the South. The seizure of Haeju by South Korea's 17th Regiment has often been used to support the North's claim that the South had started the war. The historian Bruce Cumings has pointed out that the 17th Regiment was a crack unit made up of soldiers formerly from the North who hated communism and were keen to resist attack. The capture of Haeju was therefore more likely to have been due to their initial success in combating an invasion from the North rather than the event that started the war. Yet the debate over who made the first move can detract from the context within which the invasion took place. The war had been initiated after a prolonged period of tension and skirmishes along the 38th Parallel. Both Syngman Rhee and Kim Il Sung had spoken of a desire to unite the country and both sides were prepared to use force to do so. It was possible that Syngman Rhee would have launched an invasion of the North to complete reunification at some time. His government had done badly in the South Korean elections in May, one month before the war started, and there was growing disillusionment with his rule, which Kim Il Sung could have exploited without the need to invade. Rhee may have been pleased that the North had beaten him to it as their invasion allowed him to play on western fears of the spread of communism in order to secure assistance. It also provided South Korea with the military commitment it was desperate to obtain from the USA for the defence of its country.

Traditional assessments of the origins of the war place responsibility on the North who were acting under instructions from Stalin to spread communism. This viewpoint has been challenged by those historians who see Stalin as too cautious to risk an escalation of conflict with the USA. This is supported by Khrushchev's memoirs, which state that Kim Il Sung had informed Stalin of his decision to invade the South but the Soviet leader had advised him 'to think it over ... Stalin had his doubts'. These memoirs are not an altogether reliable source but do confirm the prudence Stalin took elsewhere with his foreign policy.

The context of the Cold War: the impact of communist advances in the Far East

The USA had not always been so keen to intervene in the affairs of other states, but in the context of the Cold War, US involvement in Korea was seen as imperative. In American eyes there was little doubt that the war had been started by the North under Stalin's orders. This perception was determined by their experience of, and attitudes to, communism during the development of the Cold War in Europe since 1945. To the US government, the aggressive nature of world communism was confirmed once again.

The struggle for supremacy between the forces of capitalism and communism had been dramatically transformed by the communist takeover of China in 1949. Mao's communist forces had pushed the Chinese Nationalists out of mainland China to the island of Taiwan. The defeat of the US-supported Nationalists was a failure for US policy. There was now a large communist state in Asia, which was not only considered to be a puppet of the Soviet Union but also a base for future communist expansion throughout the region. From China, communism was ideally placed to spread into neighbouring Indochina and Korea. In the wider context of the Cold War, it had delivered a substantial blow against the USA. The stakes were, therefore, raised when the Korean War broke out the following year. The USA was determined to halt the inexorable advance of world communism.

Within the wider context of East–West conflict, the Korean War occurred less than a year after the Soviet Union announced its successful development of the atomic bomb. The era of the US atomic monopoly was over and much sooner than the US government had believed was possible. The US government thought the USSR was unlikely to develop its own atomic bomb until late 1950. The detection of tell-tale traces of radiation in the northern Pacific in August 1949 confirmed the successful testing of an atomic explosion. The atomic bomb had been viewed in the

USA as a vital weapon to deter the forces of world communism. The Soviet acquisition of nuclear technology weakened the US position in stemming the tide of Soviet expansionism.

Domestic pressures

These events in 1949 led to an increase in US concerns about the direction of world affairs and put President Truman under pressure. The Republicans accused Truman of being too 'soft' on communism and attempted to discredit his entire foreign policy. He was blamed for the loss of China. The McCarthy witch-hunt against those in the US establishment suspected of harbouring communist sympathies was evidence of the force of public concerns about Truman's approach. Within the US establishment there was pressure for firm, direct action against communism from hawks in the air force, such as Vandenberg and Finletter, who wanted to attack North Korea at the start of hostilities. When the Korean War began, Truman was under immense pressure to show he would not capitulate to communist aggression once again. The internal politics of the USA impelled Truman to take a tougher stance when the Korean War started.

The pressure on Truman to take a hard line against communist expansion had pushed him towards an acceptance of the National Security Council paper 68 (NSC-68). This document had been produced in April 1950 and recommended a much stronger approach towards the Soviet Union in order to contain communism. One of the recommendations was to increase substantially the USA's military strength. Truman agreed with the thrust of NSC-68, although he was aware that taxes would have to be raised in order for the proposals to be enacted. There was no tradition in the USA of heavy taxation to support a large peacetime army and such a measure would be politically unpopular. The Korean War provided a useful opportunity to justify the implementation of NSC-68. The invasion of South Korea was seized upon as tangible evidence of the threat of Soviet expansionism. It allowed Truman to push through the measures needed to support a more active policy against world communism without risking the loss of support from within his own party.

The hardening of US foreign policy

The international and domestic factors driving Truman to intervene in the war in Korea were considerations that produced a hardening of US attitudes towards foreign policy and the methods that should be used in combating the spread of communism. US belief in the domino effect seemed to be confirmed by the events in the Far East. The fall of China to communism now put Korea at risk. The barrier against communism had to be shored up by direct and forceful action. Truman used this argument to justify sending US troops to Korea: 'If we let Korea down, the Soviets will keep right on going and swallow up one piece of Asia after another.' The Soviet Union needed to be shown that the USA meant what it said about supporting those who, in the words of the Truman Doctrine, were 'resisting subjugation by armed minorities or by outside influences'. The strength of the US commitment to the West was also viewed with some scepticism in western Europe and proof that the USA was offering more than mere words would help stem any tendency towards pessimism and defeatism in Europe.

The impact of the military situation on US aims

The reasons for US intervention in the Korean War were to change in emphasis as the fighting progressed. The vigour with which the USA honoured its promise to South Korea evolved into a change in the aims pursued during the war. The failure of Stalin to aid North Korea or send them large amounts of military supplies (Soviet shipments to North Korea actually declined during the war) provided Truman with the confidence that the war could be limited to the peninsula. By early September 1950 the South had been saved from North Korea's forces. Truman's decision to authorise the invasion of the North marked a shift from the policy of containment towards one of attempting to roll back communism from the Korean peninsula. Horowitz, in *From Yalta to Vietnam* (1967), goes as far as arguing that 'MacArthur's whole subsequent course of behaviour was consistent with a strategy designed to provoke and then escalate a war in Asia.' The change to roll-back should not, however, be taken as evidence that the US government had always intended to pursue such a policy. It was a change that emerged from the specific situation and opportunity presented by the course of the military campaigns during the war. Truman was, in this respect, far more cautious than MacArthur and the divergence in approach led to the General's dismissal in April 1951. The intervention of China on the side of North Korea and their subsequent military success in driving the US army south was to lead to a further re-evaluation of US war aims. Instead of rolling back communism, the priority of the USA at the beginning of 1951 was to drive the communist armies north of the 38th Parallel: an aim that was to last for the remainder of the war.

Conclusions

This powerful mix of international and domestic considerations propelled the USA towards strident policy objectives. These factors conditioned US intervention in the Korean War. Despite the risk of turning a civil war into a major conflict between the superpowers, Truman was prepared to sacrifice American lives in order to ensure the USA showed its credentials against world communism.

WHAT WERE THE RESULTS OF US INTERVENTION IN THE KOREAN WAR?

The decision of the USA to commit a large number of its forces to the Korean War was to have a significant impact on the course of the war and its military campaigns. It was also inevitable that US involvement would affect the wider development of the Cold War and impact upon East–West relations.

The impact on the course of the war

The immediate result of US intervention in the Korean War was the saving of South Korea from the invasion by the North. When US troops arrived in Korea the South Korean army had been driven back to a small corner of the peninsula around Pusan. The forces of the South had disintegrated under attack and had virtually given up fighting. The first Americans to arrive in Korea were ill-prepared for action. The US forces had been reduced in size and resources since 1945 and this had left them unready for action. Michael Hickey has described US troops at the beginning of the war as, 'ill-disciplined, physically soft and dangerously under-trained'. When US soldiers engaged in fighting, their attitude was that regaining Korean soil for the South was not worth losing US lives. The result was an over-reliance on the use of massive artillery and air strikes. This was to influence the nature of the warfare in Korea. Despite the reluctance and lack of preparedness of US forces, they were able to hold off North Korea long enough for the South to survive until the landings at Inchon.

The Inchon landings of September 1950, under the code-name Operation Chromite, enabled the USA to push the North Korean forces out of the South. Brilliantly organised and implemented by MacArthur, the landings were highly successful and transformed the war. The UN forces were able to regain the territory south of the 38th Parallel and inflict a major defeat on the People's Army of the North, who were forced to retreat into North Korea to regroup. The speed of the military success resulted in the issue of whether to cross the 38th Parallel and roll back communism from the whole peninsula. When Truman authorised the decision to move into the North the subsequent rapid acquisition of territory and push towards the Chinese border altered the war. MacArthur's advance to the Yalu River sparked the entry of China into North Korea. Mao probably wanted to warn the Americans off by sending volunteers across the border. It was MacArthur's resumption of the advance after Thanksgiving in November 1950 that seems to have changed Mao's intentions and resulted in a massive Chinese invasion into North Korea. Thus, US intervention turned a civil war into a battle between the forces of capitalism and communism on a larger scale.

US military involvement in the war was an essential factor in the survival of South Korea. It provided the fire-power of tank and artillery support and a degree of accuracy that made a vital contribution in holding back the communist armies. In total nearly 6 million US soldiers served in Korea during the 37 months of fighting and over 33,000 were killed in action. They provided the vast majority of those fighting for South Korea and their contribution was a key factor in the outcome of the war. Another essential ingredient of the US commitment was its air power. The air force was involved in over a million strategic and tactical operations. It is estimated that over half of the enemy casualties were due to air strikes. The use of napalm was especially effective in destroying targets, both human and material, on the ground. Aircraft also provided much-needed cover for US troops on the ground. The aircraft carrier allowed air power to reach a greater range within North Korea than land-based planes. The superiority of US military hardware enabled the South to hold out against the greater human resources of the communist forces provided by China.

One key aspect of military technology that was raised by US intervention in the war was the use of the nuclear bomb. The US military had considered using nuclear weapons to halt the initial North Korean drive to Pusan in July 1950. The entry of China into the war raised the issue again. As early as November 1950 Truman had told a press conference that 'there had always been active consideration of its use … it is one of our weapons'. MacArthur asked for discretionary powers to use nuclear weapons in December 1950 to prevent the Chinese overwhelming the 8th Army. He was later to state that his plan had been to drop fifty

US General Douglas MacArthur at a command post close to the 38th parallel in Korea, April 1951.

nuclear bombs on Chinese targets. Ridgway, MacArthur's replacement, also supported the use of nuclear weapons but only as a last resort. US nuclear bombs were stored at Kadena air base in Japan and, although extremely cautious, he knew they were available if there was a major deterioration in the US military position. US intervention had been important in widening the range of weaponry available for use in the war and with it there was greater potential for destruction.

The impact on East–West relations

The US intervention in the Korean War made clear to the forces of communism that the USA would not stand idly by when non-communist states in the Far East were threatened. US policy towards Taiwan was altered radically by events in Korea. Before the war the USA had no plans to aid Chiang Kai Shek's Nationalist regime against a possible invasion by Mao's communist forces. Yet in 1950 Truman ordered the US Seventh Fleet to the seas around Taiwan to warn communist China that any attempt to seize the island would be resisted by the USA. In 1949 the US government had viewed Chiang Kai Shek as an embarrassment and liability; by 1950 he was perceived as a useful bulwark against the further encroachment of communism in the region. In the developing tension of East–West relations Chiang Kai Shek's reputation in American eyes had been transformed.

The emergence of China as a superpower of some potential was to have an important impact on US policy towards Indochina. The French were struggling to hold back communist insurgents in Vietnam and US attitudes to the predicament of the French were changed by the war in Korea. Before 1950 the US government preferred to distance itself from French attempts to resurrect its colonial rule in Indochina. US dislike of European Imperialism was well known. In the minds of many members of the US establishment, the advance of communism in China in 1949, followed so quickly by the war in Korea, turned the French actions in Indochina into a crucial part of the struggle against world communism. Ho Chi Minh, the leader of the Vietminh, was, to the US government, an agent of the USSR, and this led to over $1 billion a year in US aid to the French in Indochina. From 1950 the French campaign was financed largely by the USA. Thus, the change in attitudes towards the spread of communism in the Far East, which was a result of the Korean War, was to draw the USA into a gradual involvement in the Vietnam War.

US concerns engendered by Korea produced the formation of military defensive alliances in South East Asia that attempted to follow the example of NATO in Europe. The result was the conclusion of the ANZUS Pact in September 1951: an attempt by the USA to build an anti-communist alliance with Australia and New Zealand. The formation of SEATO (South East Asian Treaty Organisation) in 1954 was a bid to extend the coordination of defence of those Far East states that feared the spread of communism. In Europe, NATO was enlarged to include Greece and Turkey. US aid to NATO was increased – $25 billion was given between 1951 and 1955 – and the structure of the organisation was strengthened. Thus, the Korean War had greatly enlarged the military commitments of the USA to include the Far East as well as those already established in Europe.

The Korean War marked a significant escalation in the Cold War. It saw the first 'hot' war since the Second World War. Nonetheless, direct conflict between the USA and the USSR had been avoided and the fighting had been contained within the peninsula. The war in Korea established the trend towards the principle of limited war. In a situation where both superpowers were capable of unleashing nuclear weapons, establishing the unwritten rule of the deliberate limitation of the scale of warfare was to be an important consequence of the war. If the use of nuclear weapons was to be avoided the USA needed to develop its efficiency in a range of military tactics and the concept of 'flexible response' was developed. The Korean experience therefore produced a change in US military thinking that, in the words of the historian Bruce Cumings, 'led straight into Vietnam'.

The impact within the USA

Popular attitudes within the USA had helped push Truman into a direct commitment to South Korea but the failure to secure a quick victory against the forces of communism caused disillusionment. Desertions by US troops, one indicator of growing disenchantment, had increased dramatically in 1952. As casualties mounted so did Truman's unpopularity. UN casualties were to reach their peak in June 1953 when they rose to 23,161 for the month. Critics dubbed Korea 'Truman's War' and the President never regained his earlier popularity with the US people. Truman's presidency ended in 1953; the effects of the Korean War on the USA were to be longer lasting. The war had militarised the USA, leading to a seven-fold increase in defence spending. With concerns over the possibility of having to fight future wars to prevent communism spreading, the level of military spending would have to be maintained. The recommendations of NSC-68 were implemented. Congress voted to spend $10 billion on the army in 1950 and an additional $260 million was earmarked for the development of the hydrogen bomb. These increases strengthened the powerful interests of the military-industrial complex to the point where, by 1954, President Eisenhower raised concern at the political influence of the defence industry that was skewing political decision-making and leading to an unhealthy degree of economic dislocation.

Another disturbing aspect of the US experience in Korea was the inability of the US public and soldiers to comprehend fully what the war was about. An ignorance of the origins of the conflict in Korean terms was compounded by a failure to understand its South Korean allies, let alone the position of those in the North. This situation was also to be replicated later during the conflict in Vietnam.

Conclusions

US intervention in the Korean War had a similar impact on the US economy to that which it had on the Cold War in general. It produced a militarisation in the conduct of affairs at home and abroad. Korea marked a considerable hardening in the US government's determination towards its commitment to combating communism. It also led the USA to increase its military capacity to fight and in this respect the arms race was spurred on by the war.

After nearly five years of fighting in Korea, both sides ended roughly where they started in military terms. The ceasefire line of 1954 was little different from the line established before the war by the 38th Parallel. But for the USA the effort and losses incurred during the war had achieved important successes. They had, through the action of the UN, achieved the aim of deterring aggression and preventing the overthrow of Syngman Rhee's regime in South Korea. It had also sent a message to the forces of world communism that the USA was prepared to make a stand against communist aggression through the use of direct armed intervention. The US position contrasted with the failure of Stalin to intercede by providing direct support for North Korea. The position of the USSR as the leader of world communism had suffered a notable setback, while China had gained respect among the communist fraternity for its commitment to North Korea. The USA had shown its credentials as the leader of the free world but success in Korea was to lead subsequently to failure in Vietnam.

SECTION 8

What was the significance of the French withdrawal from South East Asia for the conflict between capitalism and communism?

The withdrawal of France from Indochina in 1954 was of enormous significance for the struggle between capitalism and communism in the Far East. The failure of French attempts to defeat the nationalist movement in Vietnam was evidence of the increasing redundancy of old-style imperialism but within the context of Cold War relations it took on a greater significance. The USA saw the French withdrawal from Indochina as another example of the onward march of communism and, as a result, the USA was drawn into the conflict in Vietnam. Attempts at old-style imperialism were to be replaced by a new type of imperialism. This was to involve the extension of spheres of influence in the battle for supremacy between the irreconcilable ideologies of the Cold War. There were important lessons to be learnt from the French experience in Indochina but, unfortunately, the later actions of the USA showed that these were lost as the events were interpreted within the narrow focus of a Cold War mentality.

WHY WERE THE FRENCH UNABLE TO REASSERT CONTROL OVER INDOCHINA AND WHAT LESSONS COULD BE DRAWN FROM THE FRENCH EXPERIENCE?

The failure of France to re-establish control over its colonies in Indochina illustrated the bankruptcy of European Imperialism when faced with nationalism. Yet after 1945 the British were able to regain control over its colonies in Malaya and Singapore, lost to Japan in the Second World War. European Imperialism, while not yet completely dead, was severely weakened. In contrast with the British policy towards its empire, the French approach to imperialism was unlikely to succeed within the situation present in Indochina in 1945. Imperialist policies that did little to meet the needs and desires of the indigenous people were no match for a strong and united nationalist movement articulating the views of a majority of the population.

Reasons for the French failure in Indochina

The strength of Vietnamese nationalism. Ho Chi Minh had been able to effectively fuse the forces of nationalism and communism to produce a movement with a wide basis of support. The French made the mistake of equating the Vietminh with the People's Army but there was more to the movement than this. The Vietminh had organisations at all levels of society, from peasants to business groups: all united in their desire to remove French colonial power. Their leaders had gained respect due to their role in the resistance to Japanese rule during the Second World War. When Japan surrendered in August 1945 the Vietminh were in a position to make a Declaration of Independence of the Democratic Republic of Vietnam. They were not prepared to swap Japanese domination for a return to that of the French.

The situation in 1945. Under the terms of the Japanese surrender Indochina was to be occupied by the British in the south and Nationalist China in the north. This arrangement would be temporary until the French were ready to resume control. In the north, the forces of the Chinese Nationalists soon returned to China to fight the communists. In the south, the British, concerned that nationalism would spread to undermine their own position in nearby Burma and India, refused to negotiate with the Vietminh, established martial law and waited for the French to return. The actions of the British Army allowed the French to restore their rule without having to make concessions to a popular revolution, which represented the majority of the people. The French were therefore given an artificial impression of the ease by which colonial rule could be re-established.

French complacency. The French government and its military leaders underestimated the Vietminh. Despite guerrilla actions, especially in the north, the French dismissed the Vietminh with contempt as 'les jeunes' and the Minister of War was, by 1946, confident enough to declare that 'there was no longer any military problem in Indochina'. The French administration refused to compromise with the Vietminh and carried on with the implementation of its intended policies. It was not until 1949 that the continued strength of Vietminh support and an increase in guerrilla action led to a change in French policy.

The failure to address the needs of the Vietnamese. The French made little attempt to win over support for their rule. The French had no intention of reducing the power of the feudal landlords who owned much of the land in Vietnam. The social status quo was to be upheld. In 1949, in an attempt to undermine the Vietminh, the French established the Emperor Bao Dai as head of Vietnam. It was obvious to all concerned that Bao Dai was a puppet of the French. He preferred the luxurious lifestyle of the French Riviera to that of Vietnam and had to be coaxed back to his native country. To make matters worse his government contained no one who had gained a reputation for fighting against the

Japanese. Bao Dai was, compared to Ho Chi Minh, a poor substitute as a symbol of Vietnamese unity.

French military failure. The reluctance of the Vietminh to engage in open warfare resulted in a lot of French frustration but little attempt to pursue a more effective strategy for combating guerrilla action. In November 1946 Jean Valluy, the French military commander in Saigon, decided to 'give a harsh lesson' to the Vietminh. The cruiser *Suffren* was sent north and bombarded the port of Haiphong. Six thousand Vietnamese were killed in an action that included a lot of indiscriminate shelling. This action summed up the inability of the French forces to adjust to the nature of guerrilla warfare. As Michael MacLear has stated, 'random action became the substitute for actual battle'. This response was to harden support for the Vietminh. The connection between winning support from the local population and military success when fighting a guerrilla war was not lost on the French but they did little to adapt this knowledge to their tactics. French forces consisted of 20,000 Foreign Legionnaires, half of whom had served in Nazi armies; and 48,000 from other French colonies. It was an inauspicious collection of soldiers, which did little to engender support. Attempts to increase the size of the French army in Indochina by conscription were difficult because of the war's growing unpopularity at home.

The role of French popular opinion. To a nation that had suffered defeat at the hands of Nazi Germany, France in 1945 was a country in need of some measure to restore its national pride. Regaining its Far East Empire could have been one method of achieving this. Yet the Second World War had also left France exhausted and inward looking. As early as 1947 an opinion poll had shown ambivalence over Indochina. Thirty-six per cent favoured the use of force to bring about an end to the war against the Vietminh; 42 per cent favoured negotiation; and 8 per cent saw immediate withdrawal as the best option. France was already a divided nation. As the fighting dragged on, French public opinion hardened against the war. With the increase in the loss of French lives, the media launched a ferocious campaign against the war. The French were to lose over 72,000 lives. The imperialist principles underlying the war were called into question. It was clear that public opinion did not see anything worth fighting for in Indochina. It was an opinion that many rank-and-file French soldiers shared by 1953.

The failure of political will. General Navarre, who took over as French Chief of Staff in May 1953, complained that the political situation in France seriously undermined his attempt to wage an all-out military effort to win the war. Political instability within France had resulted in a change of government in 1953. French politics were dominated by domestic considerations, especially over the workings of the new constitutional structure of the Fourth Republic. The war in Indochina was a low priority in French politics. The historian Lucien Bodard, who had been a reporter in Vietnam, has highlighted the failure of vision and ideals on the part of the French government. Navarre complained that the government of Prime Minister Laniel failed to give him any instructions for action in Indochina. Although it was common for the military leaders to blame politicians for the failure in Indochina, there was some truth in this complaint. The failure of political will may have compounded the situation but, as Navarre was aware, military strategy was also failing.

The Battle of Dien Bien Phu. The military defeat inflicted on France by the Vietminh at Dien Bien Phu was decisive in bringing about French withdrawal from Indochina. The battle was not, however, the turning point in the military history of the war. Navarre recognised within one month of arriving in Vietnam that the war was lost. The mobility of the Vietminh in warfare, coupled with their high level of popular support, had put victory out of France's reach by 1953. According to Navarre, the best that France could hope for at this stage was to inflict a military blow on the Vietminh to strengthen the French hand at the negotiating table. Navarre's attempt to draw the Vietminh into open battle at Dien Bien Phu was a failure. General Giap's supply routes into the area around the fortress were strengthened and, in an incredible feat of logistics, over 200,000 porters moved supplies in readiness for the battle. Giap had ensured the Vietminh were able to stand their ground in open battle as well as guerrilla warfare. After fifty-five days of heavy fighting the French were defeated. The loss was a severe psychological blow to the French army. The will of the military to continue the struggle was now gone.

The failure of allied support. Would France have won the war with support from its allies? The view that the French would have defeated the Vietminh if the USA had offered military support gained some popularity, especially in the USA, in the aftermath of Dien Bien Phu. The USA was already providing most of the money to finance the French war before 1954 and to the US government there were distinct advantages in paying the French to do the fighting rather than having direct involvement. Attempts by US President Eisenhower to form an alliance known as 'United Action' with Australia, Britain, New Zealand, Thailand and the Philippines to help France failed. The British had relinquished India in 1947 and had no desire to help France prop up its own empire. Without joint action, the US government's response to the idea of direct intervention was lukewarm. The suggestion of the US Air Force Chief that three nuclear bombs dropped strategically near Dien Bien Phu would save the French was rejected by Eisenhower. The US Congress, already war-weary from Korea, was unlikely to approve unilateral involvement. The French were left to their fate.

Vietminh moving supplies to Dien Bien Phu, 1953.

Conclusions

The military defeat at Dien Bien Phu was symptomatic of a wide range of failings, both military and political, which afflicted French policy towards Indochina. The battle provided the psychological blow that forced France to withdraw, but the war was already lost. The French had been unable to adapt to the requirements of guerrilla warfare, preferring to rely on inappropriate tactics to impose an outdated system on an unwilling people. The French experience had shown the danger of ignoring the hearts and minds of the local population when facing guerrilla warfare against a popular movement. General Navarre knew the war was lost before the final battle, 'We used our soldiers, but our adversaries were fighting a complete war in which all the disciplines – politics, the economy, propaganda – were involved.' The importance of this interaction between the military and political dimensions of waging war was the crucial lesson the USA failed to learn from the defeat of France in Indochina.

WHAT WAS THE IMPACT OF THE GENEVA AGREEMENTS ON THE BATTLE FOR SUPREMACY BETWEEN CAPITALISM AND COMMUNISM?

The Geneva Conference was, in the light of Dien Bien Phu, able to produce a settlement that brought about the withdrawal of France from Indochina. Yet, in the context of the Cold War, the Geneva Agreements of 1954 took on a much greater significance. The forces of capitalism and communism saw the agreement as part of their wider conflict and interpreted its terms as part of the next stage in the battle for superpower supremacy in the region.

The Geneva Settlement arranged a ceasefire to bring the Indochina War to an end. The French would withdraw their troops and independence was to be given to Laos, Cambodia and Vietnam: the areas that had made up French Indochina. The terms concerning Vietnam were those which were open to interpretation. Vietnam was to be divided along the 17th Parallel until elections could be held within two years to unite the country under a democratic government. It was this part of the settlement that failed to be applied because of the intervention of the USA and its concerns about the advance of communism.

Consequences of the Geneva Settlement

Independent Indochina. Independence for Indochina had placed the forces of communism in a strong position. In Vietnam, the Vietminh were able to control all territory north of the 17th Parallel. In Laos, the communist-led Pathet Lao dominated over half the country. In Cambodia, where the movement for independence had been relatively weak, the country was headed by Prince Sihanouk. Yet the success of these local movements was due to their nationalist appeal rather than any adherence they might have had to Marxist ideals.

The division of Vietnam. The original intention of the division along the 17th Parallel was to allow passions to cool. The area around the 17th Parallel was officially termed the 'provisional military demarcation line'. The French forces would withdraw to the south, while the Vietminh's People's Army regrouped in the north. Elections would be held by July 1956 under the supervision of an international commission. That this temporary division was to last considerably longer than the two years envisaged in the settlement was due to the intervention of outside powers.

The position of the Vietminh. At the time of the settlement, the Vietminh was in control of most of northern Vietnam but it had also held over 20 per cent of the south when the ceasefire was signed. In the North, it was able to start a programme of reconstruction as soon as the settlement came into being. A programme of land reform was introduced, which led to some violence as old scores between landlords and peasants were settled. The USA and South Vietnam exaggerated the level of this violence to paint a picture of a communist bloodbath. Richard Nixon accused the North Vietnam government of killing over 500,000. Historians have revised these figures downwards. Bernard Fall puts the number of deaths at 50,000; in *Land Reform in China and North Vietnam* (1983), Edwin Moise, who has undertaken the most detailed study of land reform in Vietnam, puts the figure at between 3,000 and 15,000. South Vietnamese sources have admitted the 'Communist bloodbath' was fabricated for propaganda purposes. The popularity of the Vietminh was a thorny issue for those wishing to limit the spread of communism in Vietnam. In the South the withdrawal of the French left a political vacuum. Nearly every observer of the situation in Vietnam thought a Vietminh victory in the forthcoming elections was inevitable, given the strength of their support and the lack of any viable alternative. Even Eisenhower acknowledged the attraction of Ho Chi Minh and his programme.

The attitude of the USA. The US government had been shocked by the speed of the French collapse in Indochina. Coming so soon after the Korean War the USA was not prepared to accept the situation in Indochina. It viewed the Geneva Settlement as a victory for communism and a defeat for the policy of containment. Thus, the US government overlooked the fact that the Vietminh represented a popular national revolution and saw the situation as a triumph for the forces of world communism. Ho Chi Minh was perceived as another agent of the USSR, taking his orders from Moscow. If the Geneva Settlement worked against the interests of the free world then the USA would not accept it. In August 1954 the US National Security Council stated that the settlement, 'completed a major forward stride of Communism which might lead to the loss of Southeast Asia'. In order to buttress the forces of democracy in Indochina, the USA was drawn into supporting the regime established by Diem in South Vietnam. The USA rejected elections for reunification on the grounds that they were not under UN supervision; under the settlement they were to be organised by an international commission. This disagreement over a minor detail was used by the USA to justify its refusal to abide by the Geneva Settlement. US attempts to subvert the settlement began as soon as it was signed. The US Military Mission organised undercover sabotage of communist activities by their own agents. Instead of co-operating with reunification, the USA decided to support the anti-communist regime of South Vietnam. US aid for South Vietnam amounted to $250 million in 1956 and increased in the coming years. As in Korea, the USA supported regimes that were hardly beacons of democracy or freedom. The narrow mentality encouraged by a Cold War led to a loose definition of 'democracy' and 'free world' that was to become problematic for the USA.

Diem's regime in South Vietnam. The development of the regime in South Vietnam was wholly dependent on US support. Diem was only able to survive an attempt by various religious sects and gangster mobs to overthrow him in 1955 because he received US backing. Colonel Edward Lansdale, head of the US Military Mission in Saigon, was able to buy off some of Diem's opponents with bribes. Diem would have been unable to defeat the Vietminh in elections in 1956 had they been held, but with US support he was encouraged to reject any proposal for reunification. The threat of US intervention on Diem's behalf was used to subdue guerrilla activity. The US government was willing to ignore Diem's brutal and corrupt actions due to his anti-communist stance. Thus, Diem, with the support of the USA, perpetuated the partition of Vietnam. The position of the 17th Parallel as the border between North and South was not ideal for a weak government trying to stem the spread of communism in Vietnam. South of this line lay Hué, the imperial capital city, the port of Danang and the main highway linking Vietnam to Laos. These areas had long been centres of Vietminh support and activity.

The attitude of the USSR and China. Both of the communist superpowers put pressure on the Vietminh to accept the Geneva Settlement. This pressure was important given the reservations of Ho Chi Minh concerning the number of compromises the settlement entailed. The Soviet leader Khrushchev was keen not to disturb Détente with the USA and cared little for South East Asia. Communist China was not ready to be involved in another war so soon after that of Korea (1950–3). The Vietminh would have to wait for reunification. China, and the USSR, seemed content for the moment with the gains made by communism under the Geneva Settlement. It was certainly beneficial for the USSR to ensure the seeds were sown for later US involvement in a war in Vietnam that was to become such a drain on US resources.

SEATO. Similar to the 'United Action' proposed during the battle of Dien Bien Phu, the South East Asia Treaty Organisation came into being in September 1954. This alliance was a response to the shock of the French defeat and withdrawal from Vietnam. The fear of the spread of communism was now strong enough to ensure an alliance was signed. The USA saw SEATO as the equivalent of NATO in the Far East. Building on the ANZUS Pact of 1951, it was an attempt to ensure that if the USA was drawn into a direct involvement in Vietnam in the future it would be through a joint alliance. The lesson of the Korean War was that a coalition of countries was more effective in stemming the communist tide than unilateral action. SEATO also provided the justification for future action to defend South Vietnam.

Conclusion

Instead of concluding the war in Vietnam, the Geneva Agreements provided the seeds for future conflict. There was little that was inherently wrong with the agreements. In many ways it was a sensible arrangement that had called for, and gained, concessions from all of its participants. What undermined the settlement was the manner in which the situation in Vietnam was viewed within the wider context of Cold War conflict, where any concession given away could be seen as a victory for the other side. As the historian Marilyn Young has stated, 'Each of the major powers – China, the Soviet Union, the United States, and France – had its own agenda, and a united, sovereign Vietnam was not on anyone's list.' In this respect, the Geneva Agreements provided little more than a pause in the war. The battle for supremacy between the forces of capitalism and communism was soon to be resumed in Vietnam.

SECTION 9

By what means, and for what reasons, did the USA participate in the Vietnam War?

The question of how the USA came to be involved in the Vietnam War is complicated by the nature of the USA's commitment and its gradual escalation. There was no declaration of war. The USA became entangled in what was, in essence, a civil war over the future direction of Vietnamese independence, to the point where over 500,000 US soldiers were fighting on Vietnamese soil. The mechanisms by which this escalation took place have produced a debate among historians. Did the US government get involved fully conscious of the likely results of its own actions or did it slip into a situation from which it was impossible to extricate itself without doing serious damage to US foreign policy interests?

METHODS OF PARTICIPATION AND THE REASONS BEHIND THEM

Underlying all of the methods of US participation in the Vietnam War was a refusal to see another 'domino' fall to communism in Asia. The USA saw the communist takeover of China, the Korean War and the Geneva Agreements as signs of the successful advance of communism. This trend had to be prevented by firm action. Not only was democracy threatened, but the pride and status of the USA as leader of the free world was also at stake. It was when viewed from this perspective, determined by the mentality of the Cold War, that the survival of South Vietnam was essential.

Eisenhower and the use of military advisers. The US government considered the Geneva Settlement of 1954 to be against its interests in the context of Cold War conflict. It had confirmed the spread of communism to North Vietnam and threatened the South. The USA therefore needed to devise a method of ensuring the temporary division of Vietnam became permanent. This required giving assistance to the fledgling state of South Vietnam to guarantee that it was in a position to prevent the spread of communism from North Vietnam. MAAG, the Military Assistance Advisory Group, was used to provide US military advisers to South Vietnam.

Support for Diem's regime in South Vietnam. Despite its reservations about Diem, the USA saw little option but to encourage his regime to develop into a viable alternative to communism in Vietnam. Eisenhower's administration gave substantial amounts of aid to the South in a policy known as Nation Building. The aim was to ensure Diem promoted social reform and economic development to win popular support for the regime. Nation Building remained US policy until 1960, but had little impact. Diem preferred to use the financial aid to strengthen his personal power and the advice of US advisers was consistently ignored. The US government had failed to prevent Diem's regime acting in a manner that actually lost support. The outbreak of communist guerrilla activity in South Vietnam in 1957 was a tangible sign of this failure.

Kennedy and counter-insurgency. President Kennedy continued to see the conflict in Vietnam as vital to the standing of the USA within the wider context of the Cold War. Khrushchev had given a speech in 1961 that made clear Soviet intentions to support national liberation movements in the colonial world. This raised Kennedy's concerns that US prestige was declining and hardened his resolve to reverse this trend. South Vietnam's survival was a test of the USA's determination to combat communism. Kennedy knew the situation in South Vietnam was serious. The CIA issued reports outlining the deterioration in South Vietnam. Kennedy recognised that, as a communist victory could not be contemplated, US aid needed to be increased. Thus, the irony of the situation: as popular support for the government in South Vietnam declined, the more important it became as a beacon of democracy. Kennedy's response was to increase assistance for counter-insurgency operations. The Green Berets were sent to help South Vietnam train its army in guerrilla warfare; the CIA organised Civilian Irregular Defence Groups to act as a local militia and a policy of 'strategic hamlets' was developed to separate the population from the Vietcong. A Marine helicopter division was sent to support Search and Destroy missions. All US activity in Vietnam was coordinated by the Military Assistance Command, Vietnam (MACV). Kennedy considered sending US troops to Vietnam in October 1961 but his advisers informed him that victory could be secured without a further escalation of involvement. The US government's response to the situation was based on contrary and often misleading information, and this was to have a serious impact on the methods that were chosen to participate in the war.

Conflicting information and its impact on US policy. US decision-making was based on responses to information supplied by a range of advisers and the quality of this material was often variable and contradictory. After the battle of Ap Bac in 1963, in a pattern that was to be repeated, US military sources and South Vietnamese officials continued to present an optimistic picture of the South's prospects in the war: despite an 'adverse' situation, victory was always just around the corner. This was at odds with reports from the US media who painted a more pessimistic picture of the situation. Important questions were rarely asked, such as why the Vietcong were successful in gaining support; why the government of South Vietnam failed to attract much support from its own citizens and whether additional military support would be effective. The consequence of this conflicting information was that it reinforced the process of step-by-step escalation because it gave the impression that each increase in US support to the South would be enough to secure victory. Robert Komer, a member of Kennedy's National Security Council in 1961, saw the dangers of 'getting involved in another squalid, secondary theatre in Asia. But we'll end up doing so sooner or later anyway because we won't be willing to accept another defeat.'

Lyndon Johnson, US President 1963–9.

Lyndon Johnson and new options. Kennedy had avoided making the decision about whether to leave Vietnam or commit US ground troops to a conflict that many feared could not be won. Either decision could compromise US prestige to an extent that his successor Johnson found difficult to contemplate. Yet the increasing weakness of South Vietnam made an escalation of US entanglement in the war ever more likely. In the words of the historian Robert Schulzinger, 'doing more, doing less, or doing the same all entailed enormous risks'. This was especially so for Johnson as he tried to avoid attacks from Republicans in Congress who saw all Democratic presidents as 'soft' on communism. A window of opportunity to remove the USA from the conflict with some honour arose in 1963 when the new leader of South Vietnam, General Duong Van Minh, offered to establish a neutral government of reconciliation during which the National Liberation Front would be welcome to contest elections. The offer of neutrality might have been acceptable to North Vietnam and would have allowed US troops to withdraw. The President's advisers instructed Johnson to reject the proposal. This was in the first few months of Johnson's presidency and he took their advice. The neutrality idea has been seen by some commentators as a lost opportunity to disengage from the war unscathed, but it is unlikely that the proposal, had it been taken, would have succeeded due to the political tensions amongst the Vietnamese.

Developing a flexible response. Having rejected the option of neutrality, Johnson backed the proposal of Robert McNamara, the Defence

Secretary, of adopting a flexible response. This was a criticism of Eisenhower's policy of massive retaliation, which seemed to rely too heavily on the nuclear weapons. The use of such weapons was less appropriate in a limited war, such as the one in Vietnam. By building up a range of more limited responses, from supplying new military equipment to sending task forces of specially trained troops, the USA was likely to increase the number of options at its disposal. The problem that still existed in 1963 was how to give the President the freedom to use this range of methods without enraging domestic opinion in the USA, especially during an election year.

The Gulf of Tonkin Resolution and the move towards escalation. Justification for increasing the powers of the President came with North Vietnamese attacks on US naval vessels in August 1964. These incidents enabled Johnson to pass the Gulf of Tonkin Resolution through Congress. The resolution gave the President the powers to wage war in Vietnam as he saw fit and without recourse to Congress. The strength of support for this measure was such that only two senators voted against it. Although Johnson's public statements indicated that the resolution did not amount to a change in policy, Johnson now had the authority to send combat troops to Vietnam in the future. Later events showed that many senators had been unaware of the significance of the resolution. US involvement in the war was soon increased without a debate in Congress.

The use of bombing from the air. As the communists continued to achieve success in 1964, negotiation and withdrawal were both ruled out as policy options. This created a momentum that dragged the USA further into the war. A series of coups weakened South Vietnam's government to the point where an increase in US military action was viewed as necessary. Bombing North Vietnamese targets from the air was considered, but again Johnson was cautious. He was keen to limit attacks in fear of retaliatory action that might widen the scale of the conflict. Communist attacks on US military bases in early 1965, including Pleiku where nine Americans were killed, were used to justify US air strikes against the North, which developed into Operation Rolling Thunder. The attractiveness of air bombardment was its relatively low cost in both financial and human terms. The use of superior technology would, it was hoped, bring North Vietnam to the negotiating table from a position of weakness. Yet the air war, by its very nature, required the use of ground troops. Thus, the escalation continued to gather momentum.

The use of US ground troops. The war in the air made retaliatory action against US bases much more likely. Therefore Westmoreland's request in February 1965 for marines to protect US positions was an inevitable consequence of the decision to launch Rolling Thunder. Escalation of involvement was now determined by military considerations. Once the first battalions arrived in March the crucial step had been taken. Requests for further reinforcements of ground troops followed and were accepted. Johnson deliberately underplayed the significance of these actions to give the impression that US intervention remained limited and therefore avoid debate in Congress.

The use of allies. As in Korea, the USA hoped to organise joint action with a coalition of allies in Vietnam. This method of intervention would limit criticism as well as the strain of the war on the USA. SEATO proved to be of limited use: South Korea sent 60,000 troops and Australia 8,000 but the response of other members was disappointing. Without a substantial contribution from its allies, the USA could give additional assistance to South Vietnam only by providing it themselves. Even the South Vietnamese soon came to the conclusion that the war was best left to the Americans.

In the process of getting drawn into the conflict in Vietnam, the USA had shied away from a precise and accurate indication of the level of support that was needed to save South Vietnam. Fear of how the US public would react to an increase in the military commitment to the war produced a gradual escalation that was noticed only when it was more difficult to disentangle from the conflict without the USA suffering a humiliating defeat.

What was Johnson's role in the escalation of US involvement in the Vietnam War?

In the USA, the Vietnam War was associated with President Lyndon Johnson more than any other individual. So much so that the conflict is sometimes referred to as 'Johnson's War'. This terminology stems from the fact that it was under Johnson's presidency that the USA committed itself to a ground and air war in Vietnam and, in this sense, the term has some truth. Although there were 16,000 US advisers in Vietnam at the end of Kennedy's term in office, this was dwarfed by the 500,000 ground troops present in 1968. There is evidence to suggest that Kennedy was ready to withdraw US advisers from Vietnam just before his death. Any move in this direction was dropped when Johnson became President in November 1963. Yet US involvement in the war had not been initiated by Johnson, and the situation he inherited, of a disintegrating South Vietnamese regime, limited his choices of action. Nonetheless, it was under Johnson that US intervention escalated greatly. It is therefore not surprising that attention has focused on the motives that drove Johnson to oversee this policy development.

Ideology and values. Foreign affairs had not been of major interest to Johnson before he became President. He viewed communism and the threat it posed abroad in simplistic Cold War terms. Although these views were held sincerely they were, on Johnson's own admission, not the prime determinant of his policy towards Vietnam. More important were the values held by Johnson. He saw foreign policy as a matter of honour. The USA had given a pledge to help those under attack from communism and Johnson was not prepared to break this promise. The credibility of the USA was at stake. To Johnson, 'We are there because we have made a promise.' His attitudes were influenced by his Texan background. A code of honour that saw retreat, betrayal and cowardice as unthinkable, was an important part of the cultural values of the American South. This explains his obsession with the shame of appeasement and his determination to avoid making the same mistake in Vietnam. As Johnson stated, '... if I got out of Vietnam, then I'd be doing what Chamberlain did in World War II. I'd be giving a big fat reward to aggression.' To a Southerner like Johnson, Vietnam was just like the Alamo: a line had to be drawn in the sand and held against attack. To run away was to invite shame and humiliation.

The role of advisers. As Vice-President under Kennedy, Johnson had little knowledge of policy and decision-making. This was a weakness of the government system in the USA rather than a personal fault of Johnson. It was difficult for Johnson, suddenly catapulted into the position of President, to formulate his own foreign policy. He was reliant initially on the information provided by his advisers, most of whom had served Kennedy. These advisers were not in agreement on the way forward. George Ball, the Under-Secretary of State, was the only government adviser who consistently argued against involvement and favoured withdrawal. Robert McNamara, the Secretary of Defense, and General Westmoreland argued for massive military deployment to Vietnam. It was McGeorge Bundy, the National Security Advisor, who favoured a 'middle way' of limited step-by-step assistance to South Vietnam as and when it was needed. This unhappy compromise was responsible for the gradual escalation of involvement that was to evolve. Was US commitment to the war determined by this process of bureaucratic influence rather than by the President? Ball's memoirs make clear that Johnson could have overridden his advisers and was given a range of policy ideas but he underestimates the other pressures on Johnson that limited the options available.

Military considerations. Despite the disagreements of Johnson's advisers, they all agreed that the position of South Vietnam was perilous without substantial amounts of aid and support from the USA and they made sure Johnson was aware of this. The historian Maclear argues that 'it is questionable whether Kennedy could have resisted the military dynamics any more than Johnson'. If withdrawal was unthinkable, then the military circumstances in Vietnam dictated greater intervention in the war.

Political motives. Johnson admitted to his biographer, Doris Kearns, that political interests provided the motivation behind his decisions. Johnson was a highly experienced politician by 1963 and he was a man with a mission. Johnson's vision was of a Great Society that would bridge the gap between rich and poor and black and white within the USA. Yet in order to ensure he had an opportunity to achieve his goal, Johnson needed a large enough political base to keep him in power and support his reforms. Johnson's problem was that he had become President because of the assassination of Kennedy and had inherited the Eisenhower-Kennedy stance of the USA as the global policeman for the free world. Johnson admitted, 'If we get involved in that bitch of a war my Great Society will be dead.' According to Kearns, if he let Vietnam go 'they would all be saying he was a coward. Then the conservative uprising would be so great that he would lose the Great Society either way.' Thus, Johnson saw himself in a no-win situation. He had always advised caution over Vietnam before taking office. He had, as a Senator, led the campaign against sending US support to the French in Vietnam during the battle of Dien Bien Phu. When in office, Johnson hoped to avoid debate over the increasing commitment made by the USA. He hoped this would limit any backlash over the cost of the war while still delivering the victory that conservative middle America expected. The gradual escalation of the government's commitment to the war was, in a large part, driven by Johnson's desire to secure his political position.

Personal considerations. Johnson was a man in a hurry. He had suffered two heart attacks before becoming President and feared his life could be cut short before he could achieve his aims. This factor seems to have been responsible for Johnson's constant search for quick solutions. Escalating US commitment to the war provided one method of bringing it to a rapid conclusion in order to devote more attention to realising his vision of the Great Society.

The irony of Johnson's role in the Vietnam War was that his name was to become identified with a war he had not sought. Political self-preservation and military considerations combined to accelerate the process of escalation into a war that previous presidents had seen as more central to their crusade. Johnson's reputation as a social reformer was ruined by a war he pursued in an attempt, by a man who did not have time on his side, to save his Great Society.

HISTORICAL INTERPRETATIONS

A vast array of literature on the US involvement in Vietnam has been produced. The war provoked much debate during the 1960s while it was raging and has continued unabated ever since. The predominant viewpoint has changed through time, although a range of perspectives is still evident. Interpretations can be loosely grouped into various strands.

The Quagmire Thesis. This interpretation emphasises the misguided idealism that led the USA to commit itself to the war. A failure to understand the specific circumstances in Vietnam caused the USA to take a series of increasingly bigger steps towards direct military engagement in Vietnam without an awareness of their likely consequences. As each step failed the USA was drawn further into the conflict. This viewpoint was common among government officials who sought an explanation and justification for their role in government decision-making but it is also supported by some historians. This approach is found in *The Making of a Quagmire* (1964) by David Halberstam and *The Bitter Crusade* (1966) by Arthur Schlesinger Jr.

Challenges to the Quagmire Thesis. The revelations of the Pentagon Papers allowed the assumptions of the Quagmire Thesis to be challenged in the 1970s. In a climate of increasing scepticism towards politicians and their integrity, a more critical approach was adopted. The Pentagon Papers seemed to show that consecutive US administrations were aware of the situation in Vietnam and the fact that their policies were unlikely to succeed. In *The Irony of Vietnam* (1978), Leslie Gelb and Richard Betts argue that each president did the minimum possible to avoid defeat because they knew the war could not be won. Thus, successive administrations lied to the US public about the war and US policy towards it. The 1960s and early 1970s were dominated by writers who were critical of the manner in which the USA got involved in Vietnam. This is hardly surprising, given the context within which they were writing. The humiliation of defeat was evidence of US failure and its effects were to dent severely the belief that the USA had the military power to succeed. It also led to a questioning of the USA's moral right to impose its values on other countries of the world. The late 1960s was a period of social unrest within the USA. Urban riots, often sparked by poverty and racial tension, led a large number of Americans to reconsider the superiority of their own system.

Revisionist interpretations. After the war was lost the subsequent soul searching led to revisionist studies that attempted to defend the USA's involvement in Vietnam. Guenter Lewy's *America in Vietnam* (1978) was a serious attempt to defend the morality of US participation in the war. Among those writers who defended US intervention were military officers, such as William Westmoreland in *A Soldier Reports* (1976) and U. S. Grant Sharp in *Strategy for Defeat* (1978), both of whom blamed civilians in government for the gradual escalation imposed on the US armed forces. They argue that the US military position would have been improved greatly by a full-scale commitment at a much earlier stage. The right-wing backlash of the late 1970s and early 1980s helped bring Ronald Reagan to power in 1980 and led to more strident anti-communist policies. This created a climate in which a moral justification for US involvement in Vietnam was given a more sympathetic hearing.

Post-revisionist interpretations. Since the 1980s historians have tried to take a more detached view of events in Vietnam. Less hampered by the guilt and recrimination of the immediate post-war period, the post-revisionists have been critical of US involvement. Their focus has tended to move away from looking predominantly at the determinants of US policy to consider the wider context of the situation within which US policy was operating. They see US intervention as mistaken because of a failure to understand the circumstances in Vietnam and this failure resulted in the implementation of a series of different strategies, each one as ineffective as the other. Marilyn Young, in *The Vietnam Wars* (1991) and George Herring, in *America's Longest War* (1996) have highlighted the problem of US governments perceiving the war as an element of the Cold War rather than a Vietnamese affair.

It is difficult to over-exaggerate the impact of the Vietnam War on US society. It has cast a long shadow and, despite the fact that the Cold War has ended, it can still stir strong emotions. The war was the first defeat suffered by the USA on foreign soil and it had a detrimental psychological impact on US pride. The debate and the emotions it excites are, therefore, likely to continue.

SECTION 10

What was the response of the American people to the Vietnam War and to what extent did this influence its outcome?

Most wars generate domestic opposition of some sort. What is so significant about opposition within the USA to the Vietnam War is the level of its support. Far from being a small minority of opinion, opposition reached a point where US society was deeply divided. Some commentators have talked about a 'civil war' within the USA waged between those who supported the war and those who were opposed to it. Yet this gives the impression that public opinion was polarised into two opposing camps. In reality the situation was less clear cut. Few supporters of the war were unreserved in their support and those opposed to the war were motivated by a range of different reasons and often with a sense of regret. Herein lies the reason why the Vietnam War was such a psychologically disturbing affair for many Americans: it led to a questioning of American values and self-confidence that resulted in deep divisions which could not be explained away in simple terms of left versus right or patriotism versus defeatism.

WHO OPPOSED THE VIETNAM WAR IN THE USA AND FOR WHAT REASONS?

The 1950s had been a period of consensus in public opinion towards US foreign policy. In general the US public accepted the notion of the USA's moral right to stand up against the forces of world communism. There was an agreement with the thrust of the Truman Doctrine of 1947 that 'it must be the policy of the United States to support free peoples who are resisting subjugation by armed minorities or by outside pressures'. The determination of the US people to uphold this policy had been tested by the Korean War and, as the conflict dragged on, opposition did occur. The conclusion of the war in 1953 had prevented this opposition upsetting the general consensus. The Vietnam War, because it was longer and in many ways more involved, tested the consensus to breaking point. Opposition to the war has often been stereotyped as a collection of radical, long-haired students who not only attacked the war but also the foundations of the American way of life. Detailed examination of US society and its attitudes to the war shows a more complex reality.

Attitudes to the war

It was comforting for many supporters of the war to view its opponents as radical students because it provided easy explanations of the opposition: 'campus bums', ungrateful students and communists. Research shows a more complicated picture, especially when the different forms of opposition are considered. Not all opponents engaged in active protest, many remained silent in public but privately held deep reservations about the war. A breakdown of attitudes by social group reveals this complexity.

Students. Before labelling all US students as opponents of the war, it is important to consider the nature of higher education in the USA. There were over 2500 higher education institutions in the USA in the 1960s; most of these were small and served local communities. These institutions were conservative and their students provided a bedrock of solid support for US action in Vietnam. Less than half of higher education campuses saw anti-war protests in the 1960s. Opposition was centred on the elite institutions that recruited students nationally. The ties of traditional values and family influences were more easily broken down in these heterogeneous communities of students. It was here that anti-war attitudes were often in the majority. Faculties in social sciences and the humanities provided the most vocal opposition. This pattern was reflected in the attitudes of college lecturers.

The young. Students in elite universities may have gained notoriety for opposing the war but their attitudes were not a reflection of the entire body of students or of the younger generation as a whole. According to polls conducted by Gallup, support for the war declined according to the age of the respondents. In 1965, 76 per cent of those under 30 supported the war compared with only 51 per cent of those aged over 49. As time went on, support from all age groups declined, but the gap between groups was maintained. Thus, although there were vocal opponents of the war among the young, the anti-war movement was not a youth rebellion. Many young Americans seemed to have an unquestioning acceptance of established values. The older generation, more sceptical and sometimes more cynical was, as a whole, less convinced of the morality of intervention in Vietnam but often chose not to be vocal in their criticism of the war.

Women. In all categories, such as among the young, the old and black Americans, women were much less likely to support the war than men. Their role in the anti-war movement was significant. The Women's International League for Peace and Freedom was one of the first groups to protest. Some commentators see women's traditional role as carers as the reason for their opposition to the war but this explanation is inadequate. Feminists such as Betty Friedan opposed the war as another example of conservative attempts to oppress the rights of others. The war seemed to confirm the stupidity of a policy based on traditional, outdated masculine values of strength and heroism. Some women did, however, support the war. Those women who opposed the civil rights legislation in the USA tended also to support US policy in Vietnam. The anti-war movement, like that for civil rights, was viewed as an attack on traditional American values.

Black Americans. Despite over 80 per cent of black Americans voting for Johnson in 1964, they tended to be highly critical of the war. Black women were one of the groups most against US policy in Vietnam: in 1970 only 19 per cent supported it compared with 30 per cent of white women. The reasons for opposition from Black Americans were due partly to the fact that they were more likely to live in large urban centres where traditional values were less fixed. A disproportionate number of blacks lived in or near poverty and a large section of the black community had already come to the conclusion that the US system had failed them before the Vietnam War highlighted issues of prejudice. The system of conscription, with its complex exemptions that favoured the white middle class, became an important issue at a time when there was growing awareness of civil rights in the USA. Stories of racial violence against blacks in the US army did little to ease the tensions generated by the war. When Muhammad Ali, the heavyweight boxer, refused to fight in Vietnam, he highlighted the thoughts of a large section of the black community: 'I ain't got no quarrel with those Vietcong anyway; they never call me nigger.'

The industrial workers. Many of the most violent attacks on anti-war protesters were undertaken by industrial workers. The hard hat, as worn by construction workers, became a symbol of patriotism. George Meany, the trade union leader, articulated this stridently pro-war attitude. Yet industrial workers were more evenly divided in their opinions of the war than this would suggest. Discontent among the industrial workers rose as the war progressed. The impact on inflation and rising taxes to pay for the war were the chief causes of concern. At first this discontent was subdued but by the early 1970s it had become more vocal. Although still in a minority, anti-war feeling in the labour movement was strong enough to launch an open attack on the position adopted by Meany. Poll results show that the attitudes of the industrial workers differed little from those of the middle class. Economic interests were an important determinant of viewpoints towards the war.

Religious organisations. Jewish Americans were much more likely to oppose the war than Protestants or Catholics. In 1964, 50 per cent of Jews polled favoured either withdrawal or a negotiated end to the war. This figure rose to 63 per cent in 1966. Leading members of the Jewish community and rabbis took the lead in condemning the war. This seems to have been due, in part, to the concentration of Jews in large, cosmopolitan, urban centres. These cities were less influenced by conservative values and traditional notions of patriotism. Protestants were more divided than the Jewish community. Fundamentalists tended to support the war and their publications such as *Christian Crusade* preached a strong anti-communist message, which was used to support US intervention in Vietnam. The moderate Protestant churches that had a tradition of promoting reform on issues of social concern, were more inclined to be critical of the war. Yet the majority of rank-and-file Protestants supported the war until early 1968. Catholics were strong supporters of the war because it was in defence of the Catholic community in South Vietnam. The Catholic Church was also influenced by its traditional attitude against communism. Organised Christian religion was cautious when criticising US policy in Vietnam. Anti-war organisations involving clergy tended to be non-denominational, for example Clergy and Laymen Concerned About Vietnam, which included Martin Luther King.

Intellectuals. The Vietnam War led to a revitalisation of the intellectual left. They condemned the immorality of a brutal US policy that was seen as US Imperialism at its worse. The intellectual left attracted a new generation of academics such as William A. Williams and Noam Chomsky. Right-wing intellectuals found themselves outnumbered, but they also found much to criticise in government policy towards the war: they demanded more commitment to Vietnam not less.

Reasons for opposition to the Vietnam War

Sections of the US public opposed the war for a range of reasons that varied according to social and political background and from one individual to another.

Pacifism. The view that war was immoral as a method of resolving differences was, to pacifists such as the Quakers, a central part of their system of beliefs. The 1960s saw a growth in the number of people who considered themselves to be pacifists. The potential of nuclear holocaust, brought about by an escalation of conflict, was demonstrated by the Cuban Missile Crisis of 1962. Groups, such as the Fellowship of Reconciliation, the Women's International League for Peace and SANE, renounced war as an instrument of policy and were early critics of US involvement in Vietnam.

The War in Vietnam was illegal. Critics considered US involvement in Vietnam to be in violation of the Geneva Agreements of 1954. It was therefore illegal. They also pointed out that, unlike the involvement in Korea, the UN had not sanctioned direct intervention in Vietnam. Nor was US policy in the war sanctioned officially by SEATO. Action by the organisation required the unanimous support of its members and this had not been given. These legal arguments were used during debates by intellectuals but were not the main evidence on which the bulk of the population made up their mind on the issue of Vietnam.

The nature of South Vietnam. As an example of freedom and democracy, the regime in South Vietnam did not bear too close an examination. Opponents of the war were quick to highlight the brutality and corruption of the government that the USA was supporting. South Vietnam was the product of the failure to hold elections to reunite the country after the Geneva Settlement of 1954. The state was considered to be an artificial creation, which would not exist but for US aid and assistance. Even supporters of the war were unhappy with the nature of the regime, especially when it was in the hands of Diem.

The nature of the conflict. War is a nasty business but the general population is often immune to the realities of fighting. The Vietnam War was different in this respect because of the extensive television coverage it received in the USA. Not all of the reporting was negative, but the images of the war brought home in graphic detail the reality of the war on the ground. In 1967 a poll for Newsweek revealed that 64 per cent thought the television coverage made them more likely to support the war, but this support was to fall away over the next three years. The images revealed the fearful damage that modern weapons inflicted on a peasant, agricultural-based society. Concerns were raised at the use of aerial bombing, chemical warfare and napalm. When viewing images of the war, all three methods were highlighted as weapons of indiscriminate damage and loss of life. Film and photography graphically captured the effects of napalm: the burning of human flesh, the asphyxiation and poisoning and disfigurement. These images had a strong impact on US society and many opposed the war because of their revulsion at the methods used. Even supporters of the war raised concerns over the nature in which the fighting was conducted.

The impact on the USA. As the war dragged on there was a growing anxiety that it was having a demoralising impact on large sections of US society. Commentators focused on the true meaning of demoralisation: the absence of moral constraints. Critics argued that the constant access to violence would undermine the moral fabric of society. Phrases such as 'body count' and 'free fire zone' helped disguise the horrors of war. This was especially so of the impact on young US soldiers. A sign of this deterioration in morals was the use of racist terms to describe the Vietnamese opposition. Words such as 'gook' and 'dinks' turned the enemy into anonymous stereotypes. As David Levy has stated, it was 'America's chief way of dealing with the Third World in the twentieth century just as in the nineteenth it had been the standard way to deal with American Indians'. The increase in soldiers killing their officers by 'fragging', desertion and the use of drugs was further evidence of demoralisation. So much marijuana was smoked by US soldiers on duty in Vietnam that the historian Loren Baritz wrote, 'it is a wonder that a southerly wind did not levitate Hanoi's politburo'. The seriousness of the drugs problem was highlighted by the large number of returning soldiers who had to be admitted to rehabilitation centres. Demoralisation also spread to the conduct of the USA's politicians. That the government lied to its own people was, according to critics, symptomatic of the decline in US values produced by the war.

These general reasons for opposing the war did not affect all US citizens in the same way. To those who saw the war as vital to defend US interests, they were aspects of the conflict which may have been regretted or caused concern, but they did not necessarily sway opinion from the conviction that the war was justified. For others, these reasons led them to the conclusion that the war was wrong or misguided, yet there was little unity in the anti-war movement. Pacifists wanted a withdrawal from Vietnam but liberals and more moderate opponents favoured a negotiated end to the conflict. Extreme radicals used the war as an instrument to attack the entire US establishment and the values it stood for. Thus, any generalisation is in danger of ignoring the complexity of the war's impact on US society.

Conclusion

Attitudes to the Vietnam War showed a deep division across all sections of society and it was this that made the war's impact so damaging. Both sides had their own role models: in support of the war were the actors John Wayne and Charlton Heston and the singer, Frank Sinatra; for those against there were the actors Gene Hackman, Bette Davis, Jane Fonda and Lauren Bacall, and the folk-singer Joan Baez. The entertainment business, including Hollywood, was as divided as the rest of US society. The war combined with the growing social and racial tension of the 1960s in the USA to raise doubts in many American minds about what their country stood for. The USA was not at peace with itself. Discontent took many forms: some kept their views to themselves, others engaged in protests, which included 'teach-ins', marches and demonstrations. The Vietnam Moratorium Committee took a key role in organising large-scale peaceful demonstrations; the Draft Resistance Movement took more direct action over the issue of conscription. The treatment of the Vietnam veterans when they returned home contrasted with that of soldiers from previous wars. They did not receive a hero's welcome but were abused and spat upon. In the academic year 1969–70, Richard Nixon counted '1,800 demonstrations, 7,500 arrests, 462 injuries and 247 arsons and 8 deaths'. The war had raised passions to the point where any protest could provoke violence.

WHAT INFLUENCE DID THE ANTI-WAR MOVEMENT HAVE ON THE OUTCOME OF THE VIETNAM WAR?

The connection between the strength of the anti-war movement and the failure of the USA to pursue the Vietnam War to victory is difficult to measure. Presidents and Senators in Congress needed to take into account the views of their voters at some stage but the attitudes of the US public to the war remained mixed. The consensus in favour of US foreign policy had broken down, not to be replaced by a new consensus against the war but by division.

Events such as the protests over the invasion of Cambodia and the killings at Kent State University in 1970 did put pressure on Congress to limit the powers of the president to commit more troops to Vietnam without their consent. Did the anti-war movement therefore encourage the failure of political will to pursue the war to victory by making a full commitment? This viewpoint has been put forward by commentators on the right, including some Republicans, but it can be criticised. The sequence of US involvement in Vietnam, from Kennedy's presidency onwards, indicates a failure of political nerve even before anti-war sentiment was widespread. The anti-war movement did not cause a failure of political nerve but added to the pressure that caused hesitancy in government decision-making.

There were limitations on the influence of the anti-war movement. It was badly affected by internal divisions, such as that between radicals and liberals, and it was never united in its aims or objectives. Nixon's policy of Vietnamisation, which led to the withdrawal of US troops by placing more of the burden of the war on South Vietnam, led to a decline in support for the movement. If not immune to anti-war pressure, politicians proved capable of riding the storm of protests.

What the movement did achieve was to raise the profile of the central dilemma facing the USA: how far it should intervene in the affairs of another state to protect its own interests. It was a dilemma that many Americans, from the president to the man in the street, wrestled with. It was Nixon who, as President, made the decision to withdraw US troops from Vietnam. Although made in the context of growing discontent with the war, his decision was based primarily on military considerations. The war could not be won, and by 1970 this conclusion had been reached by many of those who had supported the war.

A US soldier writes home from Vietnam, September 1967

Here in Vietnam the war goes on. Morale is very high in spite of the fact that most of the men think the war is being run incorrectly. One of the staggering facts is that most men here believe we will not win the war. And yet they stick their necks out every day and carry on.

The Marines are taking a fierce beating over here. They don't have enough men. We must have more men, at least twice as many, or we are going to get the piss kicked out of us this winter.

One of the basic problems is that Johnson is trying to fight this war the way he fights his domestic wars – he chooses an almost unattainable goal with a scope so large it is virtually undefinable, and he attacks this goal with poorly allocated funds, minimum manpower, limited time, and few new ideas.

We should have never committed ourselves to this goal, but now that we have, what should we do?

From *Dear America: Letters Home from Vietnam* (1985), edited by B. Edelman

WHY DID THE UNITED STATES FAIL TO WIN THE VIETNAM WAR?

Historical interpretations

Historians have argued over the reasons for US failure in Vietnam, with the key debate being whether it was due to political or military failure. This debate has been linked in part to attempts to apportion blame for the humiliation suffered by the USA in this conflict.

The failure of political will. Many of the military leaders who fought in Vietnam have placed the blame for defeat in the hands of politicians. General William Westmoreland saw the defeat as an inevitable consequence of the policy of gradual escalation imposed on the US military by a civilian government. Westmoreland believed that an all-out attempt to win the war would have succeeded but the government did not have the political nerve to do so. This view is echoed by that of Richard Nixon who, in his *Memoirs* (1978) stated, 'The Johnson administration pursued a policy of only the most gradual escalation of the air and ground war. What this policy actually accomplished was to convince the Communists that the United States lacked the will to win in Vietnam and could be worn down.' The bureaucratic process that led to the adoption of the 'middle way' had helped produce this gradual escalation which resulted in little discussion of the long-term consequences. Dave Richard Palmer, in *Summons of the Trumpet* (1978), highlighted the demoralising effect of government policy, combined with bias in the media and the anti-war movement at home, on the ability of the military to conduct the war. The role of the media has received special attention. Johnson had criticised the media for undermining the war effort. In August 1965, when CBS news showed a marine setting fire to a peasant's hut with a cigarette lighter, he accused the television company of having 'shat on the American flag'. The results of public opinion polls show that the influence of television was mixed and sometimes hardened attitudes in favour of the war effort. It was only after 1969 that the constant reporting of deaths and casualties seems to have helped produce a war-weariness that led to a decline in support. According to this viewpoint the military were 'stabbed in the back' by a coalition of civilian pressures. The Hollywood film *Rambo* (1985) was one presentation of the war that supported this view. The Rambo character, played by Sylvester Stallone, uses his superhuman masculine powers to counter the weakness of the liberal establishment. The film was very much in tune with the right-wing backlash of the 1980s. This 'stab in the back' thesis has been criticised for ignoring the substantial degree of freedom Westmoreland was given to pursue counter-insurgency measures. It also fails to acknowledge that previous wars had involved considerable civilian supervision and that this is an important element in a democratic state.

Military failure. Writers such as Andrew Krepinevich in *The Army and Vietnam* (1986) and William Colby in *Lost Victory* (1989) blame military rather than political failure. Colonel Harry G. Summers has drawn

One version of the USA in Vietnam. A still from the 1985 film 'Rambo', starring Sylvester Stallone.

attention to failures in military strategy in *On Strategy: A Critical Analysis of the Vietnam War* (1982). Westmoreland has been criticised for relying on conventional methods of warfare and not understanding the nature of guerrilla war. The French defeat at Dien Bien Phu in 1954 had shown that a conventional war could not win Vietnam but the US military failed to appreciate its significance. US attempts at counter-insurgency tactics failed, such as the Search and Destroy missions and the policy of 'strategic hamlets'. Air bombing campaigns, such as Rolling Thunder, were inappropriate against a rural-based economy such as that of North Vietnam. The crucial issue with guerrilla warfare is that its success depends on gaining the support of the local population. US strategy never seemed to take account of this, relying instead on its superiority in military technology. In this sense the Vietnam War has been described as a tragedy for the USA in that its military policy contained the seeds of its own failure. The war could not be won: it was merely prolonged because the US government refused to give it up.

A failure to understand the Vietnamese context. This factor has received attention from post-revisionist historians who see the misjudgement of the USA as the prime cause of defeat. This view has been presented by Marilyn Young in *The Vietnam Wars* (1991) and *The Longest War* (1996) by George Herring. The US government failed to see the National Liberation Front as anything other than a communist organisation. The powerful hold of nationalism over the Vietnamese was at best downplayed and often ignored, as was the attraction of communism to a people who had been exploited economically and lived in impoverished social conditions. In a mentality dominated by Cold War attitudes, the Americans preferred to ignore local factors that moulded the conflict in Vietnam. This attitude led them to view the regime in South Vietnam as an example of freedom and democracy, an image that contrasted sharply with reality. The USA did little to win over the hearts and minds of the Vietnamese. Cabot Lodge, the US ambassador in Saigon, told Richard Nixon in 1964, 'there's a bigger problem that can't be settled by fighting … The Vietcong draw their strength from hungry peasants, and if we want to wean them from communism we shouldn't shoot at them – we should distribute food to them.' This advice was ignored by successive US administrations and when attempts to develop the economy of South Vietnam were made they invariably backfired (see cartoon opposite). The US belief that money could solve problems was ineffective. Large sums of US money were diverted through corrupt practices and caused severe disruption to the South Vietnamese economy, which geared itself towards providing black-market goods, gambling bars and brothels for US soldiers. The culture of Vietnam emphasised past traditions and the community – the Vietnamese language does not have a word for the personal pronoun 'I'. This differed markedly from the modern,

A US cartoon from 1969 critical of imposing US values on the Vietnamese.

individualistic values of twentieth-century America. One could not be imposed upon the other.

Conclusion

The Vietnam War was a military stalemate that could not be won without radical changes in US military tactics. As long as the US government had the political will to stay in Vietnam, they could not be driven out of the country. Yet the USA could not defeat the Vietcong and North Vietnamese by arms. The communists, by combining nationalism, anti-imperialism and social and economic reform, had gained widespread support. Only a political settlement that addressed the needs of the Vietnamese people offered the USA a chance of resolving the conflict. The USA failed to ensure that there was a government in South Vietnam that could command the support of the majority of its own people. The USA never grasped the essentials of the war in Vietnam. They ignored the factors that had created what was primarily a civil war and instead turned Vietnam into merely another stage of the Cold War.

A2 ASSESSMENT

A consideration of different historical interpretations of topics is an important skill for the student of history to develop. At A2 Level this requires you to know the wider context of influences on historical writing which often fall outside the period you are directly studying. For example, interpretations of the Vietnam War have been influenced by political developments since the end of the war. The availability of new material and development of different perceptions due to more recent events has resulted in changes in historical interpretations. The historiography of the Cold War continues to develop and, despite its challenges, evaluating historical interpretations adds another level of understanding to studying topics. Awareness that historians differ in their views and that the way they approach the past is changing all the time makes history especially exciting.

EVALUATING HISTORICAL INTERPRETATIONS

As a student of history you will be expected to consider different historical interpretations, to compare and contrast their arguments, and to assess their value. It is useful to think of the following aspects when you read extracts from the works of historians and other commentators:

- What is the main **thrust** of the source? (ie. what is it saying?)
- What **evidence** is being used by the author to develop his or her argument? (e.g. does the author rely on letters, conversations or personal accounts?) How is the evidence being used?
- What **angle** does the author take? (i.e. does the author focus on one particular angle and neglect others?) It is worth remembering that two historians from the same school of history may look at the same issue from different angles.
- What is the **background** of the author? (i.e. have the nationality, date and other background factors affected the way in which the author sees the issue?)
- What is the **perspective** of the author? (i.e. which approach does the writer seem to be taking? How have the underlying principles of this perspective affected the way in which he or she has approached the topic?)

Explaining **how** historical interpretations agree or differ should be seen as a building block for moving on to consider **why**. This is what will usually be expected in high-quality answers.

Most of the questions you will be asked to consider will revolve around these aspects. Answers should always make close reference to the extracts you are asked to consider and this is best achieved by direct quotation of short phrases to support the points you wish to make. Comments such as 'see lines 8–12' are too vague and unlikely to be rewarded.

EXAMPLES: QUESTIONS IN THE STYLE OF OCR

Stalin and the Cold War

Source A: Stalin's opinion of the Polish question in 1945

For the Russian people, the question of Poland is not only a question of honour but also a question of security. Throughout history, Poland has been the corridor through which the enemy has passed into Russia. Twice in the last thirty years our enemies, the Germans, have passed through this corridor.

Source B: From George Kennan's *Long Telegram* of 22 February 1946

At the bottom of the Kremlin's neurotic view of world affairs is traditional and instinctive Russian sense of insecurity... For this reason they have always feared foreign penetration, feared direct contact between the Western world and their own ... And they have learned to seek security only in patient but deadly struggle for total destruction of rival powers, never in compacts and compromises with it ... this is only the steady advance of uneasy Russian nationalism, a centuries-old movement in which conceptions of offence and defence are inextricably confused. But in new guise of international Marxism, with its honeyed promises to a desperate and wartorn outside world, it is more dangerous and insidious than ever before.

Source C: A historian considers interpretations of American foreign policy

The initial steps in the strategy of containment – stopgap military and economic aid to Greece and Turkey, the more carefully designed and ambitious Marshall Plan – took place.

. . . Some historians have asserted that the Europeans themselves were never as psychologically demoralised as the Americans made them out to be. Others have added that the real crisis at this time was within an American economy that could hardly expect to function if Europeans lacked the dollars to purchase its products.

. . . All of these arguments have merit: at a minimum they have forced historians to place the Marshall Plan in a wider economic, social, and historical context; more broadly they suggest that the American empire had its own distinctive internal roots, and was not solely and simply a response to the Soviet external challenge.

(From J. L. Gaddis, *We Now Know: Rethinking Cold War History*, published in 1997)

Source D: Truman's speech to the US Congress, 12 March 1947

I believe that it must be the policy of the United States to support free peoples who are resisting attempted subjugation by armed minorities or by outside pressures. If Greece should fall, confusion and disorder might well spread throughout the Middle East. The free peoples of the world look to us for support in maintaining those freedoms. If we falter in our leadership, we may endanger the peace of the world.

1 a) Account for the similarities and differences between Sources A and B in their portrayal of the reasons for the Soviet Union's expansion into eastern Europe after the Second World War.

b) What do Sources B, C and D tell us about US attitudes towards Soviet actions in Europe between 1945 and 1950?

2 Consider the arguments for and against the claim that Stalin's foreign policy towards Europe was defensive.

3 To what extent can Truman's foreign policy be considered a major cause of the development of the Cold War between 1945 and 1950?

Examiner's comments

Question 1(a). This type of question is designed to test your ability to compare historical sources, both in terms of their content and their relative value. Answers will be expected to show close reference to the sources and a consideration of the overall perspective of the author. You will be expected to use clues in the extracts given to come to a reasoned conclusion about the perspective adopted.

Answers that fail to refer to the sources are unlikely to gain marks. Sound answers (Grades E and D) will contain a developed response with reference to both sources but will probably focus on the content of the sources rather than the overall perspective of the authors. Better answers (Grade C) will include reference to both areas of agreement and disagreement. Good answers (Grades B and A) will present a developed explanation with commentary on the perspective of the authors to assess the extent of agreement and the reasons for this.

The author of Source A emphasises the issue of security as a reason for extending control into eastern Europe. Stalin (Source A) is also willing to acknowledge historical factors, 'a question of honour' being a reference to Poland's past as part of the Russian Empire. This finds some agreement with the author of Source B, 'sense of insecurity'. But Kennan (Source B) sees Soviet expansion as part of 'a deadly struggle for total destruction of rival powers' and emphasises elements of 'offence and defence' in Soviet foreign policy, made more dangerous by Marxism. These differences can be explained by the background of the authors: Stalin as a communist, a nationalist or even as a neurotic leader. Kennan had personal experience of the Soviet system as a member of the US Embassy staff in Moscow but his perspective is conditioned by his American values.

Question 1(b). This question is attempting to test your skills in using and evaluating sources. Close reference to the sources is required to support relevant comments. Good answers will make use of your own knowledge to evaluate the sources within their wider context and present a developed explanation. Ensure you include a conclusion that makes your overall argument clear.

Source B emphasises the view that the nature of the Soviet system makes compromise and negotiation with the USSR pointless. Kennan's view, as expressed in this source, became the basis of the US policy of containment and the source therefore has value. This could be developed further by commenting on the misconceptions the US government had of the USSR and its foreign policy aims. Source C highlights the economic factors driving the USA towards a commitment to Europe. Soviet actions threatened US economic interests. The author Gaddis draws attention to the 'internal roots' that promoted US involvement in European affairs. As Gaddis implies, the economic argument is not wholly convincing and the reasons for this could be discussed by reference to your own knowledge. Source D gives Truman's view that Soviet actions in Greece were attempts to undermine the freedoms of capitalism and democracy. Truman was trying to justify his policy to the US Congress (and the rest of the world). This point could be developed by discussing the ideological divisions between East and West and whether it can be argued that these were the prime factor in explaining US attitudes.

Question 2. This is an essay question testing your ability to present an argument in response to the specific demands of the question. Factual information about the topic will be required to provide an evaluation of different interpretations and develop a convincing and reasoned argument. Factual knowledge that is not related directly to the focus of the question is unlikely to score a high mark. To pass at this level (Grade E) will require some relevant comment based on accurate material. Grades D and C will be gained if there is some sense of argument using a range of accurate and precise detail.

Arguments for Stalin's foreign policy being defensive include the demand for security and this would need reference to the Soviet experience in the Second World War. The attempts of revisionist and Soviet historians to defend Stalin's actions as creating a buffer zone in eastern Europe should be discussed.

Arguments against include those of the Liberal School of historians who see Stalin as wishing to spread world communism. High-level answers (Grades B and A) will be direct and well focused, with an overall argument effectively communicated by reference to thorough detail. In addition, they might consider the difficulties that contemporaries had in judging Stalin's motives in an atmosphere of mutual mistrust.

Question 3. This question is designed to test your ability to assess different interpretations and present an argument by reference to evidence. Knowledge and discussion of the most important interpretations, for example, the Liberal, Revisionist and Post-Revisionist Schools of thought, will be expected. At Grades E and D this information is likely to be sound but presented in a largely descriptive manner with limited comment. For a Grade C, sustained relevant comment will be expected.

High-quality answers (Grades B and A) will focus on the key words 'to what extent' and 'major cause' when assessing Truman's foreign policy. There is, as always, a range of possible arguments but whatever line you take, it must be supported by precise evidence.

EXAMPLES: QUESTIONS IN THE STYLE OF EDEXCEL

From Cold War to Détente

Source A: A historian outlines criticisms of Détente

A popular view in the United States is that détente was little more than an American illusion and a Soviet trick. One of the main proponents of this interpretation is Richard Pipes, who claims that détente reflected no more than a beguiling change in Moscow's tactics. Policies of confrontation which had been favoured by Khrushchev were abandoned by his successors in favour of a more subtle low-risk strategy aimed at making gains in the Third World ... By lulling the West into a false sense of security it hoped to gain access to the Western technology which was vital in its quest for strategic superiority.

(From M. Bowker and P. Williams, *Superpower Détente: a Reappraisal*, published in 1988)

Source B: An interpretation of Détente

The rise of détente can be understood as a process of adaptation in the international system and on the part of its leading members. The cold war system based upon a stark bipolarity ... began to give way to a more complex order, with other power centres developing to challenge the superpowers, at least on some issues. Furthermore, the development and deployment of large numbers of nuclear weapons by both sides made it imperative that the superpowers managed their competition in a way which prevented them from degenerating into hostilities. Détente represented a new stage in the process of adapting to these changes in the distribution of power and instruments of influence.

(From M. Bowker and P. Williams, *Superpower Détente: a Reappraisal*, published in 1988)

Source C: Brezhnev gives his view of Détente

Referring to the necessity of spreading détente to the whole world, Brezhnev expresses deep faith that the policy of peaceful coexistence will take deep root and go from success to success. 'It is still too early to say, of course,' he said, 'that a lasting foundation for peace has already been laid in Europe, let alone the world. But what has already been done and what is being done to this end are opening hopeful prospects'.

(From the official Soviet biography of Brezhnev, published in 1978)

Source D: Richard Nixon describes his meeting with Brezhnev in 1972

Brezhnev's tone was cordial, but his words were blunt. He said that at the outset he had to tell me that it had not been easy for him to carry off this summit after our recent actions in Vietnam. After he had made this almost obligatory statement, he warmed perceptibly as he began to talk about the necessity and advantages of developing a personal relationship between us.

I said that I had studied the history of the relationship between Stalin and Roosevelt. I had found that during the war differences between subordinates were usually overcome by agreement at the top level. 'That is the kind of relationship that I should like to develop with the General Secretary,' I said. 'If we leave all the decisions to the bureaucrats, we will never make any progress.'

'They would simply bury us in paper!' He laughed heartily and slapped his palm on the table. It seemed to be a good beginning.

(From R. Nixon, *Memoirs*, published in 1978)

a) Using the evidence in Sources A and B and your own knowledge, consider the reasons for the development of Détente in the early 1970s.

b) 'Despite the claims of those who promoted Détente, its achievements were superficial.'

Using the evidence of Sources A, B, C, and D and your own knowledge, explain how far you agree with this opinion.

Examiner's comments

Question (a). This question is designed to test your ability to reach a reasoned judgement on an historical issue based on an evaluation of historical perspectives through the use of sources and own knowledge.

Sources A and B give two different opinions on the reasons why Détente developed. These interpretations reflect two of the different perspectives taken by historians. The reasons for the differences in interpretation need to be examined; for example, Pipes has a right-wing perspective, Bowker and Williams in Source B give a post-revisionist interpretation. They represent part of the wider debate on Détente and your own knowledge should be used to show your awareness of this. Failure to refer to both the sources and your own knowledge will limit your marks (note the instruction in the question). Your answer needs to develop your own argument on the relative importance of the reasons for Détente within this framework. Where this argument is conveyed with precise reference to sources and your own knowledge with an understanding of relevant concepts shown, the answer is likely to be of a Grade B or A standard.

Question (b). This question requires an extended answer which can show your ability to explain and evaluate differing interpretations of a historical issue. Careful reference to the sources is required, in addition to your own knowledge. High-quality answers (Grades B and A) will show an awareness of the wider debate which the sources illustrate and how the different historical interpretations relate to the concerns, attitudes and values of the authors involved at the time of writing. There will also be evidence of the ability to assess the relative value of different perspectives to make a reasoned, independent judgement about the inter-relationship between historians and the issues they are studying.

The sources can be used to illustrate a range of different viewpoints but should also be seen as relating to different historical approaches within the wider debate on the achievements of Détente. Sources A and B can be used to develop the historical debate between the right, the left and the post-revisionists. Source C gives an optimistic view of Détente but it is from Brezhnev, one of the key architects of the policy. Source D also gives the view of one of the main players in Détente. Nixon's evidence highlights the importance of personal links between the superpower leaders but his optimism in 1972 was not always shared by other members of the US government, or by later presidents.

EXAMPLES: QUESTIONS IN THE STYLE OF AQA

The USA and Vietnam

Source A: Richard Nixon gives an assessment of Johnson's Vietnam policy

Johnson had not levelled with the American people and told them why we were fighting in Vietnam or how deeply American troops were actually involved … The price of Johnson's dissembling was high, and I was to inherit that debt: the 'credibility gap.' The government lost the confidence of the people, which I believe it could have kept had Johnson taken the risk and fully explained the war and patiently educated the people about it.

(From R. Nixon, *Memoirs*, published in 1978)

Source B

US involvement in Vietnam was not primarily a result of errors of judgement or the personality quirks of the policymakers, although these things existed in abundance. It was a logical, if not inevitable, outgrowth of a world view and a policy – the policy of containment – that Americans in and out of government accepted without serious question for more than two decades. The commitment in Vietnam expanded as the containment policy itself grew. In time, it outlived the conditions that had given rise to that policy.

(From G. Herring, *America's Longest War*, published in 1996)

Source C

There was a terrible irony in the continuing success of the NLF. Demonstrations of popular political support, which should have persuaded the United States to give up its support for an incompetent, dictatorial, minority anti-Communist government in the South, instead intensified Washington's conviction that it must do more to prop it up…the South was seen in Washington as increased instability and 'deterioration' to be halted by the application of yet new increments of force.

(From M. Young, *The Vietnam Wars 1945–90*, published in 1991)

a) Study Source B and use your own knowledge.

How valid is the interpretation offered by G. Herring of the reasons for US involvement in Vietnam?

b) Study Source A and use your own knowledge.

How reliable is Source A as evidence for the view that Johnson's Vietnam policy was a failure?

c) Study Sources A, B and C and use your own knowledge.

'Both the reasons for, and methods of, participation in the Vietnam War were misguided.'

Assess the validity of this statement.

Examiner's comments

Question (a). This type of question is designed to test your ability to evaluate an historical interpretation by reference to the source and your own knowledge. Answers will be expected to show close reference to the source and a consideration of the overall perspective of the author.

The source can be used to show Herring's view that US involvement grew out of Cold War attitudes that led to the policy of containment. You could challenge Herring's interpretation by highlighting evidence that shows the importance of the other factors Herring sees as less important, for example, 'errors of judgement', and 'personality quirks'. This would allow you to discuss the attitudes of Eisenhower, Kennedy and especially Johnson towards the war. The pressures of public opinion within the USA could also be discussed. Herring's view that the conditions that led to containment were no longer applicable could be challenged. Did Détente really mean an end to communist expansion and its threat to US interests or was it a smokescreen for Soviet penetration into the Third World? As a post-revisionist Herring tends to avoid blaming individuals, such as Johnson, for US involvement in Vietnam. Do you agree with this perspective?

Question (b). This question is attempting to test your skills in assessing the reliability of a specific source to the study of Johnson's Vietnam policy. In order to answer this question you would need to consider the limitations of the source as evidence to develop a full evaluation.

Source A represents only one view of Johnson's policy and its author (Nixon) was a staunch opponent of Johnson. Nixon criticises Johnson for not levelling with the people, creating a 'credibility gap' and losing 'the confidence of the people'. The source is a reliable indicator of Republican attitudes towards a Democratic president but Nixon is trying to blame the problems of US policy in Vietnam on his predecessor. Nixon ignores the other factors that led to failure in Vietnam, for example, military mistakes.

Question (c). This is an essay question testing your ability to present an argument in response to the specific demands of the question. As always, it is important to ensure you obey the demands of the question, and make use of the sources *and* your own knowledge.

Source A supports the view that methods were misguided but can be challenged due to the origins of the source. Source B highlights the fact that the reasons for US participation in the war were misguided, but this can be challenged by reference to evidence of communist advances in South East Asia. Source C highlights the unpleasant nature of the regime that the USA supported in South Vietnam and can be used to support the view that US policy was misguided.

Your own knowledge should include a consideration of evidence that could be used to support US reasons and its methods of participation. This could include reference to the lack of alternatives, Johnson's concern to balance the commitment to Vietnam against his policy of a Great Society, and the pressures from US public opinion.

Whatever your overall argument is, ensure you present it in an introduction and refer to it at the end in a conclusion.

ESSAY SKILLS AT A2 LEVEL

The essay skills mentioned in the AS section (pages 115–21) are equally applicable to writing essays at A2 Level but the standard expected will obviously be higher. It is therefore worth thinking about ways in which you can further develop your essay skills.

- An understanding of historiography can be used to support and develop standard essays. History is a subject which, by its very nature, involves extensive reading and, in order to make maximum use of the material you have studied, it is important to consider issues of historiography which are reflected in it. This will deepen your understanding of the topic and make you more competent as a historian. When writing an essay it is important to refer to different perspectives as this shows an awareness of different interpretations and can demonstrate that you have engaged in wider reading. Nonetheless, there are several pitfalls to avoid:
  - Try to avoid a seemingly endless list of historian's names and their books. 'Name-dropping', in itself, is of limited use and examiners are well aware that students have often never read the books themselves but are merely regurgitating learnt lists of names. It is more important that you show an awareness of the views of the different perspectives even if you have never read the books themselves and cannot even remember the names of historians involved. Showing an **understanding of the perspectives** is a higher-level skill more likely to score marks.
  - Take care in quoting from historians. A statement by an historian can be useful in summing up a relevant point or as illustrating a factor but quotes should be used sparingly. It is never advisable to use long quotations, especially in exam answers as the reward rarely compensates for the effort involved in learning the quote or the time taken to copy it out. Short, sharp quotes are preferable but think carefully about the

purpose of the quotation. Just because a historian states something does not make it a fact. In other words, be careful not to confuse opinion with fact.
  - Referring to different interpretations by historians can often result in a lapse into description rather than using the interpretation as a tool of analysis to develop your argument. For example, the answer that falls into outlining what historian A states and then goes on to what historian B states is not using the material effectively to rise above the merely descriptive. It is much better to **state whether you agree or disagree with the perspectives** covered and **why**. Ensure that you evaluate different interpretations by relating them to their wider context. For example, consider the evidence they have used, the period they were writing in and the values which have influenced them. This will enable you to show your skills in evaluation and assessment and therefore gain more marks than a merely descriptive answer, however detailed.
- Analysis and evaluation can be deepened by showing conceptual understanding. Think of how the factual information you have covered illustrates concepts and ideas and use these as tools of analysis. This technique can be an effective method of ensuring you use terminology with ease and understanding.
  - The Cold War offers many opportunities for developing conceptual understanding. Democracy, capitalism, communism, conflict, ideology, and containment are just a few. For each topic make a list of the concepts and terminology that occur and ensure you understand their meanings and the ways in which they have been applied by the main players in the events of the Cold War and by historians studying the topic.
  - Many essay questions centre on key historical concepts such as causation, which can be broken down in various ways to deepen your analysis. For example, causation can involve a consideration of long-term and short-term factors, the role of a catalyst, turning points and inevitability, immediate causes and excuses. These are all useful tools of analysis.

EXAMPLES: QUESTIONS IN THE STYLE OF EDEXCEL

Containing communism: the USA in Asia

1 To what extent was the failure of US policy in the Vietnam War a result of not learning any lessons from the military defeat suffered by France at Dien Bien Phu?

Examiner's comments

Answers without relevant comment that directly addresses the specific question will not pass at this level. Grades E and D will be awarded to essays that show sound but not detailed knowledge and tend to describe information rather than develop a direct argument. Nonetheless, they will contain some relevant comment. Grade C answers will show some development of an argument, although it may not be sustained throughout. Grades B and A answers will be well focused and supported with detailed information.

This question is asking you to assess 'to what extent' one particular factor was responsible for the failure of the USA in Vietnam. The specific focus of the question is the failure of the USA to learn any 'lessons from the military defeat suffered by France at Dien Bien Phu'. This factor needs to be considered first before the argument is opened out to discuss the role and relative importance of other factors. The following essay plan offers a direct and relevant approach to this question.

Introduction

State your view here. Outline the lessons of Dien Bien Phu that the USA is often accused of failing to learn. Is the statement true? Were there any lessons that the USA did learn? Just how important do you think this failure was? There is a range of possible arguments here from 'complete agreement' to 'completely disagree', although remember that an extreme line either way is often hard to support given available evidence. Don't forget that there is no model answer at this level, but whatever viewpoint you state you must be prepared to support it by the use of evidence. The introduction could be used to outline briefly different interpretations of US failure, but ensure your own argument is stated.

Main content:

Section 1: The lessons of Dien Bien Phu

- failure of conventional warfare
- superior weaponry does not necessarily secure victory
- victory in a guerrilla war requires support from the local population
- the strength of Vietnamese nationalism and hatred of Imperialism
- soldiers need to be convinced in the cause they are fighting for

Outline the evidence that indicates these lessons could be drawn from Dien Bien Phu.

Section 2: The failure of the USA to learn these lessons

Outline the evidence that shows these lessons were not learnt by the USA. Include detailed reference to US involvement in the war.

- The failure to adapt to guerrilla warfare. The limitations of counter-insurgency methods such as Search and Destroy, free fire zones and 'strategic hamlets'.
- The inadequacies of using aerial bombing against a rural-based society. Technology such as napalm and chemical warfare was counterproductive.
- Failure to address the needs of the people of South Vietnam. Aid for social and economic reform diverted through corruption. The nature of the regime in South Vietnam did little to address the needs of its own people. US support for Diem and his predecessors, despite their brutality and the lack of democracy.
- Underestimation of Vietnamese nationalism. USA saw the war in Cold War terms and ignored local factors that had produced the war. Failed to understand that, to the Vietnamese, there was little difference between French Imperialism and US intervention; both were foreigners undermining Vietnamese independence.
- The US soldiers were young and became more demoralised as the war dragged on. They started to question the reasons given to justify their involvement in the war.

There is an opportunity to refer to those historians, such as Krepinevich and Colby, who blame US failure on military factors. You could also develop a theme about the tragedy of US involvement: the seeds of its own downfall lay in the methods it used.

Section 3: Other factors

The essay should be widened out to consider the importance of other explanations of US failure. These should include:

- Failure of political will. Discuss the interpretation of commentators such as Westmoreland, who blamed the failure on politicians' lack of nerve and the policy of gradual escalation.
- The role of the anti-war movement within the USA and its impact on decision-making.
- The post-revisionist argument that the USA did learn lessons from Dien Bien Phu, but that they were misguided because their perspective was clouded by Cold War attitudes that were no longer applicable to reality.

Assess the relative importance of each of these factors.

Conclusion

Sum up **your** argument. How important was the failure to learn lessons from Dien Bien Phu when all these factors are taken into consideration?

BIBLIOGRAPHY

BOOKS

AS Level

Bonds, R. *The Vietnam War: the illustrated history of the conflict in Southeast Asia* (Lansdowne Press, 1983)

Conquest, R. *Red Empire* (Weidenfeld & Nicolson, 1990)

Freeze, G. (ed.) *Russia: a History* (OUP, 1997)

Laver, J. *The Eastern and Central European States 1945–1992* (Hodder & Stoughton, 1999)

Mooney, P. J. *The Soviet Superpower* (Heinemann, 1982)

Pollock, A. *Vietnam: Conflict and Change in Indochina* (OUP, 1995)

Vadney, T. E. *The World Since 1945* (Penguin, 1991)

Ward, H. *World Powers in the Twentieth Century* (Heinemann, 1985)

Young, J. *America, Russia and the Cold War 1941–1998* (Longman, 1999)

A2 Level

Bowker, M. & Williams, P. *Superpower Détente: A Reappraisal* (Sage, 1988)

Bullock, A. *Hitler and Stalin: Parallel Lives* (Harper Collins, 1991)

Chafe, W. *The Unfinished Journey: America Since World War II* (OUP, 1991)

Crampton, R. J. *Eastern Europe in the Twentieth Century* (Routledge, 1994)

Edelman, B. (ed.) *Dear America: Letters Home from Vietnam* (Pocket, 1985)

Edwards, O. *The USA and the Cold War* (Hodder and Stoughton, 1997)

Gaddis, J. L. *We Now Know: Rethinking Cold War History* (Oxford, 1997)

Graebner, N. *The Cold War* (Heath, 1963)

Hall, M. *The Vietnam War* (Longman, 2000)

Halliday, J. & Cumings, B. *Korea: the Unknown War* (Penguin, 1990)

Hastings, M. *The Korean War* (Papermac, 1987)

Hickey, M. *Korean War: the West Confronts Communism 1950–53* (John Murray, 1999)

Hosking, G. *A History of the Soviet Union* (Fontana, 1992)

Levy, D. *The Debate over Vietnam* (Johns Hopkins University Press, 1995)

Maclear, M. *Vietnam: the Ten Thousand Day War* (Thames Methuen, 1981)

McCauley, M. *Russia, America and the Cold War* (Longman, 1998)

McCauley, M. *The Origins of the Cold War* (Longman, 1983)

McElvoy, A. *The Saddled Cow: East Germany's Life and Legacy* (Faber and Faber, 1993)
Painter, D. S. *The Cold War* (Routledge, 1999)
Service, R. A *History of Twentieth Century Russia* (Penguin, 1997)
Snyder, A. A. *Warriors of Disinformation* (Arcade, 1995)
Volkogonov, D. *The Rise and Fall of the Soviet Empire* (HarperCollins, 1998)
Whitfield, S. J. *The Culture of the Cold War* (Johns Hopkins, 1996)
Yergin, D. *Shattered Peace: the Origins of the Cold War and the National Security State* (Penguin 1980)
Young, M. *The Vietnam Wars* (HarperPerennial, 1991)

FILM

The **Vietnam War** has been the subject of many films, a number of which present useful perspectives on the conflict. The following list contains some of those films that students this topic might find useful.

Apocalypse Now (1979) Dir. Francis Ford Coppola
Born on the Fourth of July (1989) Dir. Oliver Stone
Coming Home (1978) Dir. Hal Ashby
Full Metal Jacket (1987) Dir. Stanley Kubrick
Hamburger Hill (1987) Dir. John Irvin
Platoon (1986) Dir. Oliver Stone
Rambo (1985) Dir. George Pan Cosmotos
The Deer Hunter (1978) Dir. Michael Cimino

Other useful films include:
For the **Cold War**: *Dr. Strangelove* (1963) Dir. Stanley Kubrick
For the effects of **nuclear warfare:** *When the Wind Blows* (1987) Dir. Jimmy Murakami
For the **Korean War**: *M*A*S*H* (1970) Dir. Robert Altman
For the **Cuban Missile Crisis:** *Thirteen Days* (2001) Dir. Roger Donaldson

WEBSITES

There is a wide range of websites containing information on topics related to the Cold W Searching by topic will produce an extensive list. Many US universities have sites with student studies. The following websites are particularly useful:

http://www.cspresidency.org
http://turnerlearning.com/cnn/coldwar/cw_start.html
http://history.acusd.edu/gen/classes/diplo177/177.html
http://www.americanpresidents.org
http://www.pbs.org/wgbh/annex/presidents/indexnf.html

INDEX